THE NEW LIGHT LETTERS

DATE DUE

BAPTIST HERITAGE IN ATLANTIC CANADA

Documents and Studies

A Series Sponsored by

Acadia Divinity College
(Wolfville, Nova Scotia)

and

Baptist Historical Committee
(United Baptist Convention of the Atlantic Provinces)

EDITORIAL COMMITTEE

Jarold K. Zeman, Chairman
(Acadia Divinity College, Wolfville, N. S.)

Phyllis R. Blakeley, Secretary
(Public Archives of Nova Scotia, Halifax, N. S.)

Barry M. Moody
(Acadia University, Wolfville, N. S.)

George A. Rawlyk
(Queen's University, Kingston, Ontario)

Robert Wilson
(Atlantic Baptist College, Moncton, N. B.)

PUBLISHED VOLUMES

1. *The Diary and Related Writings of the Reverend Joseph Dimock (1768-1846).* Ed. George E. Levy. 1979.

2. *Repent and Believe: The Baptist Experience in Maritime Canada.* Ed. Barry M. Moody. 1980.

3. *The Journal of the Reverend John Payzant (1749-1834).* Ed. Brian C. Cuthbertson. 1981.

4. *The Life and Journal of the Rev. Mr. Henry Alline* edited by James Beverley and Barry Moody. 1982.

5. *The New Light Letters and Spiritual Songs*, edited by George Rawlyk. 1983.

The New Light Letters
and
Spiritual Songs
1778-1793

Edited by

George A. Rawlyk

PUBLISHED BY

Lancelot Press
for
Acadia Divinity College and
the Baptist Historical Committee of the
United Baptist Convention of the Atlantic Provinces
1983

v

BX
6252
.N64
N48
1983

Published and distributed by
Lancelot Press Limited,
P.O. Box 425,
Hantsport, N.S., Canada B0P 1P0

vi

CONTENTS

GENERAL EDITORS' PREFACE

The search for personal and family roots has become a popular pursuit in our days. It has also rekindled interest in the history of local churches and denominational bodies. A church without the knowledge of its history is like a man who has lost his memory. Historical amnesia is a dangerous disease which afflicts much of contemporary church life.

The purpose of the series BAPTIST HERITAGE IN ATLANTIC CANADA is to make available, over a period of years, a collection of primary sources and critical studies dealing with the historical development of the Baptist witness in the Atlantic provinces of Canada.

In the three Maritime provinces (Nova Scotia, New Brunswick and Prince Edward Island) Baptist congregations have existed for more than two centuries, and in several counties constitute the largest religious body today. By contrast, Baptist churches were introduced to Newfoundland only three decades ago. Through migration, family ties, exchange of leaders and other means of contact, Baptists of the Maritime provinces have exerted significant influence on the spiritual and cultural life in Central and Western Canada, as well as in the Eastern United States, particularly in New England. Most materials planned for publication in the series should, therefore, be of more than regional interest.

The Editorial Committee formulates general policy and

guidelines for the series, and selects works to be published. Editors or authors of particular volumes assume full responsibility for the content and quality of their work.

The publication of the series is sponsored by Acadia Divinity College and the Baptist Historical Committee of the United Baptist Convention of the Atlantic Provinces, in cooperation with Lancelot Press (William Pope). Their grants made possible the publication of the first five volumes.

Gifts for the project will be appreciated and will make it possible for the Editorial Committee to publish additional volumes without undue delays. Donations may be sent to Acadia Divinity College (Wolfville, N.S., B0P 1X0) and designated for "Baptist Heritage Publication Fund."

Jarold K. Zeman
Chairman
Editorial Committee

For
Frederick Burnett

ACKNOWLEDGEMENTS

Many people have assisted me in bringing this book together. Mr. John Perkin, of Wolfville, Nova Scotia, prepared a most useful typed transcript of many of the New Light Letters. Ms. Ann Elwood of Halifax and Kingston assisted me in finding relevant background material in the Public Archives of Nova Scotia. Mrs. Pat Townsend, the Archivist at the Acadia University Archives, did everything in her power to facilitate my research at Acadia University. For this and for her warm hospitality I shall always be grateful.

I very much appreciate the fact that the Acadia University Archives, the Public Archives of Nova Scotia and the American Antiquarian Society have granted me permission to reproduce documents from their records. And I am also very indebted to the School of Graduate Studies and Research of Queen's University for their most welcome publication subvention.

A number of scholars have read portions of this volume and their comments and criticism have been extremely valuable. They have helped me to clarify my analysis and have compelled me, moreover, not to take anything for granted. I therefore owe a great deal, more than they probably realize, to Professor Carman Miller of McGill University, Mr. David Bell, of the University of New Brunswick Law School, Ms. Marlene Schoofs of Harvard University, and to three of my colleagues at Queen's University, Sam Shortt, Klaus Hansen and Donald Akenson.

Even though he has not read one line of this volume, Mr. Frederick Burnett, of Hartland, New Brunswick, has in his own unique manner, encouraged me to take the New Lights seriously and to reexamine Henry Alline's career. This book is dedicated to Frederick Burnett; Henry Alline would have understood why.

A NOTE ON EDITING

In a particularly discerning review-article entitled "Clio and the Historical Editor," Professor J.M. Bumsted has laid down what he considers to be "the minimum to be expected from an editor." He stresses five essentials — "both from the standpoint of scholarship abstractly considered and from that of the book-purchasing public." These five essentials are:

> (1) an accurate text, and some explicit statement of the transcription style employed, (2) a complete text or some editorial explanation and justification of any omissions, (3) an editorial introduction which provides an adequate context for the printed transcription, especially for the non-specialist reader, (4) sufficient annotation to clarify obscure references in the text, including those to characters and situations given more than fleeting mention by the original author, and (5) a full index. (p. 92)

What follows is my attempt to deal with the last three points raised by Professor Bumsted. I have tried to provide a detailed historical context for the letters and spiritual songs and I have also been concerned about adding suitable and sufficient annotation as well as a "full index."

As far as the transcription is concerned, I have tried to copy accurately the original text; I have not modernized any of the spellings and I have only added in square brackets the

---

* J.M. Bumsted, "Clio and the Historical Editor," *Acadiensis*, Vol. IX, No. 2 (Spring, 1980), p. 92.

missing letters or words, which are, in my view, necessary in order to understand their actual meaning. With respect to the manuscript version of Alline's published work, I have used the Bennett version and have added, in square brackets, from the printed version, relevant missing words, sentences or verses. I have added quotation marks to all Biblical and other quotations; in the original letters the quotation marks at the end of the quotations were usually missing. As far as punctuation is concerned, I have endeavoured to replicate the original, however inconsistent it might be. New Light writing was characterized by its "stream of consciousness" quality and few of the writers had any grasp of the meaning of a comma, a period or a semi-colon. Their words flowed relentlessly in a myriad of directions as the Spirit moved them.

I have included in their entirety all the letters to be found in the Bennett volume as well as all of the available spiritual songs composed by the New Light leaders during the 1785 to 1793 period. In addition, of course, I have also included Bennett's selection of Alline's hymns and spiritual songs, his poetry, and a small segment from his *Journal*. Alline's writing not only made possible but also inspired all of the creative output of his disciples. His experience and his language, in other words his Radical Evangelical style, was deeply etched into the Nova Scotia and Maritime New Light consciousness. *The New Light Letters and Spiritual Songs*, in a very real sense, reveals the extent to which Alline's spiritual legacy lived on after his death in February, 1784.

INTRODUCTION

THE

BACKGROUND

for the

TIMES, LETTERS

and

SONGS

1

Chapter I
The Historical
Background

A little more than a year after Henry Alline's death in New Hampshire, on February 2, 1784, an intense religious revival swept through many of the Yankee settlements of Nova Scotia. It was a revival which owed a great deal to an extraordinarily able Methodist preacher from Maryland, Freeborn Garrettson. Moreover, it was a revival which energized a largely moribund Radical Evangelical movement by providing it with a coterie of new, young, energetic, and remarkably gifted leaders — the most outstanding of whom were Edward and James Manning, Joseph Dimock, Harris Harding and Theodore Seth Harding. The revival not only left in its wake a post-Alline leadership elite, but it also, almost as an afterthought, significantly exacerbated the tensions existing between the Whitefieldian orthodox elements of the Radical Evangelicals and Alline's mystical heterodoxy. The Garrettson revival, it may be argued, played a key role in polarizing Alline's followers into an anarchic Antinomian faction, on one extreme, and what eventually evolved into an Evangelical Calvinist Church, on the other. It was ironic, therefore, that a staunch Arminian from the United States would be involved in the transformation of Alline's Free Will anti-Calvinist "ecumenical movement" into what was destined to become a "closed" Baptist Calvinist Church.

I

Henry Alline was a man almost larger than life and he has cast a long shadow over the religious development of the New England-Nova Scotia region until the present day. His contemporaries regarded him as Nova Scotia's George Whitefield — as a powerful instrument of the Almighty, charismatic and uniquely spiritual. Historians in the 19th and the 20th centuries have been, almost to a person, impressed by Alline's mystical theology, his creative powers, and his unusual ability to communicate to others his profound sense of Christian ecstasy. Some scholars have regarded him as the "Prophet" of Nova Scotia's First Great Awakening and as a "Flaming evangelist" who channelled the religious enthusiasm he had helped to create in Nova Scotia during the American

4

Revolution into "neutrality".[1] Others have seen him as an "intellectual and literary giant"[2] who significantly affected the Canadian pietistic tradition and as a charismatic preacher who provided confused, disoriented Nova Scotians with a special sense of collective identity and a powerful "Sense of Mission" at a critical time in their historical development.[3]

Alline's Nova Scotia was a heterogeneous colony consisting of a number of widely scattered and isolated communities stretching from the tiny Scots center at Pictou on the Northumberland Strait, to the Acadian villages on Cape Breton Island, and then to the capital Halifax. South of Halifax, along the Atlantic, all the way to Yarmouth were located scores of New England settlements interrupted at Lunenburg by a large pocket of French and German-speaking "Foreign Protestants." From Yarmouth, along the rich Annapolis Valley to Truro and Chignecto, then to Maugerville on the St. John River, and the eastern outpost of Passamaquoddy on the St. Croix River were to be found the other Yankee settlements. And on the Chignecto Isthmus there were together with hundreds of Yankee farmers, some 750 settlers from the north of England, most of whom were Yorkshiremen, who had migrated to the region early in the 1770s.

During the American Revolutionary years, there were approximately 20,000 inhabitants in Nova Scotia, only sixty per cent of whom were New Englanders. And these "Yankees," as they were called, inhabited the "outsettlement world of Nova Scotia", a world radically different and distinct from the capital ethos of Halifax with its motley population of 2,000. Alline's world, it should be stressed, was the Yankee heartland of Nova Scotia — the fishing and trading communities between Halifax and Yarmouth and the old fertile Acadian lands in the Annapolis Valley and the eastern extremity of the Bay of Fundy and along the St. John River. And this region — "Yankee Nova Scotia" — would be the source of New Light-Evangelical strength not only in late eighteenth century but throughout the nineteenth and twentieth centuries. In most other areas of the colony, Alline and his disciples would have a limited immediate and long-term impact. 5

Alline was born in Newport, Rhode Island, in 1748 and moved in 1760 with his parents to Falmouth in the Minas Basin region of Nova Scotia. Like most young people in the settlement he was brought up in a pious and Calvinist atmosphere. There was little in his rural upbringing in Nova Scotia that would even suggest that Alline would develop into the province's most gifted preacher and most prolific hymn-writer. He was widely known in his community only because of his outgoing personality and his skill in "the art of tanning and currying".[4]

In the early months of 1775, the 27 year-old Alline experienced a profound spiritual and psychological crisis — a crisis that when resolved would provide the turning-point in his life. Alline's conversion — his traumatic "New Birth" — was significantly shaped by his finely developed morbid introspection, his fear of imminent death, and by the considerable pressure he felt to commit himself one way or another during the early months of the American Revolutionary struggle. Alline's conversion, it should be stressed, was the central event of his life and he felt compelled to persuade others to share in his spiritual ecstasy. One perceptive nineteenth century observer noted that Alline was "converted in a rapture; and everafter he sought to live in a rapture; and judged of his religious condition by his enjoyments and raptures."[5]

Alline's graphic description of his conversion experience, it is noteworthy, captured the attention of William James who, in his *Varieties of Religious Experience*, published in 1916, used it as a "classic example" of the "curing of 'sicksoul'."[6] Alline noted in his *Journal*:

February 13th, 1775, when about midnight I waked out of a sleep, I was surprised by a most alarming call as with a small still voice, as it were through my whole soul; as if it spoke these words, How many days and weeks, and months and years had God been striving with you, and you have not yet accepted, but remain as far from redemption as at first; and as God has declared, that his spirit shall not always strive with

6

man, what if he would call you no more, and this might be the last call, as it might be; what would your unhappy doom be? O how it pierced my whole soul, and caused me to tremble in my bed, and cry out for a longer time. O Lord God do not take away thy spirit! O leave me not, leave me not; give me not over to hardness of heart, and blindness of mind.[7]

For over a month Alline struggled to find peace of mind — or as he put it "to be stripped of self-righteousness." And then just when it seemed that he had reached the mental breaking point, he experienced what seemed to him to be the profound delights of spiritual regeneration. He described the beginning of his conversion experience in this way.

...O help me, help me, cried I, thou Redeemer of souls, and save me or I am gone for ever; and the last word I ever mentioned in my distress (for the change was instantaneous) was, O Lord Jesus Christ, thou canst this night, if thou pleasest, with one drop of thy blood atone for my sins, and appease the wrath of an angry God....At that instant of time when I gave up all to him, to do with me, as he pleased, and was willing that God should reign in me and rule over me at his pleasure: redeeming love broke into my soul with repeated scriptures with such power, that my whole soul seemed to be melted down with love; the burden of guilt and condemnation was gone, darkness was expelled, my heart humbled and filled with gratitude, and my will turned of choice after the infinite God.... Attracted by the love and beauty I saw in the divine perfections, my whole soul was inexpressibly ravished with the blessed Redeemer...my whole soul seemed filled with the divine being.[8]

As far as the ecstatic Alline was concerned, the black gloomy despair of his acute depression and morbid introspection had been miraculously removed. "My whole soul," he proclaimed, that was a few minutes ago groaning under mountains of death, wading through storms of sorrow, racked with distressing fears, and crying to an unknown God for help, was now filled with immortal love, soaring on the wings of faith, freed from the chains of death and darkness, and crying out my lord and my God; thou art my rock and my fortress, my shield and my high tower, my life, my joy, my present and my everlasting portion.[9]

The sudden, transforming power of spiritual regeneration — the New Light New Birth — compelled Alline to declare — and those emotionally charged words would provide the cutting edge of his Christian message until his death in 1784:

O the infinite condescension of God to a worm of the dust! For though my whole soul was filled with love, and ravished with a divine ecstasy beyond any doubts or fears, or thoughts of being then deceived, for I enjoyed a heaven on earth, and it seemed as if I were wrapped up in God.[10]

Over and over again in his *Journal* and published sermons and pamphlets and his hymns and spiritual songs Alline referred to his having been "ravished" by the "divine ecstasy," and also to his having been "married" to his Saviour by the redeeming power of the Holy Spirit. Divine love had overwhelmed him to such an extent that he viewed his own experience as being the pattern set for all others. It is not surprising, therefore, that Alline expected his followers to share the intense ecstasy of spiritual rapture — the central New Light experience — which he had so recently experienced and which he regarded as being the only satisfactory means of regeneration.[11]

Alline's traumatic conversion experience was obviously the critically important event of his life and this point merits repetition. His description of it in his *Journal*, available and distributed in manuscript form as early as 1789 and in print in 1806, and in his *Two Mites on Some of the Most Important and much disputed Points of Divinity*, first published in Halifax, in 1781, provided the pattern for his disciples to appropriate, to follow and to attempt to impose on their listeners. Alline was eager to generalize from his particular conversion experience and to make it the universally accepted evangelical norm. His audacity — some would call it "spiritual arrogance" — appealed to many Nova Scotians who were confused and disoriented by the divisive forces unleased by the American Revolution.

During his conversion experience, Alline felt that he had actually experienced spiritual life in the Garden of Eden. For a moment and for eternity — in what he referred to as the "Always Now" — he had been one of "those that are redeemed basking in the boundless Ocean of their Fathers Love...Angelic and immortal."[12] "Thro' boundless Grace" Alline had been "restored so far back as to taste but one glimmering Ray, or small Cluster of the Fruits of that Paradise which...was so infinitely Superior to all created Good, that had it been possible for me to have stood out my mortal Watch without the Enjoyments of Earth, I would never have divided the Spoil any more with the beasts." He had returned cleansed to the Edenic paradise where he had originally sinned against the "Triune God." "You have no more Reason to say," he warned his readers, "that Adam's Sin was imputed to you, than he has to complain and say, that your Sin was imputed to him." Then Alline went on to stress the fact that at the moment of regeneration "you will certainly remember your Rebellion in the Garden of Eden, as any Sin that ever you committed, yea, and as clearly as the Man remembers his past conduct, when he awakes out of his sleep."[13]

Relentlessly attacking the underpinnings of predestination, Alline stressed the importance of each individual choosing freely to return to his or her "paradisical state." This could only be done by accepting the incarnation of Christ and the indwelling of the Holy Spirit:

for that Love they now enjoy, that beauty they behold, and that glory they admire in one glimmering Ray of the perfections of God; for that Moment the Will and Choice was turned after God, they acted with God, and therefore partake of God; and thus again brought to

9

enjoy the Tree of Life, which they had lost; and are reinstated in that Paradise that they fell out of.[14]

Since God lived in what Alline referred to as the "ONE ETERNAL NOW", surely, Alline argued, the redeemed of the Lord "must inhabit the same." For the truly converted there was no sense of "Time, and Space, and successive Periods."[15] "Salvation and Damnation," according to Alline,

originate here at your own Door; for with God there never was any such Thing, as before or after, Millions of Ages, before time began, and as many more, after Time is at a Period, being the very same instant; consider neither Time past nor Time to come, but one Eternal NOW; consider that with God there is neither Succession nor Progress; but that with Him the Moment He said let us make Man, and the Sound of the last Trumpet, is the very same instant, and your Death as much first as your Birth....with God all things are NOW...as the Center of a Ring, which is as near the one side as the other.[16]

Conversion, therefore, was not only the means whereby those who had freely chosen the "Electing Love of God" were able, in a spiritual sense, to return to paradise but also the God-given instrument of telescoping time into the "Eternal Now." Regeneration was the process which destroyed artificial time and space and astonishingly transformed, for each individual, the mundane — what Alline described as the world of "Turnips, Cabbages and Potatoes" — into the cosmic and heavenly — the "Eternity you once, was, and knew."[17]

Since, for Alline, each individual was "capable of consenting to Redeeming Love," and also "the great Work of the Spirit of God" was essential in transforming the individual, he felt it necessary to trace in as simple terms as possible the actual pattern of the "New Birth" process.[18] Conviction, "bringing the Sinner to a Sense of its fallen, helpless and deplorable condition" was, he had to admit, sometimes a gradual process "altho the Work of conversion is instantaneous." The conviction of what he referred to as actual
10

and original sin operated with such power, that the sinner was not only made aware intellectually of his being a sinner but he also felt it profoundly in his own soul:

> he is convinced of his last and undone Condition in his own Conscience, without having any claim to God's Mercy or the least Favour from his Hand. He is so convinced of his helpless Condition that he finds his utter inability, either to obtain Relief for his perishing and immortal soul, or to extricate himself out of that deplorable State of Sin and Misery which he is now convinced that he has plunged himself into. He has long been trying perhaps to recommend himself to Christ by Repentance and Humility; he has been labouring with Prayers and Tears to love God & Holiness, to hate his evil Ways, and be sorry for his Sins: But the Spirit of God has now wrought so powerfully on his Heart, that he appears worse than ever. He finds his heart is hard, and his will stubborn: His Nature is at Enmity against God, and all that is good, and perhaps filled with blasphemous Thoughts against God and his Way.[19]

The convicted individual, according to Alline, feels both drawn to and repelled by the Almighty. He has "tried every possible way to flee from the Wrath to come and to recommend himself to Christ, or to prepare to be converted, but now all appears in vain, and he finds no way to step another step and all his Supporters are now gone." The disoriented sinner

> sees that to fly from his Guilt and Misery is impracticable: and to reform or make Satisfaction, as much impossible; and therefore like the four Lepers at the Gates of Samaria (2 Kings 7:3, 4) he is determined to try the last Remedy; for to stay where he is, is certain Death, and to return back unto his former State of Security, will be Death, and therefore, altho' he cannot see, that Christ has any Love for him, or Pity towards him; neither doth he see, whether He intends to have

11

Mercy on him or not; yet, he is determined to cast himself at his Feet, and trust wholly to his Mercy, and Free Grace for Salvation; and cries out with the trembling Leper. *Lord if thou wilt* (Mark 1:40)[20]

At this precise moment when the convicted individual "is willing to be redeemed out of his fallen state on the Gospel-Terms" then "the Redeeming Love enters into his soul" when Christ "the Hope of Glory takes possession of the inner Man." Instantaneously — George Whitefield had contended that "it was as easy for any adult to tell the dealings of God with their souls as to tell when they were married"[21] — the "Born-again" found "the Burden of their Sin gone, with their Affections taken off of this World, and set on things above." Moreover, "their Hearts" were "oftentimes drawn out after Christ, under a feeling sense of the Worth of his Redeeming Love; at the same Time with a sense of their own Vileness, and the Vanity of all things here below, together with the worth and Sweetness of heavenly Things, and the Amiableness of the Divine Being." Then there came "an increasing Thirst after more Liberty from Sin and Darkness, and a continued panting after the Enjoyment of God, and the Likeness to the meek and the lowly Saviour for their Hearts which before were set on Things below, are now set on Things above."[22]

Because of the mystical union with Christ, "every new born Soul is daily hungering and thirsting after its original Source, viz, spiritual and Divine Food; panting after Light and Love, from which it has been so long a miserable Deserter, and to which it is now returning." Each of "these newborn souls, being united inseparably to the Lord Jesus Christ, became Members of his Body." There was therefore a "final Perseverance of the Saints," and assurance that resulted not in Antinomian excesses but in an undefined form of "sanctified" behaviour.[23]

In conclusion, Alline contended that the Scriptures and his own mystical experience had convincingly showed him that Calvinism was a pernicious heresy. "The lesson, why those, that are lost, are not redeemed" he declared "is not because that God delighted in their Misery, or by any Neglect in God, God

12

forbid." Rather it resulted "by the Will of the Creature; which, instead of consenting to Redeeming love, rejects it, and therefore cannot possibly be redeemed." "Men and Devils that are miserable" he asserted "are not only the Author of their own Misery, but that against the Will of God, the Nature of God, and the most endearing Expression of his Love."[24]

In a particularly evocative poem inserted in his *Anti-Traditionalist* Alline attempted to crystallize the essence of his theological position. He realised that many of his readers would remember his poetry and hymns long after they had forgotten his sometimes opaque and disjointed theological writing:

> But let me turn, and with my Reader gaze
> Once more with wonder on the bloody Scene;
> Raised with the Cross they give the sudden Plung.
> To Rack his Frame sag on the ragged Nails,
> O how! good God, how canst thou yet survive!
> And why my Soul, why all this Rack of Woe?
> It is for me the God of nature Growns?
> How can I write? or dare forbear? I gaze!
> I'm lost! I believe, then doubt; the Scene so strange
> My faith is staggered by the stoop so great;
> And yet again I feel, and must believe;
> It must be true; its like the God I own.
> And near your Hearts, O reader waits the same,
> Knocking with his endearing Charms of Love.
> O hear, receive, and feel the sacred Truths!
> Give him thy Sins, receive his Grace then shall
> This Christ, the Conquest, and the Crown, be thine;
> And then eternal Ages speak his Worth....
> But O he hangs yet on the bloody Cross
> And Groans methinks, I hear but Groans for who?
> For you and me, O reader, see him Dye,
> And in his Death make sure eternal Life;
> And from his Groans immortal Songs of Joy....
> Listen O Heavens and hear ye Sons of Men.
> "Father Forgive them" Cries the dying Lamb;
> The Bleeding Victim in the pangs of Death.

13

Say O my reader dost thou hear the Cry?
Or canst thou stand against such melting Love?
And O he dies! but no my Saviour lives.
Ah lives for me, and lives to die no more.
Rejoice ye dying Sons of men, he lives,
And Crowned with all your sins, ye Mourners Crowd,
Ye sinking Millions to his Courts of grace;
His grace is free, and all is done for you;
Ye've seen him wade 'thro' all your guilt and woe
In seas of Blood thro' all his Life, or Death
A ling'ring death thro' all this servile walk
From the coarse Manger to the Blood Cross:
There won the Field in Death, then tower'd aloft
With Scars of honour to the realms of Light,
To spread for you the Gates of endless Day,
And court you to the Mansions of Delight.
O what displays of every lasting love!
Free grace the News; free grace the lasting Song,
Free grace to Jews and to the Gentile throng;
Free grace shall be the ever lasting theme;
Jehovah's product, and Jehovah's fame;
Goodness his nature, boundless love his name.[25]

Alline's "Radical Evangelical" and New Light message, it is clear, in its essentials at least, reflected what Professor Stephen Marini has sensitively referred to as "the distinctive elements of the Evangelical tradition ... intense conversion experience, fervid piety, ecstatic worship forms, Biblical literalism, the pure church ideal, and charismatic leadership."[26] And Marini correctly locates Alline at the heart of this Whitefieldian New Light framework. But there was also, of course, an important heterodox element in the volatile mixture making up Alline's theology. And many of Alline's contemporaries were aware of the potentially explosive nature of his highly mystical theology. In a particularly discerning critique of Alline's theology, the Reverend Matthew Richey, a Nova Scotia Methodist, pointed out that the Falmouth preacher's "tenets were a singular combination of

14

heterogeneous materials derived from opposite sources." As far as Richey was concerned:

> They were fragments of different systems — without coherence, and without any mutual relation or dependence. With the strong assertion of man's freedom as a moral agent, he connected the doctrine of the final perseverance of the saints. He allegorized to such excess the plainest narratives and announcements of Scriptures, that the obvious and unsophisticated import of the words of inspiration was often entirely lost amidst the reveries of mysticism.[27]

Not all of Alline's followers would be concerned as he was with neutralizing the importance of living the "good Christian life". Even during his last few years in Nova Scotia, some of his followers may have pushed his gospel to and beyond its Antinomian breaking point. But the vast majority would be content to remain traditional Allinite "New Lights," orthodox yet mystical, obsessed as was their charismatic leader with the "rapture" and "ecstasy" of the "New Birth." Such men and women, not surprisingly, sang with enthusiasm the "New Light" hymn and made it their own unique testimony:

> Come all who are New-Lights indeed,
> Who are from sin and bondage freed;
> From Egypts land we've took our flight,
> For God has given us a New-light.

> Long time we with the wicked trod,
> And madly ran the sinful road;
> Against the gospel we did fight,
> Scar'd at the name of a New-light.

> At length the Lord in mercy call'd,
> And gave us strength to give up all;
> He gave us grace to choose aright,
> A portion with despised New-lights.

> Though by the world we are disdain'd,

15

And have our names cast out by men;
Yet Christ our captain for us fights,
Nor death, nor hell, can hurt New Lights.

I know not any sect or part,
But such as are New-Lights in heart;
If in Christ Jesus you delight,
I can pronounce you a New-Light.

For since in Christ we all are one,
My soul would fain let strife alone;
No prejudice can any bear,
Nor, wrath, in those who New-lights are.

Thus guarded by the Lord we stand,
Safe in the hollow of his hand;
Nor do we scorn the New-Light's name,
The saints are all New-Lights, Amen.

Amen, Amen, so let it be,
Glory to God, this light we see;
New light from Christ to us is given,
New light will be our light in heaven.[28]

II

Not only was Alline a charismatic preacher and a controversial essayist, he was also an unusually gifted hymn-writer. He composed no fewer than 509 "hymns and spiritual songs," and these hymns contained the simplified essence of what has been described as Alline's "Radical Evangelical" and New Light message. Alline used "sensuous imagery, subjectivism, and Biblical paraphrase"[29] in his hymns to communicate deep religious truths. Alline's hymns and spiritual songs articulated religious language ordinary folk could understand and could resonate with for they

16

"represented the common denominator of plain-folk religious belief"[30] and captured the simple essence of their faith. Repetition, the use of striking phrases, the creative linking of lyrics to popular folk tunes, must have drilled into the inner consciousness of those who sang Alline's hymns and spiritual songs unforgettable experiences as well as New Light beliefs.

The core of Alline's New Light theology is to be found in the more than 500 hymns that he wrote during the latter part of his life. On the whole, these are powerful and evocative hymns,[31] and is not surprising that for many of the inhabitants of Nova Scotia and New England during and after the Revolutionary War years they contained the essential truths of the Christian gospel in graphic language which, according to Alline, "alarmed" the heart and "stirred" it "up to action, by local objects or vocal sounds." "Although persons may sing, such subjects as they have not experienced without mockery," Alline observed "by acknowledging their ignorance of, and groaning after the things they express; yet as I think it far more likely to stir up and engage the heart (especially souls enlightened and groaning for liberty) when they express the state, groans, and desires of their own souls." And consequently Alline "endeavoured to be various in many subjects, to be adapted to almost every capacity, station of life, or frame of mind."[32]

Alline's 381-page *Hymns and Spiritual Songs* — his major work — first published in Boston in 1786, is divided into five sections or books dealing with, first, "Man's Fallen State," second, "Free Salvation," third, "The New Birth," fourth, "Christian Travels" and finally, "Transporting Views and Christian Triumph." Taking into account the general confused state of Nova Scotians in the late 1770s and 1780s it is not surprising that such hymns as the following became unusually popular during and after Alline's lifetime:

> O What a heart, a heart of stone
> And Load of guilt I bear
> Seeking for help, but finding none,
> And bord'ring on despair!

I mourn beneath my heavy load,
And think I want release
But something keeps me from my God
And bars my soul from peace.

It's hard to bear these pangs of death,
And lug these heavy chains,
And yet for want of acting faith
My burden still remains.[33]

But "guilt" and "despair" were removed by Jesus Christ's sacrifice:

And dids't thou die for me
O thou blest Lamb of God?
And hast thou brought me home to thee;
By thy own precious blood?

How coulds't thou stoop so low?
O what amazing grace!
He saves me from eternal wo,
And gives me heav'nly peace.[34]

"Peace" was provided by the "New Birth" and as might be expected some of Alline's most moving hymns dealt with what he called "the New Birth and the knowledge and joys of that glorious work."

Dark and distressing was the day,
When o'er the dismal gulf I lay,
With trembling knees and stutt'ring breath
I shudder'd on the brink of death.

Destruction yawn'd on ev'ry side,
I saw no refuge where to hide,
Ten thousand foes beset me round,
No friend nor comforter I found.

I groan'd and cry'd, while torn with grief,
But none appear'd for my relief,
'Till Christ the Saviour passing by,
Look'd on me with a pitying eye.

18

He brought me from the gates of hell,
The wonders of his grace to tell
O may he now inspire my tongue
To make his lovely name my song.[35]

And in a hymn entitled, "A Miracle of Grace," Alline graphically used his own conversion experience to appeal to others:

No mortal tongue can ever tell,
The horrors of that gloomy night,
When I hung o'er that brink of hell,
Expecting soon my wretched flight!

I felt my burden waste my life,
While guilt did ev'ry hope devour,
Trembling I stretch'd with groans and strife
For to escape the dreadful hour.

But in the midst of all my grief,
The great Messiah spoke in love;
His arm appeared for my relief,
And bid my guilt and sorrow move.

He pluck'd me from the jaws of hell,
With his almighty arm of pow'r;
And O! no mortal tongue can tell,
The change of that immortal hour!

Then I enjoy'd a sweet release,
From chains of sin and pow'rs of death,
My soul was fill'd with heav'nly peace,
My groans were turn'd to praising breath.[36]

For Alline, regeneration made — as he put it — "Heaven on earth" a possibility:

Some happy days I find below
When Jesus is with me;
Nor would I any pleasure know
O Jesus but in thee.

When I can taste immortal love,
  And find my Jesus near,
My soul is blest where e'er I rove,
  I neither mourn nor fear.

Let angels boast their joys above,
  I taste the same below,
They drink of the Redeemer's love,
  And I have Jesus too.[37]

In an especially evocative and memorable hymn entitled "The great love of Christ display'd in his death," Alline captured what he considered to be the essence of his mystical, conversion experience. And many of his followers must have made Alline's vivid description their own unique experience and used his language to describe their "New Birth."

As near to Calvary I pass
Me thinks I see a bloody cross,
Where a poor victim hangs;
His flesh with ragged irons tore,
His limbs all dress'd with purple gore,
Gasping in dying pangs.

Surpriz'd the spectacle to see,
I ask'd who can this victim be,
In such exquisite pain?
Why thus consign'd to woes I cry'd?
"Tis I, the bleeding God reply'd,
To save a world from sin."

A God for rebel mortals dies!
How can it be, my soul replies!
What! Jesus die for me!
*"Yes, saith the suff'ring Son of God,
I give my life, I spill my blood,
For thee, poor soul, for thee."*

Lord since thy life thou'st freely giv'n,
To bring my wretched soul to heav'n,
And bless me with thy love;

Then to thy feet, O God, I'll fall,
Give thee my life, my soul, my all,
To reign with thee above.

All other lovers I'll adieu,
My dying lover I'll pursue,
And bless the slaughter'd Lamb;
My life, my strength, my voice and days,
I will devote to wisdom's ways,
And sound his bleeding fame.

And when this tott'ring life shall cease,
I'll leave these mortal climes in peace,
And soar to realms of light;
There where my heav'nly lover reigns,
I'll join to raise immortal strains,
All ravish'd with delight.[38]

In possibly the last hymn he ever composed, Alline
discussed his own imminent death:

Now to the pilgrims born of God,
    In Jesus' name these lines I hand,
To cheer you on your Christian road
    And point you to the heav'nly land,

When I am gone and ye survive,
    Make the Redeemer's name your theme,
And while these mortal climes ye rove,
    The wonders of his love proclaim.

Soon I shall end this rapid race,
    And tread your mortal climes no more;
But through Jehovah's boundless grace,
    Save shall I reach the Heav'nly shore....

I drink, I soar, I gaze, I rove,
    O'er the transparent scenes of bliss,
Still lost with wonder in his love,
    My soul! and what a God as this!

Ten thousand blazing realms of light
Proclaim their God, and say, Amen!
My soul still soaring in her flight,
My God is all, I drop my pen.[39]

Alline's hymns are still sung in a few Baptist churches in New Brunswick and Nova Scotia. They are not likely to be found in hymn books but in the amazing retentive memories of scores of worshippers who still regard themselves as disciples of Henry Alline. Alline's hymns are an integral part of an oral culture which still exists in the upper reaches of the St. John River Valley of New Brunswick, and in the Yarmouth region of Nova Scotia. Few may now have any knowledge of his printed sermons or treaties or have seen his *Journal*. But they do remember some of his *Hymns and Spiritual Songs*, perhaps the most lasting legacy of Alline's all too brief sojourn in what his followers frequently referred to as "this vale of tears."[40]

III

A short time before Alline's death on February 2, 1784, Hannah Adams of Boston published in her *Alphabetical Compendium of the Various Sects* a particularly discerning description of Alline and his mystical, and some would say, heretical New Light theology. Adams' treatment was the first printed New England response to the young, dynamic preacher from "New England's Outpost." According to Adams, Alline was "a man of natural good sense, and warm imagination." He had preached in almost every corner of Nova Scotia and "by his popular talents" Alline had "made many converts." He had also published "several treatises and sermons, in which he declares he has advanced some new things."[41] Alline argued, for example,

> that the souls of all the human race are emanations, or rather parts of one Great Spirit; but that they individually originally had the powers of moral agents;

22

that they were all present with our first parents in Eden, and were actual in the first transgression. He supposes, that our first parents in innocency were pure spirits, without material bodies; that the material world was not then made; but in some consequence of the fall man being cut off from God, that they might not sink into immediate destruction, the world was produced, and then clothed with hard bodies, and that all the human race will in their turns, by natural generation, be invested with such bodies, and in them enjoy a state of probation for happiness of immortal duration.[42]

The Nova Scotia tanner-farmer, morever, maintained that Christ was never, in fact, "raised from the grave" and that no human being "ever will be." Rather, "when the original number of souls had their course on earth, they will all receive their reward or punishment in their original embodied state." Alline also stressed the fact that "baptism, the Lord's Supper and ordination" were all "matters of indifference."[43]

Alline and his followers, according to the Adams' analysis, endeavoured "to support...these...most distinguishing tenents," by "alledging that the scriptures are not to be understood in their literal sense, but have a spiritual meaning." Alline had had

such influence over his followers that some of them pretend to remember their being in the garden of *Eden*. The moment of their conversion, they are so well assured of that, it is said some of them even calculate the age of their cattle by it.[44]

It is of some interest that Adams devoted more space and attention to Alline than to any other colonial religious leader — including the prophetess Jemima Wilkinson, the leader of the Universal Friends, and Mother Ann Lee, the Shaker "Christ." Alline's peculiar religious views had obviously struck a most responsive chord in Adams. But even though she was remarkably successful in cutting through the thick verbal underbush of Alline's theological writing to find

23

the core of his heterodoxy, she, unlike other contemporary observers, failed to appreciate the importance Alline and his followers placed on basic Whitefieldian New Light precepts such as the central place of the New Birth, the urgency of preaching the gospel to the unconverted, the shrewd and effective use of a distinctive pietistic language and style — "as a bare and brutal engine against the mind."[45]

The Reverend David McClure, the Congregational minister of North Hampton, New Hampshire, who had looked after Alline on his death bed, emphasized, unlike Adams, Alline's New Light orthodoxy. McClure, for example, described the Nova Scotian evangelist as "a burning and shining light in Nova Scotia and elsewhere....his christian virtues, zeal, fortitude, faith, hope, patience and resignation shone bright as the lamp of life burnt down into the socket."[46] McClure added that during the months Alline had spent in New England before being "united with seraphs and saints in their pure ardours of holy life and everlasting joy," the Nova Scotian had preached "with power to the consciences of sinners."[47] Many residents of North Hampton, though not ardent New Lights, could never escape Alline's remarkable influence. As late as 1839, for example, it was noted by the Reverend Jonathan French, one of McClure's successors, that several persons were still alive

> who saw Revd Mr. Alline while at Mr. McClures. They represent every thing in his appearance and conversation as havg been very spiritual and as become one just on the verge of heaven. He seemed scarcely to belong on earth. He passed the last week of his life at Mr. McClures, & preached on the Sabbath from "Zacheus come down etc.". Many visited his sick and dying chamber, he had something spiritual to say to everyone. Widow Hepzibah Marston, now 95, the oldest person in the town and sister of the church, was one of his watchers the last night of his life and speaks of the prayerfulness and heavenly frame of mind with which he anticipated his departure.[48]

Fifty-five years after his death, the deeply etched image of the amazing Henry Alline could not be removed from the memory of an American like the ninety-five year old Hepzibah Marston who had spent only a few days with him. For every Hepzibah Marston in New Hampshire, there were hundreds of Nova Scotians who, according to one acerbic Presbyterian critic, as late as the 1850s, believed that Alline "did more good by his labours than any minister that ever lived in Nova Scotia."[49] Most of these Nova Scotians, of course, had never met Alline face-to-face, but their positive view of the Falmouth preacher had been largely shaped by an oral culture — a culture which helped them to reconstruct an awareness of a distant past. These Nova Scotians saw Alline through the eyes of those of their neighbours who had actually seen and heard the "Whitefield of Nova Scotia." As late as 1856, for example, a ninety-three year old Mrs. Fox, a daughter of one of Alline's early converts — Benjamin Cleveland, the Horton hymn writer — still vividly remembered listening to her first Christian sermon — one preached by Alline in 1780. The sermon, she once observed, "made a deep impression on her mind;" seventy-six years after the event she still recalled Alline's text "John xii:35." It was observed that

> Mrs. Fox says she never heard Mr. Alline preach but it warmed her heart; and she heard him very often. She used frequently to travel several miles to hear him; and never heard him without there being something fresh and new in his discourses.[50]

Mrs. Fox, moreover, could still describe Alline as a man of "middling size; straight, and very thin; of light complexion, with light curly hair, and blue eyes, with a solomn expression" and his dress was "neat but plain." All of the conversation, she stressed, was "very spiritual" and Alline "would not converse about the world at all, except as urged by necessity." He "was mighty in prayer" she maintained and "was a good singer, and loved singing."[51]

Mrs. Fox and other Nova Scotians who had known Alline could only endorse with enthusiasm and conviction the last line of the inscription chiseled into his New Hampshire tombstone:

He was a burning and shining light and was justly esteemed the Apostle of Nova Scotia.[52]

Despite the fact that Alline did not always preach what one Nova Scotian described in July 1784 as *"right sound doctrine,"*[53] he was, nevertheless, widely perceived in his lifetime and afterwards as a man "sent of God" who promoted a remarkable "Work of God."[54] Amos Hilton, one of Alline's most influential Yarmouth converts, expressed in 1782 what he must have realized was a widespread view concerning Alline's so-called "heretical views." When pressed by the Reverend Jonathan Scott, Alline's bitter Congregational Church critic, on why he could accept a gospel in which "all the Revelation of God's Word is overthrown," Hilton simply replied "It was no Matter of any great Consequence to him what a Man's Principles were, if he was but earnest in promoting a good Work."[55] In other words, Hilton was arguing that it was not really important what a preacher's theology actually was. What was important was whether he was truly an instrument of the Holy Spirit and his preaching moved people to experience the New Light "New Birth."

Most Nova Scotians, during Alline's lifetime, at least, were not overly concerned with his so-called "heretical views," realizing the centrality of the New Light "Radical Evangelicalism" in his Christian message. A perceptive critic of the religious life of Nova Scotia and certainly a person who was not a New Light enthusiast, Simeon Perkins, the Liverpool merchant and civic leader, observed on Sunday, February 11, 1783:

> Mr. Alline made a long Speech, Very Sensible, Advising all Sorts of People to a Religious Life, and gave many directions for their outward walk. This is a wonderful day and Evening. Never did I behold such an Appearance of the Spirit of God moving upon the people since the time of the Great Religious Stir in New England many years ago.[56]

Perkins, it is clear, carefully fitted Alline into the orthodox New Light paradigm. Most other Nova Scotians of the time, the evidence suggests, would have done precisely the same thing.

Alline had intuitively realized that most Nova Scotians, during the American Revolution, were acutely troubled and disoriented and were desperately searching for some meaning in life and for meaningful relationships. And Alline saw that the "New Birth" provided both. It is interesting that Alline made extraordinary use of sexual imagery in order to convey something of the rich emotional texture of conversion. Conversion, in a very real sense for him, was perceived as a spiritual climax, the consummation of an intense love-hate relationship which seemed to be the essence of conviction. For Alline, conversion was, as he often graphically put it, "being married to Christ." And it was a "marriage" to the "Heavenly Charmer" which would give meaning and order to all other relationships.[57]

Women, young men and young women were particularly affected by Alline's preaching. They and other groups were almost overwhelmed by his spiritual *hubris* — his conviction that he had, in fact, seen paradise and had communicated with Christ face-to-face. The charismatic preacher had had, obviously, a unique experience; he spoke with power, eloquence, conviction and first-hand experience. None of this could be explained in any other terms than the ones he assiduously used to define his special authority. In all ages, confused, unsure people look to those who know for certain what is best for everyone to lead and to direct them. Nova Scotians in the late eighteenth century were not exceptions to this tendency. Alline possessed, as he once explained it, "an omniscient eye" to discover "a map of the disordered world" and most Nova Scotians eagerly accepted what to them was an observable fact.[58]

Young men must have been attracted by Alline's sensitivity, warmth and confidence, and also by the very sensuous manner in which he described his and the ideal conversion experience. There might have been some latent homosexual overtones to this reaction to him. But their response to Alline and his message was far more complex than this. Some may have been drawn by Alline's emphasis on the bisexual nature of God and the spiritual Christ and all those who inhabited paradise — for according to Alline they were and are at the same time both "a Male and Female."[59] Thus, in the ravishing of their souls by Christ and in the ecstacy of conversion the young men could appropriate the ultimate in spiritual and what Alline called "corporeal" experience. The spiritual and sexual thus blended to intensify the relationship between young Nova Scotians and their Saviour and also among themselves. For whether male or female they could share with one another the common experience of being "ravished with the Perfections of such a God."[60] The young males could also assert a sense of their own importance in a society which had traditionally relegated them, because of their youthfulness, to positions of subservience and deference. The "New Birth" transformed them almost overnight into influential and important Nova Scotians.

Women were drawn to Alline like moths to a lamp burning in the midst of a black summer's night. At his meetings they were encouraged to express their most deeply felt feelings and attitudes as equals. For Alline and for them, at least during the revival meetings, Christ and the Holy Spirit did not distinguish between males and females. In their homes most of the women, in their roles as mothers, sisters, grandmothers, were apparently content to be second-class citizens; in Alline's revival and in his theology they emphatically were not.

As Donald Mathews has persuasively argued in his important study, *Religion in the Old South*, conversion and revivals provided women in particular with what he refers to as "psychological and social space." Surrendering temporarily the traditional web of cultural constraints which largely conditioned their behaviour and sense of responsibility, many women sought in Radical Evangelical religion the justification for independence and collective support for what was almost universally regarded as aberrant behaviour. Moreover, the "repressed sensuality of a religion which emphasized love, care and intimate relationship with Christ," Mathews has argued, "could easily mix sacred and profane desire...into a volatile compound that provided women unaccustomed to compassionate, impassioned, even passionate men" like Alline

28

"with an emotional experience they could not quite fathom, but which they knew excited and fulfilled them."[61] Some of Alline's female converts, it seems clear, "propelled by the fervor of their own conversions," imposed their religious values on their children and their husbands.[62] This so-called "maternal evangelism" when successful, strengthened family ties when they were being threatened by the divisive forces unleashed by the Revolution. And during the years immediately after the Awakening, when they had to surrender their revival-inspired independence and freedom, many likely played central roles "in creating a narrowly maternal role and image for their sex."[63] But they, of course, would do far more than this. Even though the revival did not produce immediate liberation or equality and often disrupted society, it did provide an important push forward as women, bonded to one another "in mutual support, personal companionship and social solidarity," slowly moved "from the abstraction of emotion to the reality of exclusively female organizations" in church, community and the province.[64]

Those Nova Scotians who were converted under his preaching or by his disciples, wished to replicate all aspects of Alline's own transforming religious experience. They too wished to see Paradise; they too wished to "taste but one glimmering ray" of the "Eternal Now."[65] And they yearned for Alline's Christ to ravish them to make them one with him. They sought the mountain peak of religious ecstacy but naively underestimated how difficult it would be for them to remain there. Many would tumble to the depths of despair soon after Alline's death. But most would never forget that magic New Light moment when they, like Henry Alline, had experienced Jesus Christ and had become part of his prisitine spirituality and perfectability. They had reached out and Christ had touched them. They were certain that it could happen again — and it did, only a few years after Alline's death — as periodic revivals became a distinguishing feature of Nova Scotia's religious culture.

Freeborn Garrettson, who would trigger one of these revivals, and his American Methodist associate, the frail James Oliver Cromwell, sailed from New York in the middle of February, 1785, and after a particularly stormy passage finally arrived in Halifax. The two young American Methodist itinerants had been "set apart for Nova Scotia" by the leaders of the American Methodist Episcopal Church who were under considerable pressure from John Wesley and William Black, the Nova Scotia Methodist leader, to provide missionary assistance at a critical time in the colony's history.[66] The death of Alline had created a religious vacuum in Nova Scotia which the twenty-five-year-old Black desperately wished to fill with his brand of Methodism. And the sudden arrival of approximately 20,000 Loyalists, some of whom were Methodists, provided both a new mission field and also the means whereby, it was hoped, the Yankee New Light hegemony over much of the colony could finally be broken.

Soon after landing in Halifax, Garrettson elbowed Black aside and became the most influential Methodist leader in Nova Scotia. Garrettson was regarded, with some justification, as a "man of varied resources, a powerful preacher and capable organizer, of genuine piety and holiness of life, who left an abiding impression on the whole life of the province."[67] His influence in Nova Scotia according to J.M. Buckley, author of *A History of Methodism in the United States*, "was almost equal to that of Wesley in Europe and Asbury in the United States."[68] "It may be fairly questioned" argued his biographer, Nathan Bangs, "whether any one minister in the Methodist Episcopal Church, or indeed in any other Church, has been instrumental in the awakening and conversion of more sinners than Garrettson."[69] Garrettson was, without question, an unusually gifted minister; he was a powerful, some would say charismatic, preacher; he was, moreover, an indefatigable itinerant, a man almost obsessed with — as he once cogently expressed it — "rising higher and higher in the divine image."[70] Though he spent only twenty-six months in Nova Scotia Garretson, it has been persuasively

30

argued, "left an abiding impression on the whole life of the province."[71] Next to Henry Alline, the evidence suggests, the Maryland Methodist was the most able and influential preacher in eighteenth century Nova Scotia.

Like Alline, Garrettson had a traumatic conversion experience, an experience he too wished everyone he met would enthusiastically emulate. After listening to a Methodist itinerant and under intense conviction, Garrettson, in his early twenties, became as he expressed it, "for the first time, reconciled to the justice of God." According to the young Marylander,

> The enmity of my heart was slain, and the plan of salvation was open to me. I saw a beauty in the perfections of the Deity, and felt that power of faith and love that I had been a stranger to. My soul was exceeding happy that I seemed as if I wanted to take wings and fly to heaven.[72]

Garrettson became a Methodist circuit preacher in 1775 and only his death on July 26, 1827, brought about an end to what has been called the glorious "story of his long, heroic, and successful services in the itinerant ranks."[73]

Garrettson was a man of amazing energy which, together with his remarkable missionary zeal, helps to explain the impact he had on Nova Scotia in the 1780s. He once described to Bishop Francis Asbury a "typical" week spent in Halifax:

> Sunday eight o'clock preach in our little chapel, which will hold about four hundred persons; ten o'clock preach in the poor house, where there are about a hundred people....at twelve o'clock in the preaching house; four o'clock in a private house by the dockyard; and by candlelight in the chapel. I preach every night in the week: Friday visit the prisoners.[74]

Garrettson did not mention his frequent house visits, the time spent in keeping up his correspondence with fellow Methodists in Nova Scotia, New Brunswick, Great Britain and the United

States, his "diligence and zeal" in studying the scriptures and his exemplary "prayerfulness and watchfulness." He was, according to his biography, the antithesis of "the slothful servant."[75]

During his brief sojourn in Nova Scotia, Garrettson visited virtually every settlement, apart from Pictou. A year before his death, Garrettson described his Nova Scotia experience in the following manner:

> I began to visit the towns, and to traverse the mountains and valleys, frequently on foot, with my knapsack at my back, up and down the Indian paths in the wilderness, when it was not expedient to take a horse; and I had often to wade through the mud and water or morasses, and frequently to satisfy my hunger from my knapsack, to quench my thirst from a brook, and rest my weary limbs on the leaves of trees. This was indeed going forth weeping; but thanks be to God, he compensated me for all my toil, for many precious souls were awakened and converted.[76]

Garrettson took full advantage of the earlier assiduous missionary labour of William Black and also that of Henry Alline and his itinerating disciples; men like John Payzant, Joseph Bailey, Thomas Handley Chipman, and Ebeneezer Hobbs, a teenage New Light exhorter. But the Methodist itinerant did more than this. He not only cultivated the Yankee New Light heartland stretching from Falmouth, down the Annapolis Valley to Granville, to Yarmouth then up the southern shore to Argyle, Liverpool and Chester, but he also broke new missionary ground in the Loyalist centre of Shelburne.

Despite the opposition of some of the "Allinites," — Garrettson referred to them as being "as deluded a people as I ever saw,"[77] — the Methodist preacher attracted large attentive audiences during his visits in the spring of 1785 to Cornwallis, Horton, Windsor, Granville and Annapolis Royal. At Horton, on Sunday, May 22, over 100 people turned out to hear him "the General Cry was after preaching — if this is Methodist Doctrine, it is agreeable to truth".[78] Later that same day, in the New Light centre of Cornwallis, there was, according to Garrettson, "a Considerable moving on ye hearts of ye people." And on the following day, after a particularly emotional meeting, there was a universal "cry...if this is Methodist doctrine, I will be a Methodist." Scores of people, some of whom had first been awakened by Whitefield and others by Alline, "After meeting...Continued some time hanging round each other, inquiring what they should do to be saved". Garrettson hoped that the revival would give the Allinites a fatal and what he termed a "wonderful Stab."[79]

Preaching at a minimum three sermons each Sunday, in barns, private homes, and Baptist and Presbyterian Churches and once each day of the week, Garrettson throughout June and July continued to itinerate up and down the Annapolis Valley from Windsor to Annapolis. Then in late July he visited Liverpool from which centre in late August he made his way to the Loyalist centre of Shelburne. By the early autumn he had returned to Halifax where he took charge of the extensive Halifax circuit which included regular visits to Windsor, Cornwallis and Horton. In the spring of 1786, Garrettson briefly visited Liverpool where he observed to Wesley "Alline's small party oppose us warmly" and "The great part of the town attend our ministry, and the first people have joined our society."[80] Garrettson then made his way to Shelburne, now a town in serious decline, and to Barrington. At first, the people of Barrington were unresponsive having been warned by Thomas Handley Chipman, the New Light minister located at Granville, that Garrettson was "a dangerous 'Arminian'." Despite Chipman's warning, however, hundreds turned out to listen to the visiting Methodist from Maryland. "Between two and three hundred were awakened in a greater or less degree" reported a delighted Garrettson and "their shyness and prejudices were all removed."[81]

Scores of people in settlements along the South shore, in places like Barrington and Cape Negro, were converted, Garrettson was certain. And because of what he called "this visitation of the Spirit", Methodist churches were organized on what was then called the "Arminian plan."[82]

In the autumn Garrettson returned to Halifax and in

33

the winter months of 1786 and 1787 he was largely responsible for coaxing into existence a revival in Horton and Cornwallis. "I have had a blessed winter among them," Garrettson observed to John Wesley on March 10, 1787. "If the work continues much longer as it has done, the greater part of the people will be brought in." In Horton, especially, there had "been a divine display; many convinced and converted to God." Garrettson also noted that

> God is carrying on his work in a glorious manner in Barrington; the people flock from every quarter to hear the word: many have been convinced, and about fourteen have been set at liberty, some of whom were famous for all manner of wickedness. The fields here seem white for harvest.[83]

Despite the Nova Scotia "white fields" all "ready for harvest," Garrettson left the colony one month later for the United States. He would never return — not only because of his strong sense of being and wanting to remain an American but because as he once cogently put it "I was not clear that I had a call to leave the United States."[84] Nova Scotia Methodism would suffer greatly because of ·this decision. When Garrettson left the province, there were almost 600 Methodist Church members out of a total population of more than 40,000. The Methodists had not only made inroads in the Yankee settlements but they had been particularly successful among the Yorkshire immigrants and among the Black Loyalists. There were, in fact, ten times as many Methodists as there were Baptists and probably three times as many as there were actual New Light Congregationalists in their two organized churches, Chipman's at Granville and the Reverend John Payzant's at Horton and Cornwallis. Payzant had been ordained minister of Alline's old Church on July 3, 1786, largely, it seems, in order to neutralize the impact of Methodism in the region.

Garrettson's quitting Nova Scotia on April 10, 1787 did not, it should be stressed, bring to an end the Methodist plan to assert their spiritual hegemony over the colony. Though not yet ordained, William Black and James and John Mann,

34

Loyalists from New York, William Grandin, a New Jersey Loyalist, and "Old Mose," the Black Methodist preacher at Shelburne, continued to preach Wesley's gospel supported briefly by the sick Reverend Cromwell, who would, because of poor health, be compelled to leave Nova Scotia in May. A year later two new Methodist missionaries arrived in the colony, William Jessop, the saintly Delaware itinerant, and James Wray, a somewhat stiff, austere and some would say, overly caustic Englishman.[85] Wray was appointed by Wesley as "Superintendent" of the work in Nova Scotia; it was a mistake. Within a year Wray, who was incapable of understanding North American Methodism, had resigned. In May of 1789 the Mann brothers and Black were ordained in Philadelphia. Black's ordination prepared the way for his being appointed Wray's replacement. Moreover, and this fact was extremely important, the three newly ordained Methodist ministers could now baptize and dispense communion and thus compete effectively with the two ordained New Lights Payzant and Chipman as well as with the more numerous Anglican ministers.

Jessop could almost fit Garrettson's shoes; he was a man "of powerful eloquence," who both preached and experienced sanctification.[86] But he lacked Garrettson's enthusiasm for intinerating and this significantly limited the impact he had on late eighteenth century Nova Scotia. Nevertheless, he effectively built upon Garrettson's work in the Barrington area and firmly established the Methodist cause there before his premature death in the United States in 1795.

By the beginning of the last decade of the eighteenth century, the Methodists had four ordained ministers in Nova Scotia: Black, the Manns and Jessop and also the unordained preachers, William Grandine and "Old Mose." Five hundred and ten members were reported[87] from the colony in official records — unofficial records provide a higher number — and it seemed that the Methodists were on the verge of becoming the largest and most influential Protestant denomination in Nova Scotia and the organizational means whereby Alline's New Light movement might have been channelled into oblivion. But the Methodists had failed to take into account one important fact — the revival Garrettson had helped both to inspire and to shape had not only significantly revived the New Light movement but it had also pushed to the surface a remarkable group of young, dynamic, committed, and some would say "inspired" preachers. These men, such as Harris Harding, Joseph Dimock, Edward and James Manning would become the so-called "Patriarchs" of the Nova Scotia Baptist Church. According to the 1827 Nova Scotia census, the New Light Baptist counter-offensive had been amazingly successful. The total population of Nova Scotia in 1827 was estimated at 142,548. This included 31,199 Anglicans, 42,060 Presbyterians, 31,882 Roman Catholics, 19,846 Baptists, 9,567 Methodists, 2,970 Lutherans and 5,042 others. The Baptist percentage in 1827 was 16.0% and the Methodist 7.6%. By 1871, there were 73,295 Baptists, 18.9% of the total Nova Scotia population of 387,800 and 40,345 Methodists, 10.4% of the total.[88] Alline's disciples, in their nineteenth century Baptist manifestation, had obviously won a decisive numerical victory over the Wesleyan Garrettsonians. And they had done so in an extremely difficult demographic environment.

As late as 1776, it should be remembered, at least sixty per cent of the Nova Scotia population was of New England origin; and it was among these people, in particular, that Alline and his disciples were especially successful. But with the end of the Revolution, there was an influx of approximately 20,000 Loyalists most of whom came from the Middle and Southern colonies; and then during the last decade of the eighteenth century and first decade of the nineteenth century, thousands of Scots, Irish and English immigrants arrived to transform even further the ethnic and religious profile of the colony. By 1827, almost one-half of the estimated Nova Scotia population of 142,548 was of Scots or Irish background and this would be the case throughout most of the nineteenth century. In all likelihood, less than one-fifth of the population was of New England origin.

The fact that almost one in six Nova Scotians in 1827 was a Baptist and in 1871 almost one in five, was indeed remarkable taking into account the ethnic mix of the province.

Henry Alline's disciples had not only beaten the Methodists and all other religious competitors in the Yankee heartland in the battle for converts and adherents but they had also been successful in building Baptist bridgeheads in the Celtic fringe to the north as well as in Halifax and its environs.

V

Nova Scotia, especially Yankee Nova Scotia, had, in a religious sense, been assiduously cultivated by Alline and his disciples during the years and months immediately preceding Garrettson's arrival in the colony. Though most observers agreed with Alline that by early 1781 the "Great Awakening" had lost much of its earlier momentum in the Yankee heartland of the colony, he and Chipman and Bailey and Payzant continued to preach the Evangelical gospel in the more peripheral regions such as the St. John River Valley and the South Shore. After Alline's death, these three disciples did not stop preaching, of course. But because each was now married, with family responsibilities, and lacking Alline's example and inspiration, they began to limit somewhat their itinerating. But the Methodist offensive, organized by Garrettson, forced them to defend the Allinite New Light legacy and in the process they helped in bringing about the transformation of Alline's disorganized sect into the Baptist Church.[89]

It should be kept in mind that during the years immediately following the end of the American War of Independence, much of Nova Scotia was experiencing yet another profound, and for many disconcerting, collective sense of acute disorientation and confusion.[90] As was the case in neighbouring Northern New England, hundreds of "common people were cut loose from all sorts of traditional bonds and found themselves freer, more independent, more unconstrained than ever before in their history."[91] The coming of the Loyalists to peninsular Nova Scotia at the end of the Revolution accelerated a process of social disintegration already underway. The Loyalists, according to Edward Manning, had a "bad and...dreadful" effect on the colony and they "corrupted" societal values and made many Nova Scotians "adepts in wickedness."[92] Thus, as Gordon Wood has

37

argued, "Traditional structures of authority crumbled under the momentum of the Revolution, and common people increasingly discovered that they no longer had to accept the old distinctions" that had driven them into a widely-perceived subservient and vulnerable status.[93] And, as might have been expected, sometime "bizarre but emotionally satisfying ways of relating to God and others" became increasingly widespread phenomena as many Nova Scotians sought a renewed sense of "community-belonging" in order to neutralize the powerful forces of alienation then sweeping the colony. It was a period when, it has been perceptively observed, "everything was believable" and "everything could be doubted."[94] "Radical enthusiasts and visionaries," regarding themselves as the disciples of Henry Alline and as propagators of his tradition, became the "advanced guard" of the renewed "popular evangelical movement with which they shared a common hostility to orthodox authority."[95] By 1790 these New Lights, as they were spitefully referred to by their enemies, were a people in a delicate state of spiritual tension "poised like a steel spring by the contradicting forces pulling within it."[96] There was a mystical quality; but there was also a secular one; there was a democratic bias but also an authoritarian one together with individualism and a tendency towards communitarianism. For some, it seems clear, the seemingly contradictory forces within the New Lights would soon neutralize one another, producing apathy, indifference and disenchantment. For others, a not insignificant number, the dynamic tension would result in a renewed pietism which would become a crucial link in the chain connecting Henry Alline's First Great Awakening with Nova Scotia's Second Awakening. But for an influential minority, known as the "New Dispensationalists" by friends and enemies alike, the state of spiritual tension brought about by the coming of the Loyalists, the Garrettsonian revival, the continuing influence of Alline's legacy and growing American sectarian influences, provided a heaven-sent opportunity to stretch Alline's gospel to and beyond the Antinomian breaking point.

Critically important actors in the unfolding New Light drama in Nova Scotia in the decade or so following Alline's quitting the colony were Edward and James Manning, Joseph

Dimock, Harris Harding and Thomas Bennett. All of these men played key roles not only in breathing new life into the New Light movement in the late 1780s but also in encouraging and in facilitating for a time at least the growth of New Dispensationalism. Moreover, after the New Dispensationalists had spun off into a state of spiritual anarchy, they helped to undermine the new, divisive and embarrassing sect by, among other things, channelling the New Light majority into the Calvinist Baptist Church.

Edward Manning was born in 1766 in Ireland of Roman Catholic parents. When he was still an infant, his family moved to Falmouth Nova Scotia. At the age of ten, in 1776, he heard what he once described as "that man of God, the late Henry Alline, pray" at his father's house. "I well remember his addressing me," Manning observed over 20 years after the event, "though but a child, and the tears dropping from his face upon mine, while he exhorted me to flee from the wrath to come." Though greatly influenced by Alline's appeal, Manning "to my shame shook it off, and continued very thoughtless till the age of twenty-two." In his teens, Manning studied surveying and navigation, and was regarded as being a good scholar. But despite his preoccupation with "Singing Songs and Jesting" he could not, he once observed, escape from Alline's "sting" which "was still in [his] mind" right up to his conversion in 1789.[97]

Late in 1788 and in early 1789, Falmouth experienced what Manning referred to as a spiritual awakening and reformation. Like others in the community, he was drawn to the revival meetings where "the Spirit of God would powerfully take hold of me." But Manning resisted, exerting "every power and faculty of my soul to keep from expressing myself before the congregation." And then after the meetings he rushed to join his young friends in scoffing at the religious enthusiasm. Despite this oscillation, Manning found that by the early months of 1789, he was being particularly influenced by the preaching of Harris Harding whom he described as being "an instrument in the hands of God of alarming my mind." Harding was twenty-nine years old at the time, a school-teacher, lively, intense, sensuous and emotional; he had been converted in 1785, soon after returning to Nova Scotia from New England, after the end of the Revolutionary War. Though not one of Alline's converts, he was very much an enthusiastic disciple of Alline, and would remain one until his death in 1854 at the age of ninety-three. For Harding, according to his biographer, Alline was a unique "servant of God, and one who, if he was not infallible, had an uncommon measure of the Spirit and his writings as being the mind of God." Manning was also affected by the preaching of Joseph Bailey — "an eminent Christian" — who had travelled with Alline and though not ordained, was an effective preacher. In 1789, Bailey was thirty years old, in the prime of his life and he was able to project at Manning, with conviction, that Allinite gospel which had exerted such an impact a decade earlier.

But the preacher who actually brought about Manning's conversion was the Reverend John Payzant, Alline's brother-in-law, who in 1786 had been ordained minister of the Horton and Cornwallis New Light Church. Payzant had been converted in 1775, at the same time as Alline and with Joseph Bailey and Thomas Handley Chipman, another Alline convert, frequently accompanied Henry Alline on his preaching tours. Some time in the middle of April, 1789, Payzant, forty-years old, a tanner by trade, preached a sermon that Manning would never forget. There was more than a little irony involved in this development. In 1776, Manning's father, Peter, had been found guilty of the murder of Payzant's step-father, Malachi Caigan, and had been hanged. In all likelihood, Alline's father William, who in 1776 was a member of the "Jury of the Sessions of the Peace" was involved in both the conviction of Manning and in his execution. Payzant spoke from an Old Testament "passage where the children of Israel came to the Waters... And could not drink... by reason of their bitterness." According to Manning, Payzant "spoke with so much vision in opening the Scripture to my understanding that I was struck with Astonishment — I can't Say that the fear of Hell or the Misery of the damned terryfd me much at this time." "The World," for Manning, "wore a different aspect" and there was, for the first time, no desire to neutralize religiosity with "frolicking." Instead, Manning resolved to

40

find salvation. A concerned Christian neighbour, seeing how agitated his young friend was, gave Manning one of Alline's hymns which, as far as Manning was concerned, "Set forth my condition as it really was." The six verses eloquently captured the young farmer's spiritual predicament.

O hardened, hardened heart of mine
That loads me with distress
And doth like Iron fetters bind
My Soul from happiness.

O was there ever wretched on Earth
In such a State as I
Exposed to everlasting death
Unwilling yet to fly

Mount Sinai's Thunders doth not wake
Me from this Stupid frame
Nor can the love of Jesus brake
My Soul into a flame

The greatest grief that I indure
Or trials that I find
Is that I am destressed no more
With this unfeeling mind

I mourn because I cannot mourn
And grieve because not grieved
I think I long from sin to turn
Yet fear I am deceived

Great God Receive me as I am
And let me See thy face
And all my heart and soul inflame
With thy Redeeming grace

Manning had no trouble appropriating the first five verses of Alline's hymn as a description of his own spiritual state. But the last verse he noted "I could not Say because I know I was not willing to be converted." That evening, Manning tried to sleep, but the fear of Hell kept him awake and

41

for three days, he was morbidly melancholy. At dinner, at the end of this period, Manning "had such a sense of the State of my Soul was in" that he dropped his "knife and fork and left the house immediately." The giant of a man, six foot four inches tall, made his way to the nearby woods, with the determination never to return until he had finally been redeemed. He tramped about 1000 yards into the forest and knelt down to pray. "In the agony of my soul" the only prayer that he could utter were the six words "Lord have mercy upon my Soul." At that precise moment, Manning felt not only "a Hell in my own Breast Sufficient to torment me to all Eternity" but also a realization that God could and would save him. Yet conversion did not come but rather further intense conviction, disorientation, and a morbid fear of death engulfed him.

Then on April 26, 1789, after Payzant's sermon and the exhortation of a number of young friends, which exhortation was specifically aimed at Manning, his "heart was broken." He "could not contain" himself and "wept aloud, and came to a decision to seek the Lord." Manning declared, for all to hear, "I am determined, if I am lost at last — I am determined to go to hell begging for mercy." But the "New Birth" still evaded Manning who evidently for at least a day "endured much horror of mind." He clearly saw the "justice of the Almighty in my eternal condemnation;" this was, he realized, "a most astonishing change having taken place in my view of that justice." "It appeared" to him "that I could not but love it, even though it [justice] proved by eternal damnation." Such a realization "was overwhelming", and eventually produced in Manning a profound disorientation, so profound, that he "was lost for a season to time-things." In other words, he lost consciousness. After he "came to my recollection", the Almighty and "all creatures appeared different to me from what they ever did before" and, moreover, an "indescribable glory appeared in every thing." "As near as I can recall," he later wrote, his New Birth occurred on April 27.

But it took Manning approximately a month to be assured of his salvation. On May 25, at a special thanksgiving service for the recovery of George III, Manning was able to jettison his "melancholy bordering on despair" and replace it

42

with "a great solemnity on my spirits" and a great concern for the spiritual welfare of all the unredeemed as well as a remarkable love for his fellow Christians. For example, when Manning even thought about Harris Harding, he "immediately broke into a flood of tears and cried aloud." Manning felt an even more powerful emotional attachment to "an old christian man that I had been acquainted with before" and this sense of "nearness" drove him to cry "out louder still." From the specific, in terms of relationships, Manning moved to the general and then to the Almighty. His

> mind now turned upon the christians in general, and love kept increasing. My mind turned upon God; — an inquiry arose in my breast, whether it could be possible that God would be infinitely condescending, or could be possessed of such a nature as to have mercy upon me. I immediately discovered, that it was possible. At this discovery my whole soul was set on fire.

Manning felt, as Alline had two decades earlier, that his "soul was wrapt up in God's eternal love" and he cried out in joyous praise. Those who were riding with him heard the yells and immediately wondered what was wrong with their companion. The ever dependable Joseph Bailey rode up and asked "Edward, what is the matter?" Manning replied "O, Mr. Bailey, my soul is melted with love to God." Not having the "strength to sit up" on his saddle, Manning "leaned upon [his] horse's neck" as did Bailey who, in typical New Light fashion, was "rejoicing and praising the Lord." Manning was "intensely filled with supreme love to God," seeing "his glory in every thing." "It was not," he observed "a confidence of my own safety, nor merely a certainty of my own individual interest in his love that caused me to rejoice; but the glory and harmony of his perfections overcome me, and a satisfactory belief in my personal interest in his mercy followed as a consequence." In this manner, he "obtained liberty to [his] poor imprisoned soul" and, as might have been expected, his "happiness was unspeakable" and, as he put it, "full of glory."

Soon after what he called "this memorable day," Manning became a member of Payzant's New Light Church.

His "happiness" as a member of the church, however, was "greatly interrupted by an almost continual impression" that he "must engage in preaching the gospel". This "impression" experience was common among the New Lights. Manning was first encouraged to pray in public and then to exhort and did so in Falmouth, Windsor, Newport, Horton and Cornwallis; praying and exhorting in public only whetted his appetite further for preaching. And in September, 1789, he resolved to accompany Thomas Handley Chipman "and one or two young men to Chester;" Manning's preaching career had begun — a good distance from his home in Falmouth.[98]

Chipman and Payzant pointed Manning in one direction — what they regarded as the Allinite — New Light way — with its emphasis on traditional Evangelical tenets, and what Alline once called "true zeal." By 1789 these two men had abandoned all of Alline's heterodoxy. Harris Harding, who emphatically had not, and some of his young Falmouth-Cornwallis contemporaries, pointed Manning in quite a different direction — by stressing Alline's mysticism, his emotionalism, his indifference to Church polity, and his emphasis on the perseverence of the truly converted. But according to Alline, it should be stressed, salvation did not depend on any "act of man," as Arminianism suggested, or on "any decree of God", as Calvinism argued. Rather salvation, in its essence, was "the union ⸴f the inner man to" and "the turning of the inmost soul after God."[99] For Alline, conversion was simply:

> Christ's changing and taking Possession of the inmost Soul which is, at the time of the Change, completely sanctified. And now to show the Reason why the Man thus converted is not wholly sanctified, or without Sin, I will proceed; Man in his fallen State...consists of Body, Soul, and Spirit: viz, an animal, or elemental Body; a spiritual and immortal Body; and an immortal Mind: And at the hour of Conversion the Son of God takes possession of the inmost Soul, or immortal Mind, but leaveth the fallen immortal Body in its fallen State still.[100]

As long as one lived on earth, there would be, as Alline himself had experienced, an often bitter struggle between the sanctified "inmost Soul" and the "fallen immortal Body." "That which is born of God cannot sin" Alline contended; thus, almost despite himself, Alline reintroduced the "old Calvinistic doctrine of the perseverance of the Saints," but based it upon the "ravishing of the soul by Christ" and not upon what the *Westminster Confession* referred to as "the immutability of the Decree of Election."[101]

Alline, it should be noted, carefully balanced his stress on "perseverance" with what has been called a powerful "asceticism and bodily mortification worthy of the most austere monasticism."[102] In *Two Mites*, for example, Alline maintained that "True redemption is raising the desires and life of the inner man out of this miserable, sinful, and bestial world, and turning it to Christ, from whence it is fallen."[103] And later, in *The Anti-Traditionalist* he contended that it was necessary for the Christian to "Turn from all, Deny all: Leave all." He went on:

> I do not mean the outward and criminal Acts of Idolatry and Debauchery only: but any and every Thing in the Creature that in the least Degree amuses the Mind or leads the Choice from God. For even the most simple Enjoyments and Pleasures of Life will keep the Choice in Action, and therefore the Creature amused from God, and consequently sinking deeper and deeper in its fallen and irrecoverable State. Nor will you ever return to be redeemed until every Idol, Joy, Hope, or Amusement so fails you that you are wholly starved out, and there is not only a Famine, but a mighty Famine in all created Good.[104]

Carefully blended, Alline's perseverance and asceticism produced "true zeal";[105] the former, without the latter, led to Antinomianism. This was apparently the case in the Cumberland region of Nova Scotia in 1782 and it was certainly the case in the Horton-Cornwallis area during the years immediately following the "Reformation" of 1789.

William Black, the Nova Scotia Methodist leader, on

first meeting Henry Alline in the spring of 1780, described the Falmouth preacher as being "very zealous in the cause." "He laboured fervently, and at his coming," to Cumberland, Black stressed, "was made a great blessing to many."[106] By the time Black visited Falmouth, in June 1782, their earlier warm friendship had been replaced by a mutual feeling of bitter recrimination, hostility and ill-will. According to Black, Alline and his associates, men like Bailey, Chipman and Payzant, had maintained that the Methodist preacher "was no minister of Jesus Christ, soon after, he was no christian; and in a little while, a down-right minister of Anti-christ."[107] Black was also very concerned with what he perceived to be the pernicious growth of Alline's Antinomian-mystical gospel. In November, 1782, an obviously distraught Black noted in his journal:

> I rode over to *Tantramar*, where I was sorely grieved to find *Mysticism* and the foulest *Antinomianism*, spreading like fire; and its deadly fruits already growing up on every side. The people were informed publickly, *That they had nothing to do with God's law: that David was still a man after God's own heart; when wallowing in adultery, and murder: that his soul never sinned all that time, but only his body.* Mr. Alline himself told several persons one day that *a believer is like a nut, thrown into the mud, which may dirty the shell, but not the kernel.* That is, we may get drunk, or commit adultery, without the smallest defilement, etc. etc.[108]

Three years later, on May 22, 1785, Freeborn Garrettson had confronted in Nova Scotia what he referred to as "a people...call'd Allinites." "In General," he pointed out "they are as deluded a people as ever I saw." He went on in his journal:

> They are most all Speakers in Publick. I was conversing with one of their head Speaker (in Cornwallis). She told me she thought death would Slay more Sins for her than ever was before. And as for Sin, said she, it Can not hurt one. No Not Adultery, Murder, Swearing, drunkenness, nor no other Sin Can break yet Union

between me and Christ. They have judged and passed sentence on me, as no Christian, Nor Call'd to Preach.[109]

Moreover, the "Allinites" believed that they could "tell whether a person is a Christian at first sight" and they were absolutely "sure of heaven as if they were already there, for sin cannot hurt them."[110]

Two Anglican ministers, the Reverend Jacob Bailey and Bishop Charles Inglis also commented on what they regarded as being the peculiar heretical views of some of Alline's disciples and of many New Lights. On May 25, 1789, the often acerbic Bailey wrote from Annapolis Royal that the New Light itinerants, were creating "great confusion among the lower people" and were "of inconceivable damage to a new country, by drawing multitudes almost every day in the week, at this busy season, to attend to their desultory and absurd vociferations." Bailey went on:

> These preachers, however, agree in rejecting the literal sense of the Holy Scriptures, and the Christian Ordinances. Their dependence is upon certain violent emotions, and they discourage industry, charity, and every social virtue, affirming that the most abandoned sinners are nearer to the Kingdom of heaven than people of a sober, honest and religious deportment, for such, they alledge, are in danger of depending upon their own righteousness.[111]

Bishop Inglis endorsed Bailey's description and embellished it significantly and in the process underscored the considerable influence that Alline's theology had on the Evangelical mind a decade after his death. The New Lights, as far as Inglis was concerned, were "rigid Predestinarians" who believed "that all mankind were present, and actually sinned with our primitive parents." He continued:

> After conversion they are not answerable for any sins they commit, since it is the flesh and not the spirit which offends....Many of them deny the resurrection, a future judgement, heaven and hell, though the Elect are to be

47

happy and the Reprobates miserable after death. Their discipline is democratic. The right of ordination, dismission etc. lies entirely with the Brethren.[112]

A decade later, Joshua Marsden, a Methodist missionary in the Cumberland region noted that Alline's Antinomian legacy was still being "industriously propogated...by some new-light preachers." These men stressed four points:

> 1st. "That a believer, though he sin ever so much is still pure; — God sees no sin in Israel."
> 2nd. "That the body of a believer only sins, and not the soul; as a nut thrown into the mud is only soiled in the shell, and not the kernel."
> 3rd. "That the body of a believer may get intoxicated and commit whoredom, but not the soul; that being spiritual is not affected by such fleshly lusts."
> 4th. "That a sheep though he render himself filthy by going into the mud, and black, by rubbing against the stumps of burned trees, is a sheep still, as nobody ever heard of a sheep becoming a goat."[113]

The evidence suggests that some of Alline's followers — even during his life-time — probably spun his New Light gospel in the direction of Antinomianism. Having experienced the "ravishing of the Spirit" and the "rapture of the New Birth," these men and women could not imagine how they could lose their salvation. And their confidence and certainty of redemption was such that they became increasingly indifferent to sin and to contemporary moral standards. Most of Alline's followers, of course, were not Antinomians. But some were, for varying lengths of time, especially in the New Light heartland area of Cornwallis and Falmouth and in Cumberland and along the St. John River Valley. The most significant manifestation of New Light Antinomianism probably occurred in 1791 in the Cornwallis area. At the core of the movement were to be found Harris Harding, Edward Manning and his brother James and Joseph Dimock as well as the influential teacher Thomas Bennett and Lydia Randall.[114]

For at least one outside observer, Freeborn Garrettson, Mrs. Randall was evidently "their head speaker"[115] and according to the Reverend John Payzant, an insider, she orchestrated in May 1791 the denunciation of "all the orders of the church."[116] As far as other contemporaries were concerned, Harris Harding was the principal actor in the so-called New Dispensation movement.

Harding was born in Horton, Nova Scotia, on October 10, 1761, of Yankee planter stock.[117] Soon after his birth, his parents, like many other Nova Scotia Yankees, decided to return to Connecticut. During the early part of the American Revolutionary War, though only a teenager, Harding supported the Patriot side. He was arrested for a brief time by the British and imprisoned in a man-of-war. In 1783, at the age of twenty-two, and despite his Patriot wartime activities, Harding returned to the Horton region where he became a school teacher. Though "a stranger to experimental religion" and "famous for his love of fun and frolic,"[118] Harding began to attend New Light services conducted by Payzant and Thomas Handley Chipman, the only ordained New Light preacher in Nova Scotia — after Alline left the province in August 1783. It should be noted that Harding, despite the fact that he became Alline's most enthusiastic advocate, never met the Falmouth preacher.

Harding not only attended New Light services, he also, in 1785, according to his sister, "was much taken up with the Methodists," especially Freeborn Garrettson. Garrettson, according to Harding's sister, had stressed that it was necessary for the individual to make "strenuous efforts in seeking the Lord." "Men must do their part," he declared "and God would do his." Harding, as a result, attempted *to work hard* for salvation instead of *believing heartily* for it." He prayed no fewer than twelve times a day and he fasted every Friday, but despite this he could not "find his way into the heavenly kingdom." Instead of being part of "the great regenerating process," he found himself "plunged into despair."[119] When there appeared to be no hope, Thomas Handley Chipman nudged him in the New Light direction.

One "forenoon" in 1785, on his way to his school house,

49

Harding "seemed all at once to obtain a view of Jesus." He realized that Methodist "good works could not save him," but only his surrendering himself "to the Saviour, just as he was, to be saved 'freely by his grace,' and by that grace alone." When he arrived at his school "Joy and love transported his soul." His sister recalled that:

> He forgot the children of his charge. Eternal glory was all before him, and he stood bathed in a flood of tears. His countenance was so altered, that the children gathered around him, they likewise in tears, and thought him dying. Truly there he began to live. When he came to his recollection he thought, by the sun on the window, that he must have been standing on one spot nearly an hour.[120]

Like Alline, Harding had been "converted in a rapture" and "ever after he sought to live in a rapture" and he "judged...his religious condition" and that of others by the intensity of their conversion experience.[121] Having had a traumatic conversion, Harding, like Alline, expected that everyone else should share the same emotional ecstacy and "the ravishing of the soul" which he had experienced. Also like Alline, and most of his disciples, Harding "placed great reliance on impressions, and often regarded them as direct intimations of the divine will, which it was his duty to obey."[122] For example, in 1790, while at Horton, Harding had a memorable dream "which much affected, and made a singular impression on my mind." "I dreamed," Harding wrote,

> I was on board a small sailboat, with deacon Cleaveland, and a number of my dear Christian friends at Horton. Methought I stood upon the gunwale of the boat, having a spear in my hand. The sun shone with peculiar brightness. We were running before a pleasant breeze, at a little distance from a delightful shore. The water also was clear as crystal, and I could see the white and shining fishes at the bottom, while I was continually catching them with the spear. My friends, I thought, were sitting speaking of Christ's love to a

fallen world, their cheeks bathed with tears, and apparently filled with peace and joy. I thought the deacon said to me, 'You catch every fish you strike.' I replied, 'I miss none.' Methought I fished until I had got the boat filled and then had a delicious feast with my fellow-disciples. I awoke in a joyful frame. I visited Yarmouth soon after.[123]

The dream, according to Harding, was God's means of directing him to Yarmouth "to fish for men."

Soon after his conversion, Harding accompanied Payzant, in March 1786, to Chester where Harding exhorted after Payzant preached. Harding was obviously being tutored by Payzant and he was also being tested in the field. Payzant was somewhat concerned about the spiritual welfare of his young protege, who had wandered off reported his concerned mentor "with some of old acquaintance...he had gone with a bad crew."[124] Payzant observed in his journal that "I saw what a danger he was in if he gave way to the enemy and Satan like a Roving Lion seeking whom he may devour."[125]

But Harding was not devoured — at least at this early stage of his preaching and exhorting career. He soon began to itinerate on his own in 1789, journeying to Onslow, Yarmouth and Amherst in 1790 and back to Liverpool in 1791 and on to Shelburne, Barrington, Argyle, and Yarmouth. On his extensive travels, Harding did everything in his power to emulate Henry Alline. He tried to look like Alline — according to one contemporary observer "his form was slender, frail, and even ghostly."[126] Harding, morever, preached Alline's gospel,[127] regarding it "as being the mind of God" and virtually "infallible."[128] As far as Simeon Perkins was concerned — and he had often heard Alline — Harding's "Doctrines are much the same as was propogated by Mr. Alline."[129] What Perkins detested was Harding's "Extravagant gestures and wild motions of his Body and hands etc." which to the Liverpool merchant was "very disgusting, and the pain he seems to be in Breath, is distressing."[130]

Not only did Harding try to cultivate Alline's preaching style and physical image — he even gave the impression at times that he, too, was dying from consumption — but he also used many of Alline's evangelistic techniques and he visited those areas where Alline had been particularly successful. Harding, for example, made good use of Alline's hymns, regarding them as being especially effective with children and young people. And he even attempted to use Alline's imagery and his language and he wrote many letters to his friends in Horton and Cornwallis, hoping that these letters would eventually be published — thus making him a worthy follower of Alline. In a typical letter written on May 14, 1789, Harding observed from Annapolis Royal:

> The mighty God of Jeshurun has girded his sword upon his thigh, and is riding in the flaming chariot of Israel like a glorious Conqueror: his majesty and power are seen amongst the inhabitants of Annapolis. Some have of late felt his dying groans reach their despairing souls....I see again the immortal shore that flows with milk and honey.[131]

Harding was determined, as he graphically expressed it in 1791, to "go in the name of brother Alline's God."[132] When asked once about the publication of his letters "to the Christians" he could only answer — as he put it — "with dear dear brother Alline, God forbid I should write or speak anything but what I would publish, if possible, over the four quarters of the globe."[133] From the declining Loyalist centre of Shelburne he wrote on August 25, 1791, to Thaddeus Harris of Cornwallis:

> O brother, stand in that gospel that Henry Alline once proclaimed to your soul, and others in Cornwallis. That is the gospel that is the life of my soul, and if I am called to it will not only suffer for, but seal with my blood.[134]

Two days later Harding was planning to follow Alline to New England. "Some times I can see a man stand and call," he asserted "Come over and help us." "I assuredly believe God has called me to preach the gospel" he declared "on the other side of the flood."[135] But despite his "call", and despite his obsession with following in Alline's footsteps, Harding never made his way to New England. There is some evidence to suggest that he pulled back from going because of the New Dispensation controversy which engulfed the Cornwallis-Horton region in the summer of 1791. Some of his closest friends and associates were involved and he empathized with their concerns and aspirations; he was not eager to leave them at their moment of need. Nor was he keen to abandon the New Light movement at the precise moment that it was being challenged from within and vociferously attacked from without by its myriad of enemies.

Joseph Dimock was also absent from the Horton-Cornwallis region when the New Dispensation movement took organizational form and ideological shape. He was in Annapolis County labouring with Chipman and involved in "a blessed revival of religion, which extended from Digby Gut up to Aylesford". Dimock was born in Newport, Nova Scotia, on December 11, 1768.[136] His father was an active Baptist layman and from his early youth Joseph Dimock received a well grounded, basic, Biblical education from a distinctly Baptist perspective. At the age of seventeen, on July 17, 1785, he was "born again" when "God the Spirit was pleased to strike my soul with terrors and amazement, so that I could find no rest until I was by the Spirit presented with the Saviour, his freeness and all-sufficiency to save all that come to him.[137] In this manner, the seventeen-year old Dimock found his salvation.

Dimock possessed a "naturally affectionate disposition" and he was, his contemporaries agreed, one of the most amiable of men."[138] His associates often compared him "to the Apostle John, for his loving temper and gentleness of deportment."[139] "There was no lordliness of spirit in him," it was stressed, "no arrogant assumptions — no demand for servile attention and homage."[140] Dimock was an excellent example for many of his contemporaries of a saintly man who had humbled himself only to be exalted by the Almighty.

Dimock was baptized at Horton on May 6, 1787 and joined the Baptist Church there. He first exhorted in his immediate vicinity and then in the spring of 1790 began to preach. Dimock visited Chester in April and then again in August and later in the year he made his way to Onslow where

53

a revival was already underway. In December he wrote to a friend:

> I sometimes stand and look on the young christians, particularly children that cry "Hosanna to the son of David" till it melts my heart and eyes into tears of joy. O dear brother, rejoice with me. Methinks you are ready to join with me and say, "I thank thee, O Father, Lord of heaven and earth, because thou hast hid these things from the wise and prudent, and hast revealed them onto babes. Even so, Father, for so it seemed good in thy sight." O dear brother, pray for me, that utterance may be given me, and that I may be kept at the feet of Jesus.[141]

By the early summer of 1791, Dimock was in the Annapolis region in the midst of yet another revival. He wrote in August 20, 1791.

> Many meetings continue till almost midnight — sinners crying aloud for mercy — christians bowels yearing over poor souls on the brink of eternal ruin. Some meetings have continued all night; and O, the heavy, heart-rendering cries would answer each other, enough to pierce the stoutest heart? Nothing can I compare it to but that day when the last trump shall sound. Saints rejoice not much, for their hearts bleed over poor sinners. If you go out here just after dark, you will hear some lamenting themselves, on account of their dreadful hardened state; others mourning for others, till tears interrupt them, as though they would bring heaven down to men by groans unutterable.[142]

In September, Dimock's mind "being much exercised" about visiting the South shore of Nova Scotia, he crossed over to Digby and eventually made his way to the Acadian communties on St. Mary's Bay. After returning to Newport, he proclaimed "the Gospel with much affection and fervor in various parts of the province."[143] until September 10, 1793 when he was ordained minister of the Chester New Light Church. He would remain a pastor of this church, which

54

eventually became a Baptist Church, until his death at the age of 79, in 1846. At his funeral service, Dimock was with good reason described as a "good...and wise man...whose excellent disposition, engaging manners, integrity of heart, humility, and deep-toned piety, peculiarly fitted him for the work for which alone he seemed to live, and in the prosecution of which he died."[144]

James Manning did not possess Dimock's amiable disposition, nor did he share the Chester minister's evangelistic zeal and his spiritual maturity. James Manning always found himself in his younger brother's shadow — and never succeeded in being anything other than a competent, if mercurial, minister of the gospel. James Manning was born in 1764 in Falmouth and sometime in his late teens Alline's "preaching was the means of his awakening but the conviction he then experienced did not issue in conversion."[145] Like his brother, he was caught up in the revival of 1789 and was converted at approximately the same time. He almost immediately became a member of Payzant's church and was, with his brother Edward, apparently in the Cornwallis-Horton area throughout 1791. It was not until the following year that James began his "itinerating labours" mostly in New Brunswick and Maine. In 1798, after his baptism, he was ordained pastor of the Baptist church located at Lower Granville. He died in 1818.

Though not a distinguished preacher or overly effective minister of the gospel, Manning's greatest strength during his early years was manifested in "the simplicity and copiousness of his prayers." A close friend once observed:

> He took such a copious view of the glories of the Deity, that he seemed to sink himself into nothing before the eternal all — then he would appear to be swallowed up in the boundless treasures of grace, then he would bring before the throne, the cause of all saints and sinners in their varied circumstances. His chief excellency in prayer consisted in that holy intimacy and fervor, he evinced before the Almighty, as though he was speaking face to face."[146]

55

Manning was regarded by his associates as being "constitutionally of a melancholy temperament." During his last decade on earth, he suffered from acute despondency and "was of so modest and retiring a disposition that he seldom took part in the public enterprises."[147] Thus at the end of his life James was the polar opposite of his brother Edward who according to one critic stubbornly refused to "suffer his prerogative to be arrested from him" and who expected "that every sheaf should Bow to his Sheaf" and who stressed, morever, that he alone was "Sumbody" and all others were "less than nothing."[148] With good reason Edward was called the Pope of the Nova Scotia Calvinist Baptist Church.

VI

Edward and James Manning, together with Harris Harding and Joseph Dimock, were all intimate friends of Thomas Bennett who, in the late 1780s and early 1790s, was a schoolmaster in the Cornwallis area.[149] Bennett was a one-man clearing house for all news about the New Light revivals in Nova Scotia and New Brunswick during the 1785 to 1794 period. He received a steady stream of letters from the itinerant preachers and, morever, he was given the letters the preachers received from their converts and others. Bennett also itinerated for a time after his conversion, probably early in 1790. He took an active role in the New Dispensation movement but there is no available evidence suggesting that he was guilty of any act of immorality. In 1794 he moved to Liverpool where he married the daughter of John MacLeod and where he also became a successful merchant; he remained associated with Harris Harding, in particular, and when he died on February 19, 1800, his funeral was conducted by the Reverend John Payzant and the "Free masons walked as Mourners."[150]

Bennett obviously exerted a great influence on the young New Light itinerants; he seemed to possess a magnetic personality and probably because of this, together with his basic intelligence, he was regarded as a natural leader of men. But there was also another important leader — Lydia Randall. Randall, largely because of her spiritual gifts, had established herself as a key New Light a few years before. She had married

56

Green Randall in 1779 and with her husband became a member of the Cornwallis New Light Church. She may have been influenced by some Shaker beliefs as early as 1788 and this may help to explain why she was so determined in May 1791 to restore radical New Light faith and practice. The Reverend John Payzant described her role in the New Dispensation movement in the following manner:

> The Second Sabbath of May [1791] it was the turn to have the Church Meeting and Sacrament at Horton. Mrs. R[andall] rose against all the orders of the church and [said] that they were but outward forms and contrary to the Spirit of God. These novelties in the Church caused many to follow the same examples, which made much troble in the Church....She told me that she had seen by the Spirit of God, that Baptism and the Lord Supper, with all the Disciples, of the Church was contrary to the Spirit of God and his Gospel, and that Marriage was from the Divel. That she was determined to live sapate [separate] from her Husband, for it was as much sin for her to have children by him as by any other man and she saith that there were many that would follow her in it, that there were many young women that were converted, which she had as soon see them have children by any man; [than] to Marry.[151]

In reply, Payzant "told her that she was involving herself in an abstruse that she would find much defeculty to get out" and he "begged of her not to advance such sentiments for she had not well considered them for she would make herself an object of Rededule." Mrs. Randall quickly countered by contending that "her mind had gone farther on these things" than had Payzant's.[152]

By August, Payzant's Church was badly split; everything was in a state of utter confusion and support for what Payzant called these "fantastical notion[s]" quickly "spread from town to town and many adopted this new scheme."[153] The Church Covenant and Articles of Faith were denounced as being "not[h]ing but forms and wholly contrary to Religion."[154] The followers of Mrs. Randall stopped Payzant from serving communion. "They pretended" reported a distraught Payzant "that they were taugh[t] by the Spirit of God to go beyond all order, that they had great discoveries beyond whatever was known before, eather by the premitive Christeans."[155] Absolutely convinced of the fact that they were specially selected conduits for the Holy Spirit, and that they were divinely inspired, they manifested an extraordinary zealousness and enthusiasm for their so-called "New Dispensation" — their unique version of Christianity. They had gone beyond the New Testament; they had, moreover, moved beyond Alline's volatile mixture of Whitefieldian New Light orthodoxy and his mystical heterodoxy.

Fearing that the New Dispensationalists were planning to enlarge their influence by destroying his church at Granville, Thomas Handley Chipman, unlike Payzant proposed a quick counter offensive. He wanted all of the New Dispensationalist leaders expelled immediately from the existing New Light Churches. Thomas Handley Chipman was especially distressed when his father was finally forced out of Payzant's church by the New Dispensationalists. It was a move which Payzant was sure "made the breach wider, than it was before, for it broke up all order, at the Church meetings, which gave great strength to their Scismatical notions."[156]

In order to establish his authority, Payzant, sometime in 1792, decided to impose "Church Rules" on his disintergrating congregation. This move was vigorously opposed by James and Edward Manning who "came to the Church meeting, and begun to dispute, and condemn the Church Rules, and say that all orders were done away, and that the Bible was a dead letter, and they would preach without it and such like things."[157] It seemed clear to Payzant that Edward Manning, "in particular, was insinuating these Eronious Sentiments in young people minds.".[158] One of these young women gave what Payzant called "this fantastical notion" the name "new dispensation" and the movement continued its spread "from town to town and many adopted this new Sc[h]eme."[159] Thomas Bennett began "to burlesque the Church" and contended that "the Revd. Mr. Chipman"

58

was "a dead form" and that the New Dispensationalists "were the only lively Christeans."[160] Bennett, Mrs. Green Randall and the Mannings evidently attacked "1st Marriages 2nd all order 3ly the scriptures 4ly Ministers proving their doctrine by the Scri[p] tures".[161] They also, according to Payzant, maintained "that God had made the Elect; and the Divel had made the non Elect" and, moreover, many "gave away to carnal desire, so that their new plan took a contrary effect, for instead of living So holy as they preted [pretended] to, they were light and carnal."[162] New Dispensationalism had become a Nova Scotia and New Brunswick version of Antinomianism and as it lurched madly away from community behavioural norms, and Alline's pòsition, an understandable reaction began to set in.

At this critical juncture, Payzant decided to ask Thomas Handley Chipman to assist him "at the Church meeting and the Sacrement."[163] At the special meeting there were those who like Chipman proposed that all the New Dispensationalists be expelled from the Church especially "The Preachers...Harris Harding, James and Edward Manning, Joseph Dimock."[164] But Payzant and others opposed such a drastic move arguing that the four young men, in particular, were "ignorant in many points of Doctrine which they might afterward be convinced of."[165] Charity demanded forgiveness as did common sense and the realization that maturity would neutralize their strange and peculiar notions. As a result, there were no expulsions at this stage.

Church meeting followed church meeting as the New Dispensationalists began their counter offensive. They maintained that they alone accurately interpreted the Scripture since they alone "were lead by the Spirit of God and that their explanation of the Scriptures were all spiritual so that they were absolutely right."[166] There were endless discussions about the proper interpretation of certain key verses of scripture and the almost endless debate seemed to defuse the explosive issue. Payzant continued to oppose Thomas Handley Chipman's demand that the four "Preachers" of the New Dispensationalists be summarily expelled. Payzant's opposition continued despite the fact that

59

he realized his policy would lead to the permanent departure of Chipman's influential father from the church. Payzant hoped that "by gentle means" order and good sense and stability would return to his congregation.[167]

On October 6, 1792, the Cornwallis Church met and it was finally decided that its members "would stand by the Church Rules, and that no person should have [the] liberty, to vote, to speak, in Church meetings but those that held to her Rules."[168] At Falmouth, because of the strength of the New Dispensationalists and their continuing opposition to all "Rules", they "were denied...the ordinance." And in response, some asserted "that all the world would be Saved."

> Some said, that there was no such man as Christ; and all the Christ that there was, was what we felt in ourselves; and therefore why should they hold to Baptism, and the Supper....Others saith that the Divel made all Such as would be lost and that God made all them that would be saved. So that all that God made would go to him, and that all the Divel made would go to him, and these last sentiments they pretended to maintain from Serivture [Scripture] .[169]

The persistent struggle with his New Dispensation enemies both exhausted and depressed Payzant who in April 1793 jumped at the opportunity to minister to the Liverpool New Light Congregational Church. Two years later, Edward Manning was ordained as the minister of the Cornwallis New Light Church. By late 1793, it seems clear, the New Dispensation movement was on the decline, especially in the Horton-Cornwallis region. The Mannings and Joseph Dimock, and possibly Thomas Bennett, had been frightened and then appalled by the Antinomian excesses practised by some of their former associates. Moreover, the chaos and disorder which seemed endemic to the movement appeared to threaten seriously the already fragile underpinnings of Nova Scotia society. Short term ecstasy was one thing; permanent confusion and disorientation was quite a different matter.

It should be kept in mind that in 1791, Harding was thirty-one years old, Joseph Dimock was twenty-four, James

Manning, twenty-eight and Edward twenty-six. All were still unmarried and, the evidence suggests, physically attractive, full of energy, and convinced that they were divinely ordained instruments for the spiritual transformation not only of Nova Scotia and New Brunswick but also of Northern New England. Their preoccupation with itinerating helped considerably not only to extend the territorial boundaries of the 1789 "Reformation" but also to encourage the extraordinary growth of both the New Dispensation movement and what may be regarded as an energized New Light pietism. But by late 1793, the evidence suggests that the Mannings and Joseph Dimock had declared their independence of the increasingly Manichaen-oriented New Dispensationalists and had chosen, instead, to be at the cutting edge of a renewed and far more orthodox pietism. In other words, these men, reacting violently against Antinomian excesses they no longer could condone or control, returned to the Whitefieldian framework — but one which no longer emphasized — as it had — the importance of feelings and impressions. Harris Harding, however, continued to preach what Simeon Perkins called "the Antinomian doctrines"[170] — and he remained a principal actor in the movement until the concluding years of the eighteenth century. And there would be those in Nova Scotia who would argue that he remained sympathetic to the movement until his death in 1854. But these critics were wrong. Harding, in the nineteenth century, was not an advocate of New Dispensationalism. Rather, he continued to be an enthusiastic disciple of Henry Alline and what was frequently referred to as "Allinism."

After he had become the general factotum of the Nova Scotia Baptist Church and an ardent Calvinist and a vociferous critic of New Light enthusiasm, Edward Manning attempted to describe what he considered to be the heart of New Dispensationalism:

> Mr. Alline's lax observance of divine institutions fostered in the minds of his followers such ideas as these; that the ordinances are only circumstantials, outward matters, and mere non-essentials; that the

scriptures are not the only rule of faith and practice; and that no person is under any obligation to perform any external duty until god immediately impresses the mind so to do....Several began to question the propriety of having anything to do with external order or ordinances, and soon refused to commune with the church. ...As they had no rule to go by but their fancies, which they called "the Spirit of God," great irregularities ensued.[171]

Manning, who for the remainder of his life would be embarrassed by his close association in the 1790-2 period with the New Dispensationalists, had deftly cut to the heart of the movement's ideology. Here was a man who had played a key role in coaxing the movement into existence and who had, moreover, significantly affected its evolution. If any single person understood New Dispensationalism and its appeal, Edward Manning certainly did. As far as he was concerned, it was Alline's "lax observance of divine institutions" and his emphasis on the "Spirit of Liberty" and "individual illumination" which persuaded many of his followers to break out of the Radical Evangelical and New Light framework to enjoy what to many was regarded as "Quaker and Shaker" freedom. There was a deep desire to experiment, to shatter existing religious values, to reshape fundamentally Evangelical individualism, and to challenge frontally community norms. With the Spirit of God within them, having experienced the profound intensity and the rapture of the New Birth, having been ravished by the Almighty, anything seemed possible and permissible. Their sin had been cancelled out, once and for all, by the sacrifice of Christ, and sinning, whether in the flesh or the spirit, could not distance them from their Saviour. Instead of turning towards ascetic behaviour, as Alline had preached and practised, many New Dispensationalists, driven by the "Spirit of Liberty," and in order to test the viability of their New Birth and to flaunt their spiritual *hubris* at their neighbours, committed what Manning called "their extravagancies." Their "great irregularities" obviously served a number of interrelated purposes. They were the means

62

whereby one could both enjoy sin and appreciate salvation —
no insignificant accomplishment in any age. "Antinomian
excesses," moreover, enabled men and women to express freely
and creatively their innermost emotional and sexual desires
and drives at a time, and in an age, when such behaviour was
regarded as being sinfully aberrant.[172]

VII

It would be a serious mistake, however, to suppose that
all those individuals described by their critics as New
Dispensationalists were in fact guilty of gross Antinomian
excesses. Some were, but how many it is impossible to say. Far
more, the vast majority, inspired by the "Spirit of Liberty,"
were satisfied with questioning existing church rules and
regulations and with proposing a fundamental restructuring of
religious worship. This question of authority as well as this
actual assertion of independence was, it may be argued, a
revolutionary development. Societal values were challenged
frontally and found disconcertingly wanting. These people, in
many respects, were Allinites; they were regarded by their
enemies as disciples of the Falmouth preacher and proudly
perceived themselves in precisely the same manner. They were
carrying on his traditions in a colony which had abandoned the
principles undergirding the First Great Awakening.

During the second decade of the nineteenth century
what were then disparagingly referred to as the "old New
Lights" were still trying desperately to keep alive the essential
of Alline's gospel. These men and women were not then
regarded as Antinomian extremists; probably most never had
been. Rather, as one critic succinctly put it, they were "genuine
Christian[s]." "They had," he went on, "more experiences
than doctrine — more imagination than judgement — more
spiritualism than spirituality — more of the ideal than the
substantial."[173]

> They had no ordinances, no creed, no discipline. They
> paid little or nothing to support religion, either at home
> or abroad. To pay money for religion was with them
> one of the greatest abominations the sun ever shone

upon. But they believed in regeneration by the Spirit, in Christ as a Saviour, and in heaven and hell. But they were not uniform, or at all agreed in what they did believe. Their religion was all feeling. Every thing in the Bible, in the Old or New Testament, was but allegorical, and was what all Christians experience. Abel was nothing but the new spiritual life working in us; and his acceptable offering humility, love and faith, the sacrifices acceptable to God.[174]

According to the Reverend David Nutter "their notions about religion were...the most singular I had ever met with." Nutter was, he stressed, "exceedingly amused, not to say entertained, to hear them explain Scripture history, and Scripture characters; to notice how flexible and versatile the imagination of one can become by use and practice."[175] But despite this biting criticism, Nutter still regarded these disciples of Alline as "genuine Christian[s]."[176] They were "old New Lights" indeed and because of the challenge they posed to the burgeoning Baptist Church in Nova Scotia, they were unceremoniously pushed into a dark corner of oblivion. The New Lights were an embarrassing reminder of what so many Nova Scotia Calvinist Baptists had once been and there was a deep psychological need apparently for key Calvinist Baptist leaders to try to wipe the collective memory free of Alline's peculiar views. But in the process not only was Alline's heterodoxy excised from the Nova Scotia Calvinist Baptist mind but also much of his "Radical Evangelicalism." Thus, in their desperate search for respectability and order, the Nova Scotia Baptist leadership jettisoned much of the emotionalism and Evangelical spirituality which was at the heart of Alline's message. The result, in a particularly ironic twist of fate, was that the Baptists, in many respects, appropriated much of the theological perspective of eighteenth century Calvinist Congregationalism. There would, therefore, be some truth in the contention that the views of Jonathan Scott were as much an influence on evolving 19th-century Nova Scotia Baptist development as were those of Henry Alline. Scott's *A Brief View* had triumphed over Alline's *Two Mites* — after all.[177] Or

64

had it? On one level, it triumphed — at the level of leadership — among men like Edward Manning, for example. But at the grass roots level, Alline's influence continued to be of considerable importance. As Esther Clark Wright has correctly observed, too little has been written — in the existing sparse literature — about the significant "work of the laymen in maintaining the Baptist Churches." "The competency of the individual in religion" she has asserted, "make it possible to carry on without prophet, priest, or king — or even an ordained Baptist minister."[178] In many regions of Nova Scotia and New Brunswick, concerned lay people, many of whom were familiar with the Allinite traditions and its New Light manifestations, stubbornly resisted the seeming inexorable flow of the Baptist Calvinist mainstream.

If any one individual was responsible for the significant downplaying of the New Light influence in the Maritime Baptist tradition, it was Edward Manning. Reacting violently against his own New Light Free Will past Manning did everything in his power to ensure that the New Light legacy would atrophy into dark oblivion. Manning was haunted by his Allinite past and determined that the painful lesson he had earned in the 1790s would become his denomination's major ideological construct. Morever, he accurately linked the remarkable growth of the Free Will Baptists in Nova Scotia and New Brunswick with what he called "Allinism" which he argued made people "more confounded than comforted!" Throughout the first half of the nineteenth century until his death in 1851, Manning did everything in his power to encourage his Baptist Church to define its separate identity by behaving in a radically different manner from the Allinite Free Will Baptist enthusiasts. Manning did not want to abandon his revised version of the Whitefieldian paradigm; what he wished to do was to get rid of what he regarded as New Light excess and "extravagancy." Some might argue that this response was merely the working out of what Freud once called the "narcissism of small differences." Others would argue, perhaps more persuasively, that Manning and the Baptist "ministerial elite" remained obsessed with respectability and were eager to sacrifice an integral part of their rich historical tradition in order to become a respectable part of the Maritime Protestant consensus. They had overreacted quite understandably to New Dispensationalism by exaggerating, among other things, its appeal. Moreover, they had underestimated the broadly based popular support for Henry Alline's brand of New Light Radical Evangelicalism that the following New Light Letters and Spiritual Songs convincingly display.

New Dispensationalism, it should be stressed was, within the Radical Evangelical tradition, an abberation. And as an aberration it underlines the importance of the New Light legacy to Nova Scotia religious life. It should not be the prism through which the total Evangelical experience in late eighteenth century Nova Scotia must be viewed. Rather, as was the case at the same time in New England with a variety of fringe sects,[179] New Dispensationalism showed how elastic the parameters of the New Light movement actually were and how volatile this spiritual mixture was, in both theory and practice.

Chapter II

The New Light

Letters

and

Spiritual Songs

Henry Alline left behind him in Nova Scotia both a rich oral tradition and also a remarkable written record. During a period of less than three years from 1781 to 1783 he had published two major books, the 340-page *Two Mites, on Some of the most important and much disputed Points of Divinity, etc.* and the 74-page *The Anti-Traditionalist*, together with three sermons, and a slim volume of twenty-two hymns. It is also known that Alline carried with him to New England not only all of his published work but also in manuscript form "a number of hymns" which he had prepared to "be published"[180] as well as his journal written in a form of shorthand. Alline, the Reverend David McClure observed in 1784, had only "begun to draw off the journal of his life in a legible hand," and "had proceeded but a little way in it."[181]

Alline's hymns, all 487 of them, were published in Boston in 1786 in the 381-page *Hymns and Spiritual Songs.* His *Life and Journal*, however, was not published until 1806. But there is considerable evidence to suggest that as early as 1789, Alline's *Life and Journal* together with many of his hymns and specific poetic segments from *The Anti-Traditionalist* and at least one of his printed sermons were being circulated in manuscript form in Nova Scotia.[182] This manuscript material was apparently often passed from family to family, read and recopied, and then passed along again.

Some of Alline's letters, furthermore, were widely circulated in manuscript form as his converts enthusiastically appropriated New Testament practice regarding his letters as being as inspired as those written by Paul some 1800 years earlier. Alline was widely perceived as someone "favoured with extraordinary revelations and commissions from heaven."[183] And all of his writing, whether his *Journal*, his treatises, his poetry or his hymns and spiritual songs took upon themselves a special sacred quality.

There is no evidence, it should be stressed, concerning the existence of any popular demand for Alline's printed books or sermons. It seems that his followers in Nova Scotia were quite satisfied with the available manuscript sources as well as the rich oral culture which conveyed to them the essence of his message. They found, especially in his manuscript *Journal* and

Hymns and Spiritual Songs, all that they needed to experience the New Light ecstacy of Alline's theology.

Henry Alline had obviously established for Nova Scotia Radical Evangelicals — or New Lights — not only a popular theology but also a pattern for religious behaviour and worship. Special emphasis was placed upon experiencing a "God and Christ within" often by manifesting an "abundance of vociferous demonstrations without."[184] Intense spiritual feeling and rapture was both encouraged and demanded as Alline's followers, almost passionately, applied his paradigm of the "New Birth." They also tried to emulate his Evangelical style — by writing their own hymns and spiritual songs, by writing letters to one another which also would be read in New Testament fashion in their various churches and meeting houses, and by writing their own journals. Some, moreover, consciously endeavoured to transform themselves in a physical sense into Allines; they attempted to look like him, and respond to events and personalities as he had done as recorded in his journal and in the oral culture of late eighteenth century Nova Scotia.

Alline's New Light followers, during the years immediately following his death, circulated among themselves manuscript copies of his journal, his hymns and spiritual songs, some poetic segments from his other writings, and some of his letters. They also circulated some of their own letters — which may be accurately called the "New Light letters" — together with some of their own hymns. These letters and hymns, together with four of Alline's letters and scores of his "spiritual songs" are to be found in a rather fragile manuscript volume, eight inches long, five inches wide, and one and a quarter inches thick, encased in a fine leather binding. The volume is located in the Baptist Historical Collection, in the Acadia University Archives, Wolfville, Nova Scotia, and is entitled "Personal letters of Henry Alline, Joseph Dimock, Harris Harding, Edward Manning and others, dated from 1778 to 1793." There are now 376-pages, some may have been lost over the years, 184 consisting of letters, 192 of hymns, spiritual songs, and poetry.

Most of the hymns and spiritual songs were authored

by Alline or by Isaac Watts. There are, in fact, forty-six of Alline's hymns to be found in this manuscript — out of over 500 that he composed. All forty-six were published in the 1786 Boston version of Alline's *Hymns and Spiritual Songs* and none in his earlier Halifax volume. And, moreover, thirty-one of the forty-six hymns, came from the last two sections of Alline's volume — sections dealing with "the joys and trials of the soul" and "infinite wonders, transporting views and christian travels." The other fifteen hymns, it should be stressed, though perhaps not as personal or as "spiritual," were nevertheless concerned with what Alline called the "gospel invitation and a free salvation."

These forty-six hymns, the evidence suggests,[185] were particularly popular ones and were widely used in Nova Scotia and New Brunswick not only in the immediate post-Alline period but throughout the nineteenth century and beyond. This collection of forty-six, it may be argued, is extremely important because, among other things, it shows which of Alline's many hymns his followers actually sang. It is one thing to list all of Alline's hymns and spiritual songs; it is quite a different thing to examine a selection of less than ten percent of them — carefully chosen by his contemporaries. These hymns, it seems clear, provided at the popular level what may be regarded as the parameters of New Light Evangelical religious culture. They are included in this collection not only for this reason but also because of their intrinsic value and their influence on New Light hymnody in the post-Revolution period.

In the 376-page volume there are also a few hymns and spiritual songs written by Alline's disciples which have never been published. Of greater consequence is the collection of almost 90 New Light letters, probably the richest available source of primary documentation concerning the nature of popular Evangelicalism in Nova Scotia in the late eighteenth and early nineteenth centuries. The New Light letters and spiritual songs provide the best available reservoir of written material dealing with religion from what has been called "the bottom-up", from 1785 to 1820, for any group of Christians anywhere in North America. They deserve publication as

70

important historical documents which cast penetrating light not only on a neglected aspect of popular religion in late eighteenth century Nova Scotia and New Brunswick but also on the influence of Henry Alline's legacy on the evolving Radical Evangelical movement in the colonies. But they also merit publication for their own intrinsic mystical quality; they display, among other things, an ecstatic awareness of the divine. "New Light" Christianity is a religion of the heart not the head, and in many respects this central reality is both its great strength and its great weakness. It is also a critically important strain within the Nova Scotia and the New Brunswick Baptist tradition. It is a strain which was unceremoniously pushed to the periphery of the Baptist experience by the nineteenth century moulders of the tradition and by their twentieth century supporters.

The 376-page manuscript volume which is now to be found at Acadia University was first extensively used by the Baptist historian and President of Acadia, the Reverend J.M. Cramp, in a series of articles published in 1860 in the *Christian Messenger*. On April 11, 1860, Cramp informed his readers that "From a collection of letters in the possession of brother Bennett of Windsor, who has kindly placed the whole in my hands for the purposes of this history I take the following extracts." He then copied sections from a variety of letters written by Harris Harding stressing, in an editorial aside, "the fervour of the good man's style and manner, and the peculiar use which he mades of the language of the writers of the Old Testament."

Six years earlier, in 1854, the Reverend John Davis, who was preparing a biography of Harris Harding, was "furnished" by Mr. Thomas John Bennett, "residing at Windsor," with the "New Light" volume. Cramp used the source which his colleague had obtained six years earlier and then deposited it in the Acadia College Library. Davis made extensive use of the New Light letters in his surprisingly good, yet largely neglected, biographical study. In his "Preface" — written in October, 1865 — to the *Life and Times of the Late Reverend Harris Harding*, published one year later, Davis discussed the provenance and importance of the New Light

71

manuscript:

> These letters had been copied and preserved by the father of my friend (T.J.S. Bennett) just mentioned Mr. *Thomas* Bennett. Several of them had been addressed to himself. Other letters, from the pens of the old Ministers, contemporaries and fellow helpers with Mr. Harding, had in like manner been copied and preserved by the same gentleman. The whole collection thus obtained forms a valuable memorial of those former days in which the letters were produced. To this day I have not had the pleasure of becoming acquainted with Mr. T.J.S. Bennett; but my work shows how largely I have profited by his kindness.[186]

The manuscript volume was originally in the possession of Thomas Bennett, the key New Light leader in the Cornwallis region who, after flirting with New Dispensationalism, returned, especially after his moving to Liverpool in 1793, to his earlier New Light, Allinite position.

Neither Cramp nor Davis made any mention of the four Alline Letters in the Bennett volume nor did they mention the many hymns and spiritual songs composed by Alline and others, as well as the poetry and brief excerpt from the *Journal.* It was not until 1902 that E.M. Saunders' influential *History of the Baptists of the Maritime Provinces* referred to Alline's letters, to be found in a collection of documents originally owned by "A Mr. Bennett of Windsor, a contemporary of Mr. Alline." Saunders felt that the Alline letters reflected "a commendable zeal" and not "blind emotion and the wildest fanaticism,"[187] but nevertheless he underplayed significantly the impact of the New Light movement on the Maritime Baptists. Saunders reprinted, in carefully edited form, four of the Alline letters in his *History*[188] and Davis reprinted twelve of the Harding letters in an appendix to his volume.[189] Since the publication of Saunders book, only a few scholars have shown any interest in squeezing information from the Bennett volume and no attempt has been made to edit or publish the volume.

I have rearranged the existing letters, including Alline's, so that they follow a chronological pattern. I have included, in a separate section, forty-six hymns by Alline, together with those written by Alline's disciples. In a third section of the volume I have inserted, from the Bennett volume, what obviously was widely perceived by his contemporaries as Alline's most inspired poetry as well as the description, from his *Journal*, of his last few days on earth.

In addition, I have added two appendices. The first contains other New Light documents, including yet another Alline letter, written at the time by both central and peripheral participants in the movement. None of these documents, it should be stressed, is to be found in the Bennett volume. But they, nevertheless, are an integral part of the New Light tradition. The second appendix includes criticism of the New Lights written by two Anglican leaders, the Reverend Jacob Bailey, the Loyalist Anglican minister then carrying out his priestly function in Annapolis Royal, and Bishop Charles Inglis of Nova Scotia and by William Black, the Methodist leader. This contemporary criticism, though often unfair and inaccurate, nevertheless, is sometimes both discerning and perceptive in its response to the New Lights. And the Anglican-Methodist critique adds a certain, and some would say necessary, degree of perspective to the examination of the New Light movement in Nova Scotia in the 1780s and early 1790s.

The New Light letters and spiritual songs are not examples of sophisticated, sensitive religious literature. Rather, they are the outward and written manifestation of a popular Evangelical religious culture which was a powerful formative force in the late eighteenth-century Nova Scotia. They reveal, among other things, the remarkable continuing influence of the Allinite legacy not only in terms of theological content but also in terms of what might be called evangelical style. Furthermore, the letters and spiritual songs provide proof that in the 1785 to 1793 period Harris Harding was probably the principal New Light actor, ably supported — some might say manipulated — by Thomas Bennett.

The two ordained New Light ministers, the Reverend John Payzant and the Reverend Thomas Handley Chipman, are certainly very noticeable in the Bennett collection but only because of the relatively insignificant role they seem to play. It is as though Harding, Bennett, the Mannings, Joseph Dimock, Joseph Bailey and their correspondents were determined to push to the dark periphery these two men — both of whom had been so close to Alline. Payzant and Chipman seemed to represent an older generation — the former in 1790 was forty-one years old while the latter was thirty-four, and both were married men with families to look after. In 1790 Harding was twenty-nine, Dimock twenty-two, James Manning twenty-six, and Edward Manning twenty-three and all were still single. All were unusually warm and affectionate individuals with a powerful appeal to younger people, especially young women.

Like Alline, and apparently unlike the austere Chipman and the sour and introverted Payzant, these men were not afraid of combining, in a potentially explosive mix, the sexual and the mystical. They too, like Alline, were eager to solve all personal and social problems by the development of a personal relationship between the redeemed individual and Christ. Moreover, and this quality permeates many of the New Light letters, the four preachers and their New Light followers were drawn by what has been called the "mystery of intimacy"[190] toward one another as Christian love challenged what seemed to be a selfish, limited, almost worldly fidelity. They saw Christ in their friends and their neighbours and they wanted desperately to love their friends as passionately as they loved Christ. Some did — for a moment — and the joy experienced must have been both glorious and guilt-exacerbating. Then many came to realize that what Professor Victor Turner, the influential American anthropologist, has referred to as "spontaneous communitas" was only "a phase, a moment, not a permanent condition" as the "mystery of distancing" and the hold of tradition regained firm control of their hearts and minds.[191] But it would be a return to the status quo with a difference. For things had changed; the converts had, in fact, helped to bring about these changes. Religious life in Nova Scotia was an ongoing process, a process which would be affected by other revitalization movements, by other leaders, and by other ritual, and symbols.

Many of the Nova Scotia New Lights, during the

decade after Alline's death, revealed in their letters and their actions that they still regarded Alline's life and message as a guide for their mystical and Evangelical behaviour. Alline was a person so much like themselves; he had, in fact, been one of them. Each line of the *Journal*, each verse of his *Hymns and Spiritual Songs* and each inspired line of poetry in *The Anti-Traditionalist* emphatically underscored this fact. If he could experience spiritual ecstacy, then they could. If he could recover from his intense morbid introspection and black despair of doubt, then they could. And if an uneducated tanner and farmer, in his late twenties and early thirties, could help coax into existence a widespread religious awakening, then they could as well. For Alline had become in every sense a symbol as well as a hero; his life provided convincing proof that with God all things were possible. And many of his New Light followers for a time at least pushed themselves experimentially almost to the outer limits of Radical Evangelical possibility and a few thrust themselves through the framework of possibility into the often exhilarating realm of Antinominian anarchy.

Section I

THE NEW

LIGHT LETTERS

1.

Alline's Letters

1. *To the Church of Christ in Horton and Cornwallis*

Dearly Beloved Father & Brethren

Grace, Mercy and Peace be Multiplied to you and the Church of Christ Universal

Which I trust is the desire of all Sects & Denominations who Love our Lord, Jesus Christ among whom I trust you are Numberd. Then Surely the Cause of Christ is your Cause, his ways are your ways, and your people his people, and their Happiness your Delight — Which is a Motive must Certainly Engage your attention and ardently excite you to promote — And as this motive has already moved upon some of your minds as I have found by private Conversation and so the happiness of some of your Travellers to Zion is in some Measure dependant — — — on a Catholic forbearing Spirit. I take upon me the freedom to remind you of the Solemn Obligations you are under to make use of every Means to promote the Cause of your Lord and Master and the welfare of Precious and Immortal Souls and to remove every possible Bar or the least impedient which Otherwise would prove A fatal Stumbling Block to poor Sinners[192]   .

Now if you ask me how far you would become all things to all men, to win Souls for Christ?

I answer, not only so far as my Conscience will any way Admit, But not to Suffer my Conscience to be wounded, by the Loss of that which God never Commanded me retain — The Beloved Disciple had kept such a Close Comfort to Some particular Externals that when he saw Devils cast out in Christs Name, by some who had not Imbibed the Same principle, his Conscience was wounded and he forbade them: but, saith Christ forbid them not. — And so Peter when he saw a Sheet let down from Heaven, Containing all Manner of Beasts, and Creeping things; it was against his Conscience to eat (altho he was very hungry) Because he had not been taught the practice of Eating such Unclean food.

Now as for my part, I profess to be one of the despised followers of Jesus, who have left all to follow Christ; Not only Fathers, Mothers, wives & Children But even my own Life also.

80

And well I dare say you profess the Same.

I profess likewise to be a Stranger and pilgrim here below, Seeking a better Country whose founder and Builder is God, I profess Likewise wherever I find one of those pilgrims travelling to the Same City, to hold him not only as one of my Inseperable and Everlasting Companions; But likewise one that my God has set his Love upon and made a fellow Heir of his Everlasting favour; How dare I then refuse every possible Token of imtimacy or tie of Communion with him that I believe is receiv'd into Gods Eternal Embraces   Now Dear Brethren First I beg your forgiveness for the freedom I have taken — Secondly that none will Condemn my assertion by (only) Saying that it is wrong & unscriptural; But prove the Same by Light Administer'd from the Law, and the Testimony, which I shall not only be Willing to receive, But be thankful for their Kindness to my Benighted Mind, Thus after Beging an Interest in your prayers, & wishing all the Blessings of the Everlasting Gospel to attend you   I Subscribe myself

> Your Sincere Friend;
> And Servant in the Gospel,
> Henry Alline

Wilmot Decem   28th 1778

Argyle Octo^r   16th 1782

2. *To my Dear fellow pilgrims for the promis'd Land*

Nothing Could so sweeten my parting hours, as feeling the Inseperable, the present Ties of an Everlasting Union, and the Glimmering rays of that Immortal day: which I trust will ere long break forth, and expel every interposing Shade.

Therefore it is in that I at times rejoice, & will rejoice, Altho our Labour in the Vinyard shou'd Divide & allot us the four Quarters of the Globe.

But O from Jesus let us never part. —
I trust I'm borne on the Arms of your Faith & prayer, as one of your fellow Servants on the Masters Important Errande.

When we Came to Cape Sue, [Forchu] we found some Impatient to hear the Message of the Lord; while others Judge themselves unworthly of Eternal Life. We preach'd every day until Friday last, and see some favourable Signs of Jacobs Deliverance; Then Brother Chipman[193] Embark'd for St. John (May the Lord go with him) I preach'd that Evening and the next day; Still heard some Hebrews groaning Under the Bondage of Egypt — The Next day I preach'd two Sermons after which there was a Cry, What Shall we do to be Saved? by a Number for about Two Hours, when two poor Sinners were Deliverd; And I cannot but remark what the Apostle saith of the Harlot Rahab *"perish'd not with them that Believ'd not"* when she had Receiv'd the Spier with peace: The two brought out was the wife and Daughter of one M[r] Rogers;[194] who had left M[r] Scotts[195] church And was look'd on (as A Troubler in Israel) to vindicate the Truth; five or Six more of other familys, And two more of his Travailing in Birth, & appear near deliverance.

A Sabbath Evening I preachd again, and three times on Monday, Tuesday came here, and found Some Souls deliver'd since I left this; and here to this afternoon; The people seem Thirsting for the word, O that God would give me A Message for the deliverance of many!
I cannot yet inform you how far, or where I Shall be call'd to; but expect to travel as the Cloud appears to move, around this shore, and it may be I Shall have my hands full for A Time: but will endeavour to inform you of my Travels as often as I Can.

And O let me intreat a people near my heart to Keep near your Glorious Leader; that you may be both happy, and usefull; I Know there is no need of Telling you *he is All in All,* and that without him all is Vanity and vexation of Spirit; O then what Can possibly find place in your souls but Jesus that Infinite Lover! can fears, or frowns, prosperity or adversity, Crowns and Kingdoms, Life or Death break your hold, or Steal your affections from him that is So Strong, so worthy of your Love, Who Brought you so dear? Remember that in the Lord Jesus is your worthiness, Strength, life, Joy & reward.

O the unspeakable happiness those must enjoy who walk near the lovely Jesus! Surely it must be great indeed when one who Travels at so vast a distance As I do, Enjoy so much from the Glimmering Rays, that I now and then Attain of the hem of his Garment.

O Linger not, Linger not, Dear Fellow Travellers as I do: But keep near the Morning Star; For altho I love your Company, Yet I Ask it not at so expensive a Rate as your waiting for me;

No, go on, go on, Elijah, with your eyes fix'd upon your approaching Chariot, But this Know this, as God liveth and thy Soul liveth I will not Leave thee (or Sight of thee) untill I receive my double portion.

Let them Advance O Thou Adored Name
But Thou bring up the Rear & help the lame
And let me yet (tho Dead) Advance & See
The promised Land, thy Children, Lord & Thee.

Henry Alline

3. *H. Alline to Jacob Brown*[196] *at Falmouth*

To the Pilgrim on the border of his Everlasting Inheritance

> I hope Dear Sir that the name of Jesus is still your Joy
> and continual confidence while lingering on the
> confines of the grave & bordering on the Promis'd Land

And if I see you no more on this mortal Stage O may you
conclude your days with joy, & Awake (O shall I say) in the
Likeness of him, whose worthy name has been our theme many
an evening and happy Hour And O shall on the same them[e]
bask in Heavens Eternal Day

Ah' soon those bright Immortal Plains
We'l tread and Join Seraphic Strains
While he, Ah' he, the Slaughters Lamb
Shall be our Joy and all our Song

2

Hark, Hark methinks the Angels Say
Welcome to Immortal Day
While we with Songs Triumphant Come
To welcome our Eternal home.

Blessed be God I am well! (at times) And have much to Say to
one so near my heart; but scarcely time to put pen to paper, &
I'm Just now going to preach A Lecture.

O that you might share with me in the Blessings of the
Gospel this Night. Ah if you Enjoy him you need no more, Live
with him, talk of him, & walk with him continually

Remember your Absent Bro[r]
H.A.

Nov[in] 29th 1782

4. *Henry Alline to William Wells[197] of Halifax, [1783]*

It is well for me Dr. William that God Dwells in the Flesh, and gives me to Drink of the Rivers of Life. For although I'm Like a Bubble on the water, & my Mortal Life almost exhausted; yet Bless'd be God, all is well. Ah' that Religion which I have profess'd in Health, not only Supports But makes me Happy in Sickness; O the worth of such a Friend: how it sweetens my trials, & lifts me Above the Fears of Death.

Altho the Carnal world & dry Pharisee, will account all pretensions to a felt knowledge of Christ, & the Joys of the Holy Ghost as vain. Yet it is the only Joy & Life of my Soul, not only in prosperity, But in these Trying hours when Earthly friends, Comforts Joys and all Created helpers prove abortive. Ah When all things else shall fail Jesus is a friend Supporter, Comforter, & Everlasting portion & reward. I have been sometimes so weak in body I could Scarcely Speak, & O my Soul could mount up & Rejoice. Jesus made me Strong in his Grace.

O William, it is a Religion that the world despises But it is Joy unspeakable & Life Eternal to the Despised followers of Jesus.

Ah that Christ that you have heard me recommend to poor Sinners is all the Happiness I want in Life or Death; I am so much Confirm'd in that Glorious Gospel that If I had Strength I would proclaim Thro the world; Yea and if I Recover let it be for nothing Else, But to preach & enjoy a Risen Christ in the Heart, the hope of Glory.

I want to see you and my Friends in Halifax but it is to me Uncertain when.

But nevertheless while I feel the Rock all is well: If I recover Jesus will Stand by me, And if I'm dissolv'd Jesus will never forsake me. But Support me thro the small Conflicts of my exit, and hand me, Ah Safely, to those Realms of Light & Life where Sin & Death is known no more.

O William Shake off the world Untill your Soul is alive, & Strong for the Cause of Jesus in that Dark land where you resid·

And O, intreat Mrs Wells from me her Soul s friend & well wisher, to arise, look about her, and make sure the one thing needfull!

O that Jesus may Bless you both with much of his love, & if I See you no more in Time that I may meet you Both in Glory.

O take the advice of your Servant who is both Sick and well.

Henry Alline

5. *Henry Alline to Henry Ferguson*[198] *at Halifax* [*nd*]

May the Best of Blessings Dr. Father attend you and yours, & Let me be cloth'd upon with humility as with a Garment & exalt the Redeemers name! whose goodness to me is so great that innumerable favours must forever remain unsung: but howsoever I may forget or Neglect his Goodness past. Yet, Let my hungry Soul forever Stretch forward & pant for greater Manifestations of his Love & displays of such Unbounded Goodness!

Surely I pray the Lord is Good yea my Jesus is Goodness itself And if I know the choice of my Soul is more to me than Ten Thousand Tongues Can Express.

He is my Strength, my Life, my Joy, Supporter & Leader thro all the Trying Scenes & Unexpected Vissisitudes of this miserable disordered Stage — Ah late have I found him A hiding place from the wind A [unintelligible] from the Tempest as the rivers of water...

Note: The rest of the letter is unintelligible.

2.

The New
Light Letters

I
1785-1789

6. *Sarah Brown to* —

Newport 12th Oct   1785

Dear Bro^r 199

You know not how much Contempt you cast on the God of the armies of Israel When you Spoke to one of his followers in the Manner you did Yesterday to M^r   Young.200 What doth Christ Say to such as offend his Little Ones it was better that a Millstone was put About their Necks and were cast into the Sea than to offend one of these, O be Carefull how you treat the Children of God for your own Souls sake, for I believe it touch'd every One that experienced the love of God in their Souls for your own Sake O Be intreated to Adhere to the Lovely Charms of the Gospel, O Hear and your Soul shall live, O dont be displeasd to hear the Children of God recommend what the Lord has done for their Souls for it is a great work and none but God Can do it, Only that he makes them instruments in his hands to convince the Ignorant and unlearn'd, And Who are they perhaps you will Say! I will tell you, if the Lord assists me, which I make No Scruple he will for he has promis'd never to leave nor forsake those that put their trust in him, Why they are those that have Eyes and See not, Ears and hear not, Hearts and Understand not, For the God of this world Has Blinded their Eyes that they Cannot See And by having a proud heart and a Stubborn Will they will persecute the Lord of Life and Glory and put him to open Shame, Why the Children of God can boast of nothing of themselves, NO! Bless'd be God for the more he makes himself known to them the more they see of their own unworthiness and find Christ to be their Stay and Support, Great peace says the Psalmist have those that love thy Law And nothing Shall offend them tho' they may be reprochd and their Names cast out as evil by an Ungodly World, He Says my Son be of good cheer I have Overcome the world, *Ah thanks be to Our Lord Jesus Christ*, that giveth us the Victory, O I Can say by faith what a glorious Redeemer theres provided, for every one that Believes he is precious Dear Brother take these things into serious Consideration and examine yourself wither or not you dont find within your mind that something Convinces you, your Heart is not right with God, And When you speak reproachfull of any of these people

89

that you think is deluded dont you find Something afterwards that makes you feel Sorry, And if you do I Can tell you that it is the Spirit of God telling you it is wrong, And if you'd adhere to that Still Small Voice it would presently discover to your Understanding what a Lost Situation you are in by Nature Then you will discover by Faith that you must be Born of the Spirit of the living God, for we must become as little Children And willing to become Nothing, That Christ may become all. and in all, That is to find him Prophet Priest and King to rule in and over us, We Must be as willing to be ruled by his Laws as Loved by his merits. I fear I shall weary your patience O take it not amiss my writing you for your Everlasting all lays at Stake and the desire of my heart is that you would come to the Knowledge of the Truth And Judge for yourself for I Can Say I never Saw A Moments peace till my hope was Staid on the *Mighty God of Jacob*

O Lord grant for thy Own Names Sake that many may come to the Knowledge of these truths, And to thy Great Name Shall be the praise

These from your Frd & Sisr

Sarah Brown[201]

Windsor Augt   5th 87

Dear Sister Charlotte

Have you the honour to suffer Persecution because you will follow the despised Nazarene! Rejoice then dear Sister that you are counted Worthy; follow and keep close to the Gallilean's King; Under his Almighty wings shall you find protection; in his lovely Arms shall you find rest, While looking on his Pierced Hands and feet beholding how he has Lov'd you, and has been Wounded for your Sins, you will be constrain'd to Cry "My Lord & My God!" — Ah! Sister does he not Say to you "It is I, be not afraid. I have been wounded that you might be healed, I have been despised that you might be honoured... to sit at my right hand! I have been dejected and Sorrowful that you might Rejoice, & be Glad! Yes; I suffer'd myself to be Crown'd with Thorns, that you might be Crown'd with Glory! I have Drank of the bitter Cup of Affliction that you might drink the New-Wine with me in my Kingdom."

But how can I point out any Idea of the Unbounded, Unmerited, Unparelel'd Love of Jesus to you my Dear Sister! Since Gabriels Tongue would fall short. Blessed be God; the Day is Approaching near, when we shall begin Eternity with the Soul-Transporting Theme —

"Thro all Eternity to thee
A grateful Song I'll raise
But O! Eternity's too Short
To Utter all thy Praise"

This makes us willing to Suffer, Bleed & die, for Christ if call'd to it for his sake; This Love makes us count all things else but Dung and Dross; And this will make us to be willing to quit the thousand disorders of Our fallen State; And break forth in sacred Strains in the Courts of Paradice
Shouting "Worthy is the Lamb that was Slain"

Yours Eternally in Jesus

H. Harding

Windsor 5th Augt   1787

8. *H. Harding to Jacob Brown at Falmouth*

Dear Father in Christ

Nothing on Earth can Certainly rejoice your Soul
more more than to See or hear of the Prosperity of Zion. And
the New Jerusalem coming down out of Heaven like A Bride
Adorn'd for her Husband — Some of the Saints I have heard
blowing their Trumpets of Salvation and Crying the Sword of
the Lord And of Gideon — In Cornwallis the pow'r of God
Shakes the whole place, Numbers are prick'd in their Hearts
Crying "Save or I Perish" — Mrs Lockwood[203] I think has
found the Lord God of Elijah, one or Two more have found A
hope, but I fear not A Christ. — O Father Brown I Long at
times to finish my course & receive that Eternal Immortal
Crown of Glory eternal in the Heavens — O My Aged Brother
nothing but the Lord God and the Lamb shall eternally
enlighten our Immortal Souls — I hear the Blessed Sound at
times — Behold the Tabernacles of God is with men — I see
the Heavenly ladder reach'd down to the Earth, and the Top to
the Glorious Paradice — The Lord God of Abram Still
waiting above to receive our Souls into arms of Everlasting Joy
— You have Father Brown almost enter'd into the Glorious
rest, And will be soon bowing-with the Twenty four Elders
before the Throne of the Dear Lamb for Ever.

Perhaps you can now say with old Jacob "It is enough
Joseph is yet alive, I will go and see him before I die" Well now
pray for your Brother who is Eternally United to you in Christ
Jesus

H. Harding

9. *H. Harding to Jacob Brown at Falmouth*

My Dear Bro^r in the Slaughter'd Lamb

I often think of our discoursing on the Nature of that Eternal Unchangable Jehovah, whose delight is in displaying his Goodness, and Shining into our Souls with the immortal rays of his Paradisical Glory, wherever there is A Crack or A Crack or crevice to receive it. Hear, how quick the great I Am Speaks: & with his Heavenly Voice Stops our rebellious Souls from Eternally Sinking, Saying "It is not Good for man to be alone, I will make him an help-meet" And Blessed be God. Thro this Everlasting help (The Seed of Woman) Our Souls have enter'd the Heavenly door, and Shall walk up and down in the midst of the Glorious Pearls clothed with Perfect Robes of Paradise; And strike an Immortal Note of Praise with the Harps of God in Angellic Day; The Clogs of Mortality thrown off — The Curtains of Time drawn — Opening Regions of Immortal Life — The Kingdom deliver'd up to the Father, Our Souls shall fly from Darkness and Sorrow into the Bosom of Gods Everlasting Love, And Begin with Abraham Isaac & Jacob, Samuel David & the Prophets who have been there many hundred years; and all Strike as one that Soul Ravishing, Soul Transporting Theme.

"The Lord God Omnipotent Reigneth"

But I must break off because I am on the Earth — But keep I could on the heavenly Theme, & Sometimes think I Should follow old Brother Elijah in the Gospel Chariot of Israel — I must tell you the Kingdom of God has come to Chester, to One Soul in Particular, I Believe who was one of the most Abandon'd Wretches in the Place, But now feels little else but Heavenly Joys Continually — He was Converted before I Came. Jesus meets with us — The Christians rejoice & Some Sinners Tremble; If Jesus Permit, I go from this in three or four days — To proclaim the Everlasting Gospel of Christ who has made me your Everlasting Brother.

Harris Harding

10. *H. Harding To Thaddeus Harris*[204] *at Cornwallis, To be Communicated*

Annapolis 14th May 89

Dearly Beloved in the Lord Jesus,

I know it rejoices your Souls to hear of the Prosperity of Zion, therefore I could not refrain from letting you know that the Mighty God of Jeshurun has girded his Sword upon his thigh, Is riding in the flaming Chariot of Israel like a Glorious Conqueror: — his Majesty and Pow'r is seen amongst the Inhabitants of Annapolis — Some has felt his dying Groans to reach their despairing Souls of late; Some of the great in the worlds esteem bows, (and I can but believe) Melts down before the Everlasting Gospel of A despised Jesus — Col. D'Lancys Daughter[205] and some others at the Lower End of Annapolis is under distress of Soul, I must stay A little Longer for my Lord is bringing them home I think —

O bear me on your minds to Jesus that I may have Strength of Soul to Sound the Trumpet of Salvation — Keep near Daniels God, Shout Victory, Victory, thro the Blood of the Lamb — Remember the Nazaritish Covenant — "Little children Love one Another" — O Strengthen each others hands in God — Methinks I am now with you — And can see you as it were Burst into A flood of Tears — Saying to each other — O my Bror O my Sister, be Encouraged, I see you again the Immortal Shore that flows with Milk and Honey — I feel, I feel my Bror O my Sister, be Encouraged, I see you again the determin'd to know nothing but Christ here Amen Amen, my Bror my Sister, my Soul Joins you, I think I Can Say I feel encouraged to Press thro Storms to Angellic Day — I Am Dear Pilgrims yours Eternally in the Righteousness of Christ
H. Harding

II
1790

11. *Helen Grant*[206] *to Harris Harding*

Annapolis March 1790

Dr Bro^r

Glory Glory to God for what he has done for the fallen race of Adam, Glory to God for what he has done, and is still doing, for Annapolis Sinners, *Glory to God* that ever I had a Name and portion among the Despised followers of *Jesus* I think it is the highest honour that could be conferr'd on me to make me worthy the Name of a New Light, Glory to God that ever my feet trod Nova Scotia Shore that ever I heard the Sound of the Gospel — O my Dear Brother the Lord is on his way he is once more passing thro Annapolis Calling poor Sinners home: Three I trust in the last week was brought out rejoicing there is a Number of Souls born to Jesus in this place since you left us as I Suppose Brother Chipman has inform'd you O he is a Dear Servant of Jesus yould love him better than Ever was you now to see him he is very much Engag'd, The Christians Seems in General awake and some are very much Engaged; Old Mr Tupper is on the borders of the Heavenly Jerusalem, And Sometimes ready [torn] away, For these two months every meeting Christians are very happy and some long

Note: A page is missing from the book, and the next page begins in the middle of a letter from Hannah Webber to Joseph Dimock.

96

12. [*Hannah Webber*[207] *to Joseph Dimock, beginning in the middle of the letter*]

...told my mind much better than I Could have told it myself: I thought somebody had been a telling you my mind when you was a talking with me; I have Seed myself so wretch'd before Now I would have been glad to Changed Conditions with any body in the World, Man or Beast, I cant tell you the Horors of Conscience I felt in so small a volme But Nothing remains Yet but Horor as I see Sometimes I think I feel Something of the Love of God but dare not rest there, The other night I woke out of my Sleep Saying these words most Beautifull

> "There I Shall Behold my Saviour
> Spotless innocent and pure
> Sure to Reign with him forever
> For he's promis'd me Secure"

And I felt pretty well all the Next Day, And the Next Night following I awoke up Saying those words — "God is my all I hear his Voice His Love makes all my Soul rejoice" — My Soul did rejoice for Some time but as soon as that was gone I Thought it was nothing but a Delusion of the Devil; I have a great many Scripture promises applied to my mind but a heard and unbelieving heart dare not lay hold of them. Sometimes I think that all Christians has forgot me and that they have no desire

[Here the bottom of the page is torn and the last line is missing]

Sometimes I think I must part from all the Dear Children of God How can I bear to part from those that Call'd me so often and much More from Christ Thats always Calling of me I Love every Body in the World that I think Loves God, I think I can count Christians as the excellent of the Earth, Indeed they dont know What they Enjoy they dont tell of a Christ half as much as they ought to do, I think they are Not half so much Engag'd in their Masters Cause as they Ought to be, I think if I Could Say that Christ was mine it would be my Delight to tell of his Goodness to an ungodly world, But Little Hopes of ever being

One. Ah while I write I tremble for fear it will all be to my Condemnation I think all the race of Adam I am in the dreadfullest state, Once I could read & pray with delight, and so I Can now Sometimes, but very seldom, Sometimes I go out with this Intent, well I'll go and fall at the feet of Jesus I'll give myself up to him, but when I get there I have no heart, Well I think how can I give myself up to thee, I shall never be more willing to receive him than what I am and so I shall never obtain Mercy, then I try to pray but Cannot say one word then I go and take the Bible thinking to find Something there to comfort me But that like a pointed Dagger to my Heart; well there is not One promise there for me, this is the way I Spend the chief of my Days, in this Sad Melancholy State, mourn with me, pray for me But I Know it will all be of no Service — Unless the Lord Speaks peace to my Soul, I dont think you'l have the patience to read the Half of what I have wrote, for I am sure it will give you no manner of Satisfaction But it Seems as if I wanted to write more than I did when I began but must conclude with a Heavy Heart But a Word or Two more I must Say, pray dont think I mean to tell you my Experience NO NO Because I have none to tell you for I never was Convert'd, therefore I have nothing to Tell, If ever I Should be So happy as to be brought into Liberty it would be well worth my while to write out all from the first to the Last, I could set and write this fortnight and never tell half that has pass'd thro my mind. Since I was awaken'd it is going on five years under the Rev d Mr Chipman And so much the more it distresses me when I think How Long the Lord has been calling me, The more I write the more I want to write But must Conclude — May the Lord Strengthen you to go on your way rejoicing may he pour out his Spirit upon you And enable you To preach the Gospel to poor Sinners, and that Many may be brought out under you, if I never Should be a Christian myself It is my Souls desire that ev`ry Body else Should be — Dont forget me in your prayers: I doı.t forget you in mine, So I remain with the most perfect Lov.

Year 90   Your Unworthy Friend
Copy to Mr
Joseph Dimmock   Hannah Webber

          pray dont let no body see this paper

13. *Elizabeth Prescott*[208] *to Joseph Dimock*

Chester Ap^l   1790

Dear Bro^r

Help a worm of the Dust to praise the Name of *Jesus*,
He is precious yea he's worthy of all praise, & adorations O he
is my Life, my Strength, and my Only Joy: I Want words to tell
you his Goodness to me the most Unworthy of all his
Creatures, he did Indeed pluck my Soul as out of the Jaws of
the Devouring Lion, And from the lowest Hell, And hath Since
been with me in the fiery furnace, in the Lions Den, and in
passing thro Deep Waters. I have been very Ill almost all
Winter so as at times to be depriv'd of my reason, Yet I have
enjoy'd the presence of *Jesus*. And often found his Love to
transport my Soul Beyond itself, Yet was not without Many
Dark and Distressing hours. But about 3 Weeks ago I was in
the greatest distress of Soul that Can be imagin'd. The Enemy
made me Believe I was past all recovery, He told me I had had
my days, And had pass'd it; That I had been Exalted up to
Heaven, and so with the greater Vengance should be thrust
down to Hell. He told me I had sold my Saviour, and denied
the *Lord* that Bought me, that I had been Inviting others to
Christ and Should myself be a Castaway, And that I Should be
Eternally Banish'd *from the presence* of *the Lord.*

Eliza^h   Prescott

Not finish'd

To M^r   Joseph Dimock

14. *Charlotte Prescott to Sarah Brown*

Chester 23rd May 90

Dear Sister in Christ

For So I trust, through Rich, free, and Sovereign grace I may call you; and tho' we are Strangers in person yet not in heart but Join'd in the Everlasting Love of Jesus, which I find at times to draw my mind away from all Created Good, and which I trust will Eer Long carry my Soul Beyond Death and the Grave to those Bright Mansions of Eternal Glory which our Dear Redeemer hath prepar'd for all that Love him O that I could Live to him that has Died for me Dr Sister that I may be able to follow the Good advice you give me in your letter, for which I return you many thanks. I think I feel new Desires to follow my Bless'd Master thro Evil as well as good report, But O I find a Heart that is deceitfull above all things Desperately wicked, prone to wander from Heavenly friend and often do in by and forbidden paths, Yet like a tender parent does he bring me back and Cause me to Rejoice in his Unchangable Love which I find to be the Same yesterday, to Day, and for ever *O How Rich* my Dear Sister are those that have *Christ* for their friend and portion. Well might the poet Say

> Theres Life, Theres Joy, Theres solid peace
> Theres Friendship that can never Cease
> A Rock that Cannot move —

O Can it be that my feet is placed thereon; yes Bless'd be God I I trust they are; tho I Cannot Say my mind is in that happy frame that I have in times past, Yet I know he is faithful who has promis'd never to leave me nor forsake me time will not permit to add more at present — Your unworthy tho' I trust Sister in Christ

Charlotte Prescott

15. *Joseph Baily[209] to H. Harding*

Dear Brother

I have seen the going of our God in his Sanctuary The power of God falls in the assemblies — And many times I Cant but Say this is no less than the gate of Heaven. I found in this place a Number who were Thirsting for the Waters of Life who receiv'd me with Joy, And Could rejoice in Soul to See the thing which we see Never was I more Convinc'd of Gods Sending me to any place than here, I have been in the place a fortnight Tomorrow, O I Can Say Dear Bro[r] Bless'd be *God* that I ever knew the wonders of his grace. O this is my Meat and my Drink to Declare the wonders of his Dying Love to Immortal Souls. O I See the Chariots of Israel appear and his Children Shout for Joy. O I trust you find your Soul on the Mount and the Cause of our God is your Eternal Theme, O that he dwells in the Bush may Send his Angel before you and prosper your Way. — There Seems a great attention given to the Word here at present, and a Number Seems concernd what they'l do to be Saved, O that he would give them quick relief Before the Land Beyond recovery — If you feel the Cloud move to come to this place, I think it would be for the Salvation of Souls — And I trust you cant but come remembring the Lambs of the Flock who are near your Soul in that Covenant which is Stronger than Death O I Can tell you, I feel as I write, for this is the Cause of your God and my God, your Father and my Father. M[r] Blair[210] and Family give their Kind regards to you, longs to see you with many Others, I see a Need of your Coming Soon as I am bound to leave this place (if the Lord will) On Monday next, I Should been rejoicd with Moses to have Seen Aaron my Brother before I left this place. But the Day is at hand Dear Brother when forever we Shall meet in our Fathers Kingdom,

I am in great haste

I rem[m] your Bro[r] in Christ

Joseph Baily

Betsy Blair[211] gives her respects to you, And tells me She has Cause to Bless the Day to all Eternity that ever God Sent Salvation by you to her Soul —

To M[r]   Harris Harding
          Cumberland

16.   *Thomas Lynds[212] to Joseph Dimock*

Onslow July 12 1790

Dear Bro[r]

        I rec'd your lines by the Serv t of Our Dear Lord and Master who is rec d as the ambassador of Christ And Comes in the power of the Everlasting Gospel which I trust will be to the Salvation of Souls — The Powers of Darkness Shakes and trembles — The Waters are troubled And Souls are Stepping in, O my Dear Brother I find you near my Soul, O may we stand for the Cause that Stands Nearest our hearts, Methinks that there is Such A Door open'd for you to Sound the trumpet of the Everlasting Gospel of peace amongst us That it will be your Duty to Come as soon as You Can, I think it will be for the Advancement of Christs Kingdom. There seems to be a Thirsting for the waters of life amongst us, O that my fellow pilgrims might Stand for the Cause of My Bleeding Saviour. Let us go forth therefore unto him without the Camp bearing his reproach. My Dear Brethren let our Souls ascend to God for poor Sinners. Its a time amongst us of the Outpouring of Gods Holy Spirit — Saints Rejoicing and Sinners Crying for Mercy — Dear Bro[r] in Christ Communicate these lines to my D[r]   Brothers and Sisters in Christ.

Tho[s]   Lynds

To Joseph Dimmock

102

17. *Charlotte Lusby[213] to Thomas Bennett*

Amherst Aug t 4th 90

Dear Sir

I take this Opportunity of Writing to you, I hear you have a Letter for One of us from M^r   Manning, I Should be very glad if you would Send it the first Opportunity. I Want to Know if you are happy Now a Days, you never write to me, We have lost M^r   Harding And we Seem alone, for we have no body to talk with; I want to See you and talk with you Sometimes; But I am so bad I Cant think of Nothing that is good, when I think of you and how much your Engaged and I so Careless for it Seems to me that I dont think of my Soul or Nothing Else, Sometimes I think I am resting Short of Christ O and... unconcerned about my Soul, And then I Set down and Cry, and begin to look at my self And think what an unworthy Creature I am, of the least of Gods Mercies, for it Never Can be that I Should be a Christian for I think I have the most Temptations and Trials and trouble of any One on Earth; Sometimes I think I Shall be a Christian and at other times I think it is Impossible, for I have Greiv'd Gods Spirit so often that he will not have Mercy on me, but I hope I Shall Struggle along if I Never get quite through. Write to me, the first Opportunity. No more at present but rem^m

Your H. Sev^t   till Death

C.L.

18. *H. Harding to Thomas Bennett*

Onlsow 17th Aug^t   90

D^r   Bennett

Has the Dear Emmanul Brought you into the Fulness of his Gospel, So that out of Your Soul Flows Rivers of Living Waters I hope you can say *"I am sick of Love"* — If so, O how does the Blessings of the New Covenant pour into your Soul. — And whilst the Shadow of his Wings of *Love* overspread you, *O how* Sweet is his Fruit to your taste! But if you Cannot yet Say *My Lord and my God!* yet Dont be Discourag'd, He will Come and will not Tarry. I know after I had waded thro them trials for 8 Months, Sometimes had Almost despair'd of seeing him And quite Sunk down with Discouragements, the day Broke, the Sun of Righteouness arose at Last And O my Dear Thomas How did my Soul walk in the Light of his Bless'd Countenance   I really thought I Never felt trouble, And Ah I feel while I write this that this *Jesus* will bring you there too, Write   as soon as possible to yours *Ever Ever* in Christ Jesus

Harris Harding

To M^r   Thos   Bennett   Remember me to my dear Friends
Sackville   in Sackville

19. *H. Harding to Thomas Bennett* *Communicated*

My Dear Dear Brethren

Jesus that Worthy Bless'd Everlasting *Name*, has brought *Salvation* to a Number of your Souls — You are the Purchase of his Tears, Dying Groans, And precious Blood. O therefore remember you are not your own but his — I have (Bless'd be God) been an Eye Witness to the outpouring of his Spirit upon you; Surely you must Say he has been Gracious to Sackville, You Acknowledge you made it a place of Merchandise, But O Behold *Jesus* hath made it a *Bethel*. O Keep near, Keep near the Dying Lamb: And follow him wherer he goes — I hope Soon to meet you on the Immortal Fields of *Canaan*

These I Suppose will be handed you by Bro^r Dimmock, who I hope will be a Blessing in the Gospel to your Souls

Let no man Despise his youth
I am Everlastingly Yours In Ch^t Jesus

H. Harding

To Thomas Bennett
to be Communicated to the Church at Sackville

Onslow 17th Aug^t   90

Dear Sister

Thro' the Goodness of God I am what I am, Bless'd be his name who hath Caused me to rejoice in his Unchangable Love And Shall have ever to adore his Bless'd Name, for his infinite condescension to one of the most Unworthy of all his Creatures: By O I can Say he is my God, He is my Shield and Everlasting defence against the Ungodly world; Tho Sinners Rage, and Devils Blaspheme, I find a Determination to stand for that Bless'd Cause, And am willing that my Name should be Cast Out as evil, for I know that all them that is truly his must suffer persecution, And Bless'd Bless'd are they that is found worthy.

I have Cause to bless and adore him for what he is in himself infinitely Holy in all his ways and Righteous in all his Judgements. O go on in the Strength of your Lord and Master Stand in that Bless'd Cause which is Stronger than Death, For Methinks The happy day hastens when our Souls shall be disentangled from the Clogs of Mortality and we Shall awake in his Likeness And be Satisfied — O Can it be possible that Worms of the dust will be so ravish'd with his Beauty — Thou art fair my Love, Thou hast doves Eyes. O Soul Transporting Word, *God Man Mediator* "The Bright and Morning Star that leads the way" Methinks my imprison'd longs to be gone, But O why Should I think the time long when I feel his Love and will Carry me thro all my Trials, And how fair is my love, my Sister, my Spouse. When I feel his Smiles I Can Say he is my friend in time, and will be thro Eternity; And why Should I be Impatient to be gone for he has promis'd me never to leave me nor forsake me, O that he may Empty me out of Self, for I know this Bless'd Robe of Righteousness will And that, and that alone will stand when Heaven and Earth shall pass Away.

Dear Sister for so I trust to Call you by the Acquaintance Brother Harding has had with you, which gives me Boldness to write to you, hoping You will not take it amiss; and should be glad of a Letter from you the first Opportunity.

O Dear Sister go on, if we never meet in time, we Shall Spend an Eternity together; Stand the Storms a few Moments more — And you Shall Safely Reach the happy Shore — There you shall reign in Everlasting Light — Your name is there in the bright Worlds above And theres your portion in Unbounded Love — *All Glory to the Lamb*. Give my love to all the lovers of *Jesus*. They seem near my heart who so are his followers. Tho I never saw none of your faces, I trust we are united in the Bond of the New Covenant never to be broken, I Can Say as the Angel to Mary, *Hail ye that are highly favour'd of the Lord;* for the Lord will crown you with Everlasting Joy, your peace will be as an Overflowing flood. Nothing to annoy you, Tho you might be tried in a furnace, *Daniels* God will deliver you and bring you off Conqueror, O Amazing Condescension and wonder, O ye Saints of Joy, Shout the wonders of the redeeming Love — for Behold Oh Soon, I trust thro' Boundless Grace with you to bear my part in that immortal Note of praise, *"My Peace I give unto you, but not as the World giveth."* Must conclude and Subscribe your Unworthy Sister in Christ

                                                        Betsy Blair

To Elizah Lusby

21. *Betsy Blair to Joseph Dimock*

Onslo Augt 20 1790

Dr Bro^r

Tho' we are absent in Body yet I find you near my Soul, O go on in the Strength of the Lord God of Abraham Isaac and Jacob, Go Spread Redeeming Love from Shore to Shore, And bid a Guilty World Welcome to Christ, Heal the wounded and feed the Hungry with immortal food, Go on with Joy to face a frowning world, turn not aside to Court the Worlds applause, But spend your Breath in the Redeemers Cause, Withstand the storm a few Moments more, And you shall Safely reach the peaceful Shore, There you Shall reign in Everlasting Day, — your name is there in the Bright World above — Theres your portion in Unbounded Love — And this is that Mystery of Mysteries God manifested in the Flesh And dwells with the Sons of Men — This the Eternal Word which became Flesh This is he that was made a Curse for us Who Hath born our Griefs and Carried our Sorrows This is he that had the Weight of the fallen World upon his Shoulders and was press'd as a Cart is press'd with Sheaves. This is he that groaned upon Mount Calvary and Shed his Blood for the Sins of the Ungodly to redeem Immortal Souls O this is he that will One Day appear in Glory to Judge both the Quick and Dead Saints And Sinners — Angels and Men The Only Name by which Salvation is found in, This is that Christ Which I Declare to my fellow Mortals until my Expiring Breath and this is the doctrine which by his Grace I am willing to Seal with my Blood Dear Brother go and the Lord Shall prosper Your ways O go on in the Strength of your Lord and Master Stand for that Cause that is Stronger than Death for methinks the Happy day hastens when our Souls shall be disentangled from the Clogs of Mortality and we shall awake in his Likeness. O Can it be that Worms of the Dust will be so ravish'd with his Beauty, Thou art Fair my Love, Thou hast doves Eyes, Thou hast Ravish'd my Heart with one chain of thy Neck I charge you O ye Daughters of Jerusalem If ye find my belov'd that you tell him I am Sick of Love My Beloved is mine and I am his Methinks

108

my imprison'd Soul longs to be gone But O why Should I think the time long when I feel his Smiles, I Can Say he is my friend in time and will Carry me thro all my Trials. And why Should I be impatient to be gone, for he has promis'd never to Leave me nor forsake me, O that he may Empty me of Self, I know that his Bless'd robe of Righteousness will, O Tho' you might be tried as in a furnace, yet *Daniels God* will deliver you and bring you off more than Conqueror, O Amazing Condescension — May peace I giveth unto you but not as the world giveth — Least I Weary you must conclude and Subscribe Myself

Your Unworthy Sis^r in Christ

Betsy Blair

To
Mr Joseph Dimock
Cumberland

22. *Sarah Brown to Joseph Dimock*

Dr Bro^r

  I Can tell you that I have had a View of the Promis'd
Land, and my Tongue fails to Express the Views of Eternal
Glory — It Causes my Soul to Sore aloft in Angelic Day; O A
field of divine Light, transports my Soul to a paradice of Joy,
and wonder, and praise to the great *I AM* The Ancient of
Days, O Transporting View, A look within the Veil where
Angels Bow, and Seraphic Armies Bow, Crying *Holy Holy
Lord God Almighty* was and art to Come; the great *I Am.* Be
astonish'd O Earth at the wonders of redeeming Love, O my
Heart throbs, and Beats: Burns with Seraphic fire, O Brother
be determin'd to know Nothing Save *Jesus Christ and him
Crucified* O Stand with that drawn sword in your hand and
Salute No man by the way; I feel that Life that will never die, O
Love transporting, I feel you near my heart Dear Brother,
Stand the Storm a Little longer, for a Little while longer and he
that shall come, will come and shall not tarry — Dear Lord
hasten the wheels of thy Chariot, And while I am adrinking of
the waters of Shiloh, methinks I long to tell Sinners what I have
found in the God of Elijah, O Sinners: I Can tell you that there
is Joy in Heaven over One Sinner that repents Blessed is the
God of Abraham and Jacob that ever I poor mortal knew the
Blessings of the *Lamb* I beg that you would not shun to
Declare the whole Counsel of God, and may the God of the
Armies of Israel be with you, is the External desire and prayer
of your unworthy Sister in the Lord

Sarah Brown

To Mr Joseph Dimok

Give my Love to all the Dear followers of Jesus, it seems as tho
I Can see them Stand firm as the Everlasting Hills never to be
Moved.

23. *Joseph Baily to Joseph Dimock*

Onslow Augt 22nd 1790

Dr Joseph

I have got to Cobiquid and found Brother Harding on Mount Zion proclaiming the Everlasting Gospel   Our hearts were one in Jesus, and the place where we Stood were Shaken; the hearts of his Children were burning with Love to God. I Expected to have Seen you here, but found you were gone, I Send you these lines hoping they will find you in that Cause which is your Life, your Joy, and Everlasting portion; O Let your Soul ever be awake to God, ever remember the Morning Star goes before you, The Shepherd of Israel shall not depart, ever Let your mind dwell on the great things of the Kingdom of God, Ever remember you are to Salute no man by the way: But endeavor to Bear the Dying marks of a Crucified Saviour and may the God of the Armies of Israel be with you And give you Utterance to make Known his Dying Love to the Sons of Men, My heart has Ever been with you, May Jesus Bless you

I'm in haste

Joseph Baily

To Mr Joseph Dimmok

24. *Susy Lynds[215] to Joseph Dimock*

Onslo Sep^r   1790

D^r   Bro^r

I take this opportunity of writing you, to let you Know that the Dear Lord is making up his Kingdom in this place. How is your mind at present? Are you determin'd to Stand for the Cause of Christ! O Stand for that Blessed Cause! And trust we shall soon meet one another face to face. Sometimes I long to take my flight out of this world into a world of Joy. My Dear Brothers And Sisters are yet in the Gaul of Bitterness and Bond of Iniquity. O pray for their Conversion And not for them only but the whole world. O Come poor Sinners Share a part, give this Bless'd Christ your heart, We will take you by the hand, Go with us to Canaan's Land. O poor Sinners take no rest untill the Lord appears for your Souls — O Be Encourag'd My Dear Brother we have but a few Moments more to Stand the Storms of this World, Then we Shall with Jesus Dwell in Joys Beyond what Tongue can tell

O may the Lord Send you here to proclaim the truth to your poor fellow Mortals

Yrs

Susy Lynds

To Mr Joseph Dimock

This is wrote by A girl about 12 years Old

25. *Geo Boyle*[216] *to Tho*[s] *Bennett*

Windsor 19th Sep 90

Dear Sir

I Expected to have heard from you ere now but Since you I Suppose forgot Writing I Cant help Embracing this Opportunity to express the Satisfaction and happiness it has given me to hear you have put on the Lord Jesus *for your Righteousness*, and by what I have heard I dont in the least doubt but you have made a happy & a Glrious Choice for time and Eternity Well then I bid you A Thousand Welcomes to my Dear Jesus O Methinks I hear you tell he is altogether Lovely. O Eternal praises to his Dear Name that ever so unworthy a Wretch as me was Brought to hear the Joyfull Sound of Salvation sounded in my Ears and apply'd to my poor Sorrowful Soul *O Glory to the Eternal God* that Brought and conducted my way to this part of the world to see a New Heaven and a new Earth — O Brother I Cannot express half my feelings, my Love, my gratitude to the Eternal prince of peace, who Condescended to Bow the Heavens and Come down to redeem poor Wretched perishing Christless Souls from that Unfathomable Gulf of Woe and Misery they had plung'd themselves into *of whom I am Chief* — O Brother Bennett invite poor Dying souls to come to Jesus in my name

Room Enough in Realms above
Jesus Courts them to his love

Bless'd be God a full fountain for all Judea and Jerusalem may Come And have their Blackest Sins and Iniquities Wash'd away in the all attoning and purifying Blood of Jesus.

O I wonder how any Soul can hold out or refuse such endearing Love as the dear Redeemer offers them, but alas they Cannot See any Beauty or Comeliness in him — but you my Dear Sir that has found him to be precious invite intreat and beseech them to come and be Married to your Lord and Master. O Methinks I hear you do so in the Soft and Melting Language of your Soul.

O I Long to See you very much that we may Sweetly

113

converse together on them Unspeakable Joys & Glories which will be our happy theme to all Eternity, paper will not admit my writing much more   Must Conclude desiring my Love to Mrs Chandler and all the tender Lambs of God and to all that Love the Name of Jesus

I am Eternally Y^{rs} in Ch^{t} Jesus

Geo Boyle

To Thomas Bennett   Please write first   opp^{y}
   Cumberland

26. *Charlotte Lusby to Thomas Bennett*

Dear Sir

Yours I receiv'd which gave me great Satisfaction to hear from you; You write your unwell in Body, and dont Enjoy much in mind; As for my part I dont know any thing about myself or any Body Else; Every Body here Seems dead in Religion, I think religion is as far off from me as from them that was never under any Conviction, I think Sometimes I have got all off my Mind and Sinking to Everlasting Misery; O I wish I knew what or where I am, I Sometimes wish I was where and as I was when you used to come to our house last Winter, I wish I could see such a Winter as we then had. Remember me to all Enquiring Friends, Especially to them that loves Something Better than this present world, I Should be glad to See you over at Amherst for when you are not here I have no body to talk to — Excuse a heavy heart and hand

I am your Friend till Death

C. Lusby

Amherst
Novr 3rd 1790

27. *Charlotte Lusby to T. Bennett*

S^r

I take this opportunity to write to you to let you know Something of my Mind I Can tell you how Stupid I am It Seems to me that I am more hard and Stupid than ever I was in my life, I dont know that ever I felt any thing of the Love of God in my life, I doubt it greatly Sometimes and do at present, I thought Once and more than once that I felt happy, But I am so Stupid and hard that it Seems I am unmovable, It Seems to Me I have got Secure and Insensible, And In a manner Contented; for I feel Such a Wicked Heart that is almost Reigns Master, You must pray for me when you Can And when you are happy you must write — I was at Meeting this day And I felt my Heart as hard as a Stone Could any one feel so that ever was happy Before, for I am so uneven it Seems to me I must be a Stumbling block to poor Sinners, I realy wish Sometimes I was out of their way for I do hurt, Remember me to all the Girls over there, I must Conclude least I weary your patience

I Conclude y^{rs} C.L.

28. *Joseph Dimock to Thomas Bennett at Horton* [*1790?*]

Dear Bro^r

I take pen in hand to tell you that the Lord that directed the Patriarchs of Old to Labans House is going before me whether I know not, & will prosper my way; thro him I shall gain the Conquest, Ah! Dear Bro^r   I feel it already gain'd. Yesterday there was the most of the Power and Life of Religion that I have seen these two Months past; The Gospel roll'd like Waters of Shiloh.   The Saints of the Living-God look'd in Countenance like the Stars of the New-Jerusalem treading [   ] their different Orbs; Some of them declar'd the Lord was going with me And O let Bonds & afflictions abide me if it be for the Cause of my GOD, and I will rejoice in ten days tribulation   O my Dear Brother tell all my Bro^{rs}   & Sisters by name that the Angel of the Everlasting Covenant is once more determin'd to divide the waters of the great Deep, the ransom'd of the Lord shall pass over with Songs to M^t   Zion — Sinners shall be brought by the power of the Holy Ghost to Join the Saints of God to Sing "Thus shall we draw Waters out of the Wells of Salvation." I feel some of you going with the Young Stripling who is determin'd to lay his life at the feet of Jesus

[The remainder of this letter is obliterated]

29. *Joseph Dimock to Thos Bennett*

Dr Brother

    My heart is full and must write to tell you, that our Glorious Master is Carrying on his work in this place — Sometimes I feel my Stammering Tongue in Some Measure loos'd to Speak in the Name of Jesus, And O I Can Say I am more & more determined to Stand in his Cause to live And Die in his Gospel — And Blessed be God I know he will Stand by me Tho the Powers of Darkness rage against me —

    I Sometimes Stand and look on the Young Christians particularly Children that Cry *Hossanah to the Son of David* 'til it melts my Heart and Eyes into Tears of Joy. O Dear Brother — Rejoice with me Methinks you are ready to Joyn with me and Say I thank the Lord God of Heaven and Earth that he has hid these things from the wise and prudent and has reveal'd them unto Babes. For so it Seem'd good in thy Sight, O Dear Brother pray for me that Utterance may be given me and that I may be kept at the feet of Jesus O Dear Brother above all things pray for the Cause of God in this place — O pray for poor Sinners, Sometimes I think I Can see you on your Bended Knees with Uplifted groans and Tears rolling down your Cheeks whilst the worth of Immortal Souls lies at Your Heart — So go on in the Strength of Jesus — And rem^r yours in Christ

Joseph Dimmock

Onslo 18th Dec^r   1790

III

January, 1791

to

July, 1791.

30. *Joseph Dimock to Tho^S Bennett*

To be Communicated

Dear Brothers & Sisters

I take this Opportunity to inform you that I am well thro the Goodness of God: O that I Could tell you of the Goodness of God in this Place, But would Just inform you that the Lord is working wonders in this place, Many poor Sinners are Brought to the Arms of Jesus, Saints are rejoicing in their Dear Lord Several of the Brethern Stand as Public Ministers for God

O Dear Brothers and Sisters stand in the Cause of your God, O Witness by your lifes and Conversation that you have been with Jesus, O Let your Light so Shine Before men that they Seeing your good Works may glorify your Heavenly Father; O *Keep near Keep near to your Dying Agonizing Lord*, O Tell of Goodness, tell of his Love O Stir up your pure minds by way of Remembrance, O take Care not to Wound the Cause of God; I Know you have Enemies, within and without, But O Watch above all that are within thạt Causes the mind or Desire to wander away from God. O Keep your Souls alive to Jesus — Labour for a Continual Nearness to Jesus Stand the Storm a little Longer And you will fly Beyond all your Sorrows, and with Joy awake in Abrahams Bosom, There my Dr Bro^{rs} & Sisters, (If I never meet you in time, I Expect to meet you on the Happy Shore Joyn'd Heart and Soul in the Eternal Jehovah; (I feel Something of that Union which is Stronger than Death, Even while I write my Soul is United to you by ties Divine, Soon, Soon Certainly I Shall meet you on the Immortal fields of Canaan

Y^{rs} Everlast^y

Jo^h   Dimmock

Onslo Jan^y   11th 1791

31. Dr Bro^r Bennett

How do you do, I hope you find your Soul wrapt up in the Nature of the Eternal Jehovah. O I Long to hear of your Standing in the Liberty of the Everlasting Gospel, Witnessing Both to Small & great the Wonders of the Eternal love of the great Jehovah: O be encourag'd to press forward. Jesus Leads the way Tho The Devil is Engaged to distress the Children of God all that is possible, yet the Lord is our friend O Lean upon him, Stand for his Cause fight under his Banner

   And So I Remain Yrs

   J Dimock

I would be glad of a Letter from you, I Suppose the People here will Send for you Soon.

32. *Mary Freeze*[217] *to Edwd Manning*

Dear Sir

         I Cannot call you Brother at present, I Love the Christians and think I Could give my life for them — And I don't know but I Shall be Seperated Eternally from them; I have Thought I was sorry I had ever set out for the Kingdom, If I never have had to set out I knew I was wrong, But Now I do not know where I am going to: I am one of the Vilest of all mortal mortal beings, It cannot be possible that I am an heir of Glory, I have Such a Nature as no one was ever posses'd with; Oft I have thought I would give up my hope but I Cannot, Sometimes I think I would Change my State with Any One, If I am an heir of Glory I would be engaged both Night and day and Encourage my fellow pilgrims who are travelling thro this world of Sin and Death. Though we are Seperate in Body yet I Believe I Shall Spend an ever ending eternity with you, If I was in your State I would Not care for men or Devils, O ye Worlds fools, go on ye Bless'd of the Lord you are going to Eternal Glory where you Shall Sing the Victors Song, Write to me all Opp^{ys}

   I remain allways yours

Amherst January 16th 1791

121

33. *Edwd Manning to Thos Bennett*

Onslow Ap^l 19th 1791

Dr Bennett

   After many trying Scenes outward And inward I am permitted to Come to Onslow, where I behold the outpouring of Gods Spirit upon the inhabitants thereof. Some I verily Believe has found the Lord to be their Everlasting portion; Others have taken up with Something Short and I fear will Eternally perish; Some groaning for Liberty, The Angel still Continues To Trouble the waters, So that it may be Said indeed that Onslo is a place highly favour of the God of Heaven, His Tabernacle Certainly appears, And O he dwells with them, Walks with them, and has Certainly become their God in an Everlasting Covenant: We have Blessed Meetings the Christians Seem to grow and are willing to have their name cast out as evil for the cause of their God; Its a Blessed Sight to See the Young Christians Leaning upon their Dear Jesus going hand in hand to Glory it would do you good to see them, I dont doubt but it will to hear of it, I hope youve seen happy times your Soul Brought into that Liberty which you long'd for so much; O Dear Friend, that God who has Brought you so far, will bring you & your unworthy friend to those Regions of Unspeakable Joy where we will doubt his Goodness no more

I am Y^r Bro^r in Christ

Edwd Manning

34. *H. Harding to Dorcas Prentice*[218] *and [Keturah?] Whipple*[219] *at Horton*

My Dear Sisters in Christ Jesus

Chester 24th May 1791

My Soul is bound with you to the Choice vine and no length of time nor Space I'm sure, will ever break that Everlasting Union I feel with you in the Dying Messiah — I need not tell you of his Gracious Dealings with my Soul for you have not only been Eye witnesses of his Resurrection in me, but likewise in your Secret hours have often (Ah and Jesus has recorded it) Born me in your mind to his Gracious Throne — Yet I Love to tell of his calling me; Altho least in my Fathers house to feed his people Israel — I was no Prophet, nor Prophet Son, yet he Saith; "Say not you are a Child, for I am with thee to deliver thee" — And Ah my Dear Sisters I believe it Shall be as 'twas told me. I often feel him near when declaring the truths of his Gospel And I Can truly Say I'm determin'd to be Spent in his Cause

Yesterday I was walking across the field weeping and praying for the Dear Christians in Horton, when all on A Sudden, my Soul view'd A bleeding Dying God — I Lean'd over a fence & cry'd aloud for a Sinking Dying world — O my Dear Dear Sisters if I had a Thousand Lives I would wear them out Spreading the Everlasting Gospel — I know it is your Meat and Drink to see his Kingdom come.

O think if I could only see you one half Hour, what Sweet counsel would we have together in Christ Jesus — But I must away and proclaim my Saviours free Salvation to my poor fellow-Mortals There seems to be some Moving upon the face of the Waters in this Place — Adieu my Dear Sisters; The Boat waits for me; If Jesus permit I will write you, and the rest of my fellow Disciples in Horton by every opportunity

Lord Jesus be with their Souls — farewell

H. Harding

35. *W. Freeman*[220] *to Tho*[S] *Bennett*

Dear Dear Brother

Amherst 28th May 1791

Glory, Glory to god in the Highest Last Saturday my Brother Sam[l] was Brought out into the Liberty of the Gospel. In the Morning he went on the Marsh by himself, while he was there, he said his mind was Soaring away to God; he fell Down on his Knees to pray, and was so fill's with such Love to God, and his fellow Mortals as is inexpressible — He remain'd so about 3 Hours, and it then left a Solemn peace, He then came off the Marsh where I and others were at work; I look'd round and Saw Heven & Glory in his Countenance; I went to him and Said, Brother I know the Lord has redeem'd your Soul; he said yes; I Believe he has pluck'd me as a Brand from the Burning. O I know the Lord has Redeem'd my Soul, He is my Eternal Portion. My Mother hearing him, Ask'd what was the Matter. He Said the Lord has Redeem'd my Soul from Hell. O Did you but know what Love I feel in my Jesus, and unless You Experience the same God you are undone forever — She said "Don't Cry so loud the people will hear you" — he answer'd "O that the whole world could but hear! O did they but know what Love there is in Jesus! O my God! my God! What Beauty I See in my God!" & Continued the Language. My Father being some distance off, Little Philip ran and told him Sam[l] was Dying, he Immediatly ran to him (and Martin Dawlin a Christian standing by) my father said to him I heard Sam was dying. The other Replied No, NO, *he is alive and liveth for ever more* — It struck him so, he Said, I Believe it for the very work Sake. It seem'd Like Heaven upon Earth, Some of us Rejoicing, the rest crying, & Weeping; this Continued about 2 hours. Methinks it makes your Soul Leap for Joy that one Soul is Born into Zion.

O tell the world there is Room Enough and to Spare Since such an Unworthy worm as me have found Mercy — But I trust If I never see you in time we shall Meet before the throne of God, there to Spend a Long and Never-Ending Eternity together with all the despis'd followers of Jesus.

124

Your Unworthy Bro^r

Willm   Freeman

To Thomas Bennett at Horton

Betsy Lusby is Sick, the Girls as Usual. Low in Religion at Tantramar.

36. *H. Harding To Jacob Brown at Falmouth*

Liverpool 24th June 91

My Dear Aged Father in Christ Jesus,

My Soul, I think I can say dwells on the Plains of Mamre, and often Views the City of Palm-Trees, O tis there where all the Sons of GOD Shout for Joy, And the Morning Stars sing together; I Expect to meet my Dear Aged Brother in a few Moments more — Ah' my Dear Sir, the Ark passes on before us, and soon, Ah' Soon shall the flaming Chariots of Israel appear that our Heavenly Joseph shall send for you and I — and won't your Spirit revive, at the Sight — I think I can almost see you lifting up your Eyes with unspeakable Joy, Crying out it is enough, Joseph is yet alive — I can truly Say I often find you near my Soul: But I must Away & Proclaim the Everlasting Gospel —

The Lord is often in our assemblies

H. Harding

37. *H. Harding to Nancy Brown*[221] *at Horton*

My Dear Sister

Jesus holds me in the Hollow of his Bleeding hand — Since I have seen you my Soul has rejoicd seeing how the Holy Ghost has (at times) fell upon the Assemblies; but I see some trying Moments too, Sometimes for an hour or two it seems as if all Hell arose to withstand me; But it so far from moving that thro Jesus I thread them down with ease — for I know he shall Sling out my Enemies as out of the middle of a Sling, for I am bound in the bundle of Life with his dear Children — O how my Soul has pray'd for you and the dear Saints in Horton, I never felt them so near (I think) in the Gospel before.

O Nancy God has certainly told me that he would be certainly near you and a present help in a time of trouble — O my Dear Sister, he looks on while you read with Compassion and Love — I know he Witnesses these truths to your Soul by his Spirit. I Can almost see the Tears Start in our Eyes while you look over these broken Sentences & hear you say with the Poet

"I Love the Windows of thy Grace
Thro which my Lord is Seen
And Long to meet my Saviours face
Without a Glass Between"

Remember me in the kindest manner to your dear Parents, Charles & the rest of the Family, O that I might meet them all in Glory if never more here,

Adieu my Sister for the Sake of Christ my Blessed Master,

I am

Your Blessed Servant & Brother

H. Harding

Liverpool 9th July 91

38. *H. Harding to Benj*^a *Cleveland*[222] *at Horton:*

To be Communicated

My Dear Bro^{rs} & Sisters

   I dont doubt but you Offer your Sacrifices upon the Alter, which you took up out of the midst of Jordan, where the feet of the Priests stood that brought Salvation and bore the Weight of the Cause upon their Shoulders; that said unto Zion, "Thy God Reigns:" I know you never forget the day that he roll'd the reproach of Egypt off your Souls when you was made to drink from the Rock and Eat the Old Corn of the Land — O my Dear, Dear Brothers & Sisters Edom shall be for A possession for your flocks and feeble Lambs. & I feel it in my Soul, that Israel shall do Valiantly, for the Mouth of the Lord hath spoken it. And O Blessed be God that ever A dispensation of the Gospel was committed by the Bleeding hand of Jesus to me the least in all my Fathers House, who seperated me from my Mothers womb to bear his Name before Gentiles & Rulers, & counts me Worthy to Suffer shame for his Gospel Sake wher'er I go.

   I think I can almost see you standing around leaning on Each others Shoulders, the Tears rolling down your Cheeks While Jesus stands in the midst Saying — "Lord thou hast now Answer'd my Cries for his Soul when he was under distress, that he might be brought out to Witness for thy Gospel" — But O his Goodness is hardly discover'd in what he has done for me!

   There are some Joyful days here among the Saints. I think about 6 or 7 among near 30 that have got hopes of late in this place, can say Shibboleth; and the Lord often searches Our Assemblies with Candles. I hardly have got Liberty Once since I came away but I have been with you. I am going to Shelburn the first opportunity, and from there If the Lord permit to New England. But will see you again in the Body if God will — if not we'l meet in Immortality

   Liverpool 26th July 91

127

IV

August 1791

39. *Jo^h Dimock To Thomas Bennett*

Granville 20th Augt 1791

Dear Bro^r

I rec^d yours with great Satisfaction, to hear that the Children of God shout for Joy, And Sometimes the wings of the Immortal dove is Spread over your head. Not want of will or regard but want of time hath prevented my writing to you; And now was I to write A Volume I could not tell you half what I have seen, for I Can tell you all I ever saw before is small in comparison of what I have seen here; Surely the Lord hath Triumphd Gloriously, Grey headed Sinners shaken from their Supinity, brought to have their eyes renewed like an Eagle. Many heads of young familys in full pursuit of the world never turn back to bid Houses, Land, wife, or Children farewell, and Determind to have Christ or die Soon Brought to Sing the Song of Moses and the Lamb . Young Men and Women turn their backs upon their Companions, and against the Rage of Earth and Hell (with parents also) are Brought off Eternal Conquerors Through the Blood of Christ — Some Children 14 to 16 years old Brought to rejoice in him that is Invisible. Thus Fathers have Known him that is from the beginning — Young men have overcome the wick'd One — And little Children have known the Father. Many meetings Continue till almost midnight — Sinners Crying aloud for Mercy — Christians Bowels yearning over their poor Souls on the brink Of Eternal ruin — Some meetings have Continued all night, And O the heavy, Heart rending Cries would answer each other enough to pierce the Stoutest heart. Nothing Can I Compare it too, so much as that day when the last Trump Shall Sound. Saints Rejoice, And Sinners Tremble; Tho Saints Rejoice not much for their hearts bleed O'er poor Sinners. If you go out here Just after dark you will hear some lamenting themselves their dreadfull hardened State. Others mourning for others, till tears interrupt them; then Sob and Cry — then begin again, and Cry aloud for them as tho they would bring Heaven down to men, by groans unutterable.

And I Can Say Dear Brother it warms my Heart while I

129

write to think the Kingdom of God is come with Power, while you read your Soul longs to be here

I Remain Y^{rs} in Christ

Jos^h Dimmock

Write soon.

40. *H Harding to Lavina D'Wolf*[223] *at Horton*

Very Dear Sister

Shelburn 20th Augt 91

Yesterday Morning I attended Davids Meeting, where as soon as I Came I found about Twenty or Thirty made White in the Blood of the Lamb — Singing Hosannahs to the Son of David, Several of them frequently was oblidg'd to Stop and rejoice, soon after David Began Prayer, But was so overcome with Joy Was Likewise obledg'd to Stop, and turn'd to me with many Tears like Brooks Running down his Cheeks desiring me to Call upon that worthy Name that was like Ointment pour'd down upon the Assembly. — My Soul was upon Mount Zion — And I Saw Whosever worked Righteousness was accepted by him.

O Vina, I feel that Gospel you often heard me proclaim to be my Meat and Drink — I See the fields all white before me and Believe Im Going to reap a Glorious Harvest — All my mind Seems Drawn away to New England

I Can But Believe if ever I Should Return, I Shall Bring my Sheaves with Joy — Remember me in the Kindest manner to year Dear Mother whose wrestling Groans I think I often feel with me in the Everlasting Gospel

If ever God gave me a Union with, And A Heart to pray for any one in his Spirit, he has for her —

Remember me Likewise Affectionately to your Dear Father, tell him I should indeed be heartily Glad to See him Believe me to be, My Dear Sister, You Everlasting Bro^r

In the Dying Lamb,

H. Harding

41. *H. Harding to Betsy Grimes & Nancy Smith*[224] *at Horton*

My Dear Sisters

Shelburn 20th Aug[t]   91

I doubt not, But you often feel Jesus's Everlasting Arms Beneath your Souls — Is he not altogether Lovely, dont you find his ways Pleasent: dont you Enjoy an hundred-fold here — And *Ah* my Dear Sisters Eternal Life is Before you, O therefore Be not Discourag'd by reason of the way — My God will certainly Send his Angel before you, You'l Soon, if not Before these lines reach you, pass over and posses the Fields that Flows with Milk and Honey

When you feel your minds Soaring away: dont fear to let them go — dont think you have got as far as you can go when you feel your Enemies under your feet and are made to Shout aloud for Joy — O my sisters Launch out into the Great *Deep* of Gods *Nature.*

You dont know how near you are Sometimes of passing over Jordan — There the Glory of God and the Lamb enlightens the City — There the Voice of the Turtle is heard all the year There Dear Betsy and Nancy you'l be far from Doubts and fears — for these things shall not Come near you, In that day shall the Lord roll off the reproach of Egypt from you, and you shall Eat the Old Corn of that Land — Ah my Sisters, there you shall drink of the well Rehobath And the Lord will make room for you — And you shall be fruitfull in the Land

I have had many happy moments Since I Saw you Ah Blessed be God the Ark passes on before me. And I am Going to see greater things than those —

Yours in the Groans of Christ

H. Harding

132

42. *H. Harding to John Payzant*[225]

To be Communicated to the Church at Cornwallis

My Dear fellow Desciples

Shelburn 23rd Augt 91

Never, Since JESUS united my Soul to you in the New Covenant, have I found a Greater Union, and Oneness with you than I have at times since I Came away; My Soul has wept and pray'd in Secret places for Cornwallis — There, it was my Soul first heard the Voice of the Bridegroom, There it was my worthless name was wrote in the records of the Everlasting Gospel And there, O my Soul, have I annointed the pillar, and left my Eternal vows, and Sworn by the Mighty God of Jacob, that if he would be with me, in the way that I go, and Bless me, & return me again there, to my Fathers house in peace, the Lord should be my God.

You are his witnesses my Dear Dear Bro^{rs} & Sis^{rs} of what he has done for my Soul — when my Life drew near the Grave; My Iniquities o'erwhelmd me, I sunk in a place where there was no Water, and my Soul fail'd for thirst; Then it was I first heard the Joyful Sound — "Deliver him from going down to the pit: I have found a ransom!" — Then did he take me from following the Ewes Great with Young, to call Sinners to repentance Judging me faithful, putting me into the Ministry; Shewing me how great things I must Suffer for his Gospel sake — Ah! Blessed be his worthy name! he goes with me, And has let none of my words hitherto fall to the Ground — I have seen happy hours since I saw you as ever I did, and Distressing Ones too I have seen Saints Shouting aloud for Joy And Sinners Crying for Mercy But none as I know of Converted — people in this place think I bring strange things, Because I preach JESUS and the Resurrection — GOD I think is certainly going with me to New England, pray that I might go in the name of Brother Allines God — My Soul is full — I know not how to Leave writing — I think I can see you Stand Around with the Tears rolling, falling on Each others Necks, Saying Come, L. Jesus

133

Even so Lord   let thy Kingdom Come,

H. Harding

43. *H. Harding To Daniel Welsh*[226] *at Cornwallis*

My Dear Dear Bro^r

Shelburn 23rd Augt 91

I Can tell you I am determin'd through grace to be spent in my· Fathers Gospel — and it seems as if I was going to see greater things than ever I have yet. For there Stands a Man of Macedonia I think I can sometimes see — Crying "Come over and help us" I think God has Certainly call'd me to preach the Gospel in New England on the other side of the flood, If his presence only goes with me, It's all I want, O' my Brother! I Can Bless God from my Soul that ever I Saw Cornwallis; But O above all that ever I heard there The Voice of Bride-Groom, And was Sent to tell poor Sinners that Jesus Reigns. O I think, if I could be with you again how would we go from house to house breaking of Bread — Dr Bro^r keep sight of the Star And dont miss any opportunity of speaking for him-Who plead your Cause and mine before Pontius Pilate

      Encourage those feeble Sheep & Lambs that he has purchas'd with his own Blood — You'l see Joyful days in Cornwallis: I have not the least doubt Our Dear Lord has told me in my retir'd, moments that he would certainly be your strength, and Bless you — O then let none of you be discourag'd because of the way that you go-for the Angel of the Lord stands over against you with his Sword drawn to fight your Battles, O be Strong and O of Good Courage for Israel shall do Valiantly. The Angel that has redeem'd my Soul out of great Tribulation will certainly bless you and shall surely carry up his Bones with you

I am yours

H. Harding

44. *H. Harding to Amasa Bigelow*[227] *at Cornwallis*

My Dear Dear Fellow Pilgrim

Shelburn 23 Aug[t] 91

I often feel my Soul united with You in our Fathers Gospel, and think Sometimes, if I could see you one half hour, O what Sweet Counsel we would take together — Well, the time is at hand, now Dear Brother that we Shall see the Lamb stand on Mount Zion with his Despis'd followers — And you and I shall Surely stand amongst them there —

O Amasa I hope the Lord my Righteousness is still your Song, And that you feel such an application of it that your going on making mention of it Continually — O I Can bless God that ever I heard the Sound of your voice and others declaring in the Power of the Holy Ghost, the words of Eternal Life, which was a Great means thro Boundless Gra[ces]of my Eternal Redemption

I have heard the Voice of the Angel out of the Bush; calling me to feed his Sheep and Lambs since I saw you — I have seen Also the Reproach of Egypt roll'd away from Israel, and numbers eating the Passover in   haste, while the Ark of the Lord pass'd on before them —

But thro' Great Tribulation I shall Enter the Kingdom of God; yet, O my Brother, his Grace shall be Sufficient for me.

Its likely that many (if not all) among whom I've been preaching the Kingsom of God, may See my face no more — Well, if so; — I Can Sing with dear dear Bro[r]   Alline

"If I am but near God
All is well tho far abroad"
Always at your Fathers Throne Remember

H. Harding

45. *H. Harding to Thadeus Harris at Cornwallis*

Shelburn 23 Augt 91

My Dear Dear Brother

The Everlasting God of Na[hor?] my Shield and my great reward, he makes me to Drink living Streams, out of the Rock of Eternal Ages — Many times since I have seen your face, I have Seen the Saints of God so overcome with A Sight of their Inheritance, that they have Cryed "I'm sick of Love" — others say the Latter Day of Glory was now Commencing, Crying out My Father, My Father, the Chariots of Israel appears and the Horsemen thereof — O Brother, stand in that Gospel that Henry Alline once proclaimed to your Soul, and others in Cornwallis — that is the Gospel that is the Life of my Soul; and if I'm Calld to it, will not only Suffer for; But But Seal with my Blood — O D^r , D^r , Bro^r — He that call'd our Dear Father Abraham out of Urr of the Chaldees, Calls my Soul to declare his Righteouness made Known to me in Zion — I have often, since I Came away felt a witness (when in my retir'd moments) from the Holy Ghost, that GOD would Bless you in Cornwallis

O how my Soul has been united with you since I came away. O my Brother dont be discourag'd with the darkness of the Children of God, they'l come out like gold tried in the furnace, for the mouth of the Lord has spoken it — My voice is almost gone, as it appears; But as long as I can whisper out one word, I'll declare his Salvation — I find him with me in this Dark place I'm going; I think, with the Glad Tidings of my Dear Master's Gospel to New England. But if Jesus Keeps me in this Vale of Tears, I'll see you again; but if not I'll meet you with unspeakable Joy in Immortality

Yours in C. Jesus —

H. Harding

136

46. *H. Harding to Lebbeus and Mrs. Harris[228] at Cornwallis*

My Dear Dear Bro[r] & Sister

Shelburn 23th Aug[t] 91

    I am Surrounded by many who are Saying by every appearance, "We would know what this strange Doctrine would mean wherof thou Preachest... — But thanks be to God he Stands by me And hitherto has been my helper — My Soul has often drank of those Pleasures that flow from the right hand of my heavenly Father Since I've seen you Many of the Dear Saints have heard the Voice of the Turtle in the Land, And have often Cried out in Meetings — "If you see him tell him I'm sick of Love" O Dear Uncle & Aunt, I have A happy lot in God s house, and he that is Mighty has done great things for me "Lord not unto me, not unto me, But unto thy Blessed name be all the Glory" — O that you might Both grow like the Cedars that the Lord has planted, and walk like Zecharias & Elizabeth in all the Ordinances of the Lord Blameless

    Beg of Lydia in my room not to reject Christ any longer, lest the Summer should be ended his Spirit forever gone, then A great ransom Cannot deliver her. O that Jemmy Elisha & my Dear Cousins might meet me at his right hand

    I Am my Dear Uncle & Aunt yours in Christ

    H. Harding

47. *H. Harding to Judah and Mrs. Wells*[229] *at Cornwallis*

My Dear Brother & Sister   Shelburn

25th Augt 91

Last night while I was trying Behold the Bridegroom cometh-to an assembly in this place-Numbers gathered about the door, their Countenances Spoke their opposition against the Gospel They rail'd and raged in a fearful manner 'till at last a young Man espous'd the cause (as he thought), by carnal weapons, Several join'd him: And the Riot & darkness increas'd so powerful, the people of the Meeting, after Seperating them Shut the Doors — They Still continued making disturbance.

I gave out   dear Mr Allines Young Mans Song Dismiss'd the Meeting — and went peacably home.

Satan's Kingdom being disturbed, And the Holy Ghost giving me some utterance in Speaking is the only signs I see of Christ's Kingdom coming among these Strangers

Though Bonds and Afflictions Abide me in every place, yet Blessed be God None of these things move me, My Life I Can truly Say is not dear to me; for I believe thro Boundless Grace I Shall finish my Course   and the Ministry of Jesus Christ with Joy — O Dear Bro^r & Sis^r , you don t know how near in the Everlasting Gospel you and the Children of God seem in Cornwallis

While I'm writing I as it were see the ears Start in you Eyes for Joy that we shall Soon meet in Abam's Bosom Pray for me my Dear fellow pilgrims that I may be Spent in his cause who has Bought us with his own Blood

Adieu it may be till we meet   in the Kingdom of my Father, and your Father My God and your God

H. Harding

48. *Harris Harding to M^r & Mrs Lockwood*[230] *at Cornwallis*

Dear Bro^r and Sister,

Shelburn 25 Augt 91

I hope you are on Mount Zion Beholding the Everlasting Fields Towards the Sun's Rising, many A Time Since I Saw you Jesus has taken me to the Top of Mt. Moriah where I have seen the Lamb that was Slain from the foundation of the world to Redeem us unto God O the happy hours I often Enjoy proclaiming my dear Lords Gospel. Dear B^r & Sister you dont know how Cornwallis seems to me of late. There have I set up my Ebinizer & often there has his Angel helped me, there the Waters were turned into Wine, & my Soul addorned to preach the Gospel of Jesus Christ O blessed be God that ever I was born to be A dispised Messenger of Salvation that ever he said to me feed my Lambs and Now I go bound in Spirit to New England not knowing the Things that Shall befall me there I cant Say I know that among all of you whom I have gone preaching the Kingdom of God Shall See my face no more, but I will Return again to you if God will — & I hope Strengthen you in God — O pray for Brother Payzant and others who Labour among you in the Gospel — and O bear my Labours in your minds to his Gracious throne where we soon will bow come L. Jesus,

always yours, H, Harding

49. *H. Harding to Asa and Mrs Dewey*[231] *at Cornwallis*

Dear Dear Bro[r] & Sister

Shelburn 25th Aug[t] 91

Although we are seperate in Body, yet not in Soul, for I Often feel you near my Heart when I get near my Blessed Master

O I have seen some Joyful meetings, and moments since I left you; and many times when I have been declaring that Gospel that brought our Souls to Zion Christ has sent his Angel before me-And divided the Sea before his Saints and Caused them to Sing Hosannahs to the Son of David — Blessed be God that ever I went with the Joyful news of the Gospel to a Lost world, O that I might wear out in the despised Cause.

Dear Brother & Sister you felt many Groans for my redemption and often wept over my Sinking Soul before Jesus appear'd for my help — but Glory to the Lamb that was Slain, Altho my feet had well nigh slipp'd he has now set them on the rock that never can be moved: Altho the Star appear'd before, yet it was under your roof where the Sun arose upon my Soul; I never shall forget it — I Believe it is recorded in the Book of Life — O what things has he shew'd me since of his wonders in the Deep. I expect to set out on my way for New England next week to tell my Dear fellow men that *Jesus is Risen*. But if I stay in this Vale of Tears, — will see you again if God will — O, Glory to god that ever my Lot was cast among you — That ever I was made a Doorkeeper in his house —

Go up and look·towards the Sea: for I think there is a Sound of Rain again in Cornwallis. It is certainly coming

O Rejoice for there shall be A performance of those things told you from the Lord —

In whose cause I Am

Your Brother for Ever

H. Harding

50. *H. Harding to John Payzant*[232] *at Cornwallis*

Shelburn 25th Augt 1791

My Dear Dear Brother and fellow Labourer in the Vinyard of GOD, My Soul is united with you in the Despensation of the Gospel committed by the bleeding hand of our Dying Lord — My Soul
has wept and Pray'd for your Joyful Success in the Ministry often in Secret Places since I Saw your face — GOD has my dear Brother placed you in A Pleasant place, Surely you have a Goodly heritage —
As to my own part since I came away, I have seen some trying moments too — The Church at Liverpool are (I Believe) more united than they were Some time Past — I think Six or Seven in the late reformation there are Savingly Converted, They would be exceedingly glad to see you. I wrote Pressingly to Bro^r Dexter the other Day, in the name of Jesus to go up the Bay
Many attends our Meetings in this Place, at different times, with great opposition — If my Dear Master permit I expect to go to Barrington next week on my way to the States — Remember me in the Bowels of Jesus Christ to your Dear Wife, & all the followers of the Ark, I Am my Dear Bro^r in the Gospel & Righteousness of our Blessed Master.

Yours forever

H. Harding

51. *H. Harding to Julia [Swigard]*[233] *at Cornwallis.*

Shelburn 25th Augt 91

My Dear Dear Sister

The Blessings of him who was Separated from his Brethren, does not depart from my soul, still he is with me, whose I am, And whom I serve — And O Julia He that took David from following the Ewes great with young, Amos from gathering Sycamore fruit, And Peter from his Nets To feed his Flocks and Fathers inheritance, the purchase of his Blood — Also has taken me, that I may not only see that Just One, But Be a Witness to all he Sends me of his Resurrection, both of those things that I have seen, and in which he will appear unto me

O my Sister, that Cry "My God, My God, why hast thou forsaken me" — Has Call'd my Soul from all Created Joys, to Sound Aloud the dying Groans of the worlds restorer; I feel the Eternal Bleeding truth while writing, And must call my Sister to Behold what manner of Love the Father has Bestow'd, that we should be call'd the Children of God — O Lord, My God — is this the Love that Enterpos'd the Everlasting Rebellion of Sinking Millions; & treads the wine-press alone — O thou Everlasting Shephard, who hath laid down my Life for the Sheep; Remember the purchase of thy Blood in Cornwallis: and Lead my Sister to the Top of the Mount with thy Bleeding hand, to behold with Joy the Land of promise, unto the utmost bounds of the Everlasting Hills —

I See the fields white — all ready for Harvest & expect to return again to Cornwallis (if God will) from NEW England, bringing my Sheaves with Joy

Yours in the Righteousness of JESUS

H. Harding

52. *H. Harding to Susa Eaton[234] at Cornwallis*

Dear Sister in Christ Jesus

Shelburn 25 Augt 91

That Angel that Redeem'd our Souls Out of all Tribulation, goes before me, and fights my Battles, and many times when I'm declaring his Gospel he stands at my back, and Witnesses to the truths I'm Speaking

O Susa! once you remember'd I was in darkness, the Shadow of Death, But now Light is sprung up in my Soul, My Dr Sister — Ah! thro his poverty I'm made Rich — And the Excellency of Carmel is my portion for ever — I well remember the night when the first born was Slain, when he Sprinkl'd the Blood upon the door-posts of my Soul, that run from the foundation of the world for my crimes; Then it was, O my Soul, I heard the Joyful Sound of the Hebrews release, Beheld the Bright and Morning Star, followed the Cloud of Immortal Glory, the ark of his Strength, Singing Hosannahs, Blessed is he that Sitteth on the Throne of my Father David, Hosannah in the hightest — Yes my Dear Sis^r , When you   also fill'd with the Holy Ghost, Spake out with a loud voice, My Soul doth exceedingly rejoice in God my Saviour, who has helped me in remembrance of his tender Mercy whereby the day Spring from on high has visited my Soul — O Susa, I hardly know how to stop writing, I feel the Kingdom of God within me like an Overflowing fountain — I Shall soon reach the fields of Immortal Beauty, where an Exceeding weight of Glory from the right hand of God shall be pour'd upon my Soul

There you'l certainly meet again

H. Harding

53. *H. Harding to Marven Beckwith*[235] *at Cornwallis*

My Dear D^r B$_r$o^r

Shelburn 26th Augt 91

I often think of you, And long to meet you again on this Mortal Shore, But if not Dear Marven we'l soon meet upon the Immortal Plains, there thro Boundless grace is my Portion and my rest, and my Worthless name recorded, O my Brother keep in Sight of the Morning Star, take care of Contenting yourself Without A Sense of Religion, Because, you think you can get alive easy by only Looking to Jesus, Many children of God, have had their Locks Shav'd off, upon this enchanted Ground (who were once as Strong as Sampson) by getting Asleep in Delilah's Lap: And when they have try'd to shake themselves, as they often had done before, from Earthly Enjoyments; their Strength is departed; the Glory of Israel is gone; and they are bound in Prison; their Eyes being put Out; they have been ready to follow every wandering Star of Natural Passion for Religion, Which only gather more Blackness and Darkness

But my Brother, you have not so Learned Christ when you receiv'd him he was all, And in all your Actions, in all your Behavior, in all your Works more or Less, & in all your words declaring plainly to Saints & Sinners, you Sought A Better Country; that is an heavenly So walk in him my Brother, And you shall grow like the trees of Lign-Aloes whom God hath planted with his own right hand beside the Waters, In that Name that has often ravish'd my Soul; Since I left you, And will be our Joy when time is no more

I Am Still, And ever yours

H. Harding

54. *H. Harding to Fally Bent[236] at Horton*

Shelburn 27 Aug 91

My Dear Dear Sis[r]

The Angel that Redeemd my Soul out of all Tribulation
with his own Blood is with me and upholds me with his own
right hand, I have had many Joyful meetings Since I wrote
you last, Jesus I find is with me in this place. And O my Sister,
He that call'd me to be a Witness of his Resurrection before
Gentiles and rulers opens my mouth, altho but A Babe, and
enables me to declare the things I have seen & heard before
many Witnesses in this place — Sometimes my Dear Fally the
Lord leads me to Horeb the Mount of God, where by Faith I
Can see you Stand with ten thousand times Ten Thousand of
his followers Singing that Song that none can learn But those
whose names arc in thc Book of Lifc. O my Sister my Sister, my
Soul leaps while I'm writing to you and thro Faith in his Name
attains the Promise — My Grace is Sufficient for thee   If my
Dear Grand Father, and Grand Mother are Journeying in
Earthly Tabernacles; Tell them I'm well Soul and Body, and
Expect Soon to meet them in Immortality, if not here before —
O Fally, I Can I think, See the Tears of Joy Start in your Eyes,
as you Read, for Jesus tells me while I'm writing he'l be near
you when you receive these lines; O my Sister, my Soul is full of
that Love that make me your Everlasting Unchangable Friend,
And Brother

Harris Harding

To Miss Fally Bent

Horton

55. *H. Harding to James McClanan*[237] *at Horton*

D[r] Bro[r] McClanan

Shelburn 27th Aug[t] 91

How do you Seem to be in your mind, Can you openly Confess before men that Jesus has Bought you with his own Blood? I hope Before this, you feel the Spirit of God almost Continually Crying *Abba Father*, O my Brother, that Christ who made the Wilderness Blossom around you is still your great reward Ah, he it is that Sends his Angel before me wherever I go — And enables me to Declare his Deeds among the people,

When I first came to Horton my Dear Brother my Soul was in Darkness & in the Shadow of Death: But O JESUS Behold me when a great way off —

All Heaven Bow'd with Love to my Poor Soul; he met me in the way to Destruction with arms extended, And told me he had appear'd to me for this purpose to make me a Witness for his Name unto the Gentiles to whom he has since sent me — Then was a time of Love indeed — his Dear Children receiv'd me with open arms; and told me, that Jesus who had appear'd to be in the way, had Chosen me as the one to feed his Sheep & Lambs — And O I Can tell you My Dear Maclanan I was not disobedient to the Heavenly Vision; And tho Earth and Hell are engaged against me, yet thro the help of God I'm more and more determined to Spend my last Breath in his Cause,

H. Harding

56. *H. Harding to Dorcas Prentice at Horton*

My Dear Sister

Shelburn 27th Augt 91

If I knew how your Letter Engag'd my Soul for the sake of our Dear Lord, you would soon write again, There is not a Day for some time past but my Soul has been Engag'd with you in Zion, — O my Sister many times while I have been declaring our Fathers Gospel since I came away from you, He enabled me to put whole Burnt Offerings upon his Blessed Alter, and Accepts the works of my unworthy hands in his Cause

It would have done your Soul Good to have been at some of our Meetings at Liverpool — Some of the Dear Children of God, Crying out "This is the Gospel that brought Salvation to my Soul under Henry Alline;" others, at times, Dropt their Old forms Caught the Mantle and Smote the Waters, Crying out in the Assembly with a Loud voice "Where is the Lord God of Elijah" — Dear Sister Gorham you would have thought sometimes would have gone off in a Chariot of Fire to glory — But I had some Sore Trials there too, with the Dear Children of God who seem'd to be more united before I Came away — Dr Sister, I hardly know that I'm writing, it seems as if I was Conversing with you face to face as I Used to when we were Sitting together in Heavenly places in Christ Jesus — My Dear Sis^r go and Sit down by my Dear Dear Grand-Parents (if they be with you) And tell them the Joyful News the Bride Groom is Coming

Always yours in Christ

H. Harding

57. *H. Harding to Green and Lydia Randall*[238] *at Horton*

My dear dear Bro^r & Sis^r

Shelburn 27th Augt 91

Altho I have Seen many poor Sinners taken hold of, and made to tremble, yet I know not any are Savingly converted where I have been since I Came away, But the Dear Saints of God have been Led to the top of Moriah and Seen the Lamb that was Slain from the foundation of the world, The Voice of the Bride-Groom is heard among them — Ah Blessed be God that Love that first led my Sorrowful Soul to Zion and Sent me to Sound the Hebrews release to my fellow prisoners of hope has often loos'd my Tongue and caused me to Cry aloud in the Great Congregation *Jesus is Risen.* O My Dear Brother and Sister, That fountain of Free Grace that Interpos'd the Everlasting Rebellion of Sinking Millions flowing in Infinite Goodness like rapid torrents towards a Lost world I Can truly Say is all my Joy That Righteousness is all my Song — And them Streams Gladdens my Heart — I expect to set out for Barrington next week on my way for N. England with the Rod of God in my hand, that wrought wonders in the Land of Ham and Smote Egypts first born — I BELIEVE O Lord my God that it will divide the Sea before me and bring waters out of the Rock — Sometimes I Can See A Man stand and call "Come over and help us" — I Assuredly believe God has call'd me to preach the Gospel on the other side of the flood. If God will indeed be with me in the way that I go give me food to eat and raiment to put on and Return me again to my Fathers house in Peace the Lord Shall be my God

H. Harding

58. *H. Harding to Fally Harding*[239] *at Horton*

Shelburn 28th Augt 1791

My Dear Dear Sister

My Soul is united with you in the Gospel of Jesus *Christ*, beyond what my Tongue or pen can describe — I think if I Could only see you how would I with tears my Dear Sister intreat you to remember him that Deliver'd you out of the Paw of the Lion and the Bear, who in remembrance of his tender Mercy has redeem'd your Soul out of great Tribulation that you might Serve him in Righteousness all the days of your Life — Your Dear Sister is now Singing Eternal Hallelujahs upon the Immortal Plains whose happy Translation to Glory was one great means of your Souls redemption — But my Dear Fally, is Israel converted. He Lay for a good while with weight upon my mind; I wish I knew from GOD where he is I fear if the Lord has chosen him, Some of the Dear Children of God may hurt him, if they are not guided by the Holy Ghost in telling of him he is Call'd to Speak — before Jesus tells him so — I Long to See him as well as the rest of them that Professes Christs Gospel — I am with you in Spirit almost every day, And when natural affections is done away — I am your Brother forever In the Everlasting Patience of Jesus Christ

H. Harding

149

59. *H. Harding to David and Mrs. Harris at Horton*[240]

Shelburn 28th Aug^l 1791

My Dear Bro^r & Sis^r

I hope you feel your minds in the Kingdom of God — remembering that every foot of Land you tread upon is yours to possess here; Ah! the Land that old Abraham was led to behold with Joy, the fields of Immortal Beauty; where you shall drink of the River of GOD — and hear the Voice of the Angel Preaching the Everlasting Gospel to them upon the Earth, Ah! Methinks, the Sound of his Gracious Voice, while you read, make you cry out with me "How Beautiful upon the Mountains is the feet of him that says unto Zion thy God Reigneth" — And it is this Name that's my Joy, my Strength, and Salvation; that I'm determin'd thro grace, to make my Theme thro this waste and howling Wilderness; And O my Dear Brother and Sister you need not be afraid of his Faithfulness for this is he that was with the Church in the wilderness, the Children in the Furnace, Daniel in the Lions' Den Ah' he it was that reprov'd Kings for their Sakes, And what O What shall I more Say the time would fail me to tell of Gideon, of Barack And Japhthat   & O my Soul of his wondrous works that I have been an Eye and an Ear Witness too — Ah and as long as this GOD is my Friend, I need no other whether I may see you again in the Body or not, Its no matter, If we are only in his Cause

Adieu it might be till I meet you in Glory

H. Harding

60. *Harris Harding to Nancy Brown[241] at Horton*

My Dear Dear Sister in Jesus

My Soul rejoices to think in a few Moments I shall meet you on the plains of Immortal Glory — Often since I saw you my Soul has been drawn out to pray for Immortal Blessings to be pour'd down upon You, and my Dear Horton Brethren

I Receiv'd all your Letters, as well as from the rest of the Dear Saints in Horton.

Being Surrounded by the powers of Darkness, & Beasts of Ephesus in this place, I Shut myself in a Room, Sit down, began to read, and Cry, and pray — Sometimes I would Stop and rejoice, And O you cant think Nancy how the Children of God appeared, My Soul Ascended the Mount with Unspeakable Joy And I Saw Israel abiding in their Tents According to their Tribes And could hardly help Crying aloud Several times, How Beautiful are thy Tabernacles O Israel —

I have been in this place about Two Weeks and the Longer I Stay the more Liberty   I find in proclaiming that Name which you and I have found Salvation in.

Unspeakable opposition and Darkness arises from almost all quarters against the Lord and his Christ.

I Expect to Leave this in a few days for New England, but if God will I'll see you again in the Flesh in about a year, But if not, Dear Sister, we'l Soon meet on Canaans fields, I Expect my Work will be Soon over, I fail, and Bleed at my Lungs — But never was more Confirm'd in the Gospel than Since I have Seen you.

Remember me Affectionately to your parents And tell your D^r   Mother My Soul is Entering thro Tribulation the Kingdom of God where I Expect to meet her with Joy — Adieu my D^r   Dear Sis^r   I must away to   Meeting

Never forget your Unworthy Brother in the patience of JESUS

Harris Harding

Shelburn 29th Aug^t   1791

151

61. *H. Harding to James and Nancy D'Wolf*[242]

Dear Brother & Sister

1791: Shelburn 29th Aug[t]

I Cannot help writing a few lines to encourage you on your pilgrimage — It does my Soul Good thus to converse with the Dear Children of God tho at a distance, I am now in one of the darkest places I ever yet Saw, their opposition against the Gospel is Amazing but the Strength of Israel is with me, and I Can truly say I find some Liberty in Speaking in his Cause — O Dear Jemmy and Nancy you Cant think how I feel the dear Saints engag'd with me, I do Believe and often think they pray for me

My Soul often leaps at the thoughts of Sounding his name in N. England, Jesus will Surely send his Angel with me and Prosper my way, And my Soul shall possess the Gates of my Enemies for the Mouth of the Lord has spoken it — The Lord was with us (many times) of a truth at Liverpool, and we Saw his goings in his Sanctuary, and his Foot-Steps in the Great-deep, The waters divided before his people And the Ark of his Strength came into the Camp — O my Dear Dear Bro[r] & Sis[r] I m determind To conclude my mortal Notes in Sounding that Gospel that caus'd me to Leave my Father House to be a doorkeeper in his Courts.

O know nothing but a Christ Crucified to the world — Its unspeakable Loss in the Christian to Look at the darkness of their Brethren — Keep your eye on the Star

from your absent Brother

H. Harding

62. *H. Harding to Thomas Bennett at Horton*

My Very Dear Brother

Shelburn 31st Augt 91

I think I can often say with Dear Bro^r Alline — A Land in possesion is better than one promis'd — Surely he that is mighty has done to me great things and given me a Goodly heritage in Zion, I have Indeed my Dear Brother seen the waggons of Joseph and the Sceptre arise in Jacob since I Came away — I have had happy moments and Meetings and by Faith sometimes rejoic'd in that day that Abraham glad[?] — O My Brother I Can Bless God that ever I was made a door-keeper in his Courts, And to thread his Sanctuary with the Joyful news, Jesus is Risen.

I made my Soul glad to receive a Letter from you Especially when I read of your having new displays of Eternal wisdom made Known by the Spirit of God to your Soul; O that you might still Continue thro the Length and Brea[d] th of the Land for I know that God has given it to you as he swears unto Abraham — Still my Bro^r Keep your windows open towards Jerusalem

My Soul is often with you, and the Dear Saints in Falmouth, Rejoicing and Beholding your order in the Blessed Gospel

In two days I'm to set out on my way for New England. The thoughts of Declaring to them that Jesus Lives makes my heart leap — If not in Glory before — you may See me again probably within a year

I Am Still in the Death & Resurrection of Jesus,

Your Ser^t & Bro^r

H. Harding

P.S. Remember me in the Bowels of Christ to my Dear Dear Bro^{rs} & Sis^{rs}

V

September, 1791

to

October, 1791.

63. *Harris Harding to Joseph Dimock at Horton*

Shelburn 1st Sepr 91

My Brother

My Soul rejoices to hear the Lord goes with you, & makes his Blessed Work Prosper in your hand, I have felt my Soul Engaged with and for you, O' Go on, Go on from the Bottom of my Heart I wish you GOD Speed, & can pray if I never see your face again in the Flesh, that the GOD of Abraham may send his Angel before you, And that being in the way the Lord would direct you with Success, & cause you always to return with Joy, bringing your Sheaves with you to your Fathers house

My Dear Brother I'm now in one of the darkest places in the Province — Theres no appearance of A reformation unless it is their Unspeakable opposition against the Everlasting Gospel (I Mean Among the White-People). Davids Church[243] appears at times like A woman clothed with the Sun — I had some Joyful Meetings at Liverpool: I think Six or Seven in the Last Stir there were Converted — they would be Glad & Something expect to see you there Soon

I Set out (with Gods Will) tomorrow on my way for New England — Pray for me my Dear Brother, And always remember — I Am yours — In the Death Resurrection & Eternal Conquest of the Worlds Restorer

Harris Harding

P.S. I want   to know those who have Lately Enter'd the Kingdom of God in Annapolis. H.H.

64. *H. Harding to Frederick Fitch*[244] *at Horton*

My Dear Dear Bro^r

Shelburn 1st Sepr 91

That faithful Covenant keeping GOD, who has bought you and I with his own Blood is Still with me, & is my Shield and great reward, O Frederick why did he bring you to Zion? Ah! after you had Rejected his calls, quench'd his Spirit, And turn'd away his Ear from his Gracious Invitations; he still followed you with Eternal Blessings, And at the Expence of his Dying Groans reinstated you again in the Paradise of his Everlasting Love — O my Bro^r make his Righteousness now your Song, Ah' Sing thro this waste and Howling Wilderness — I'll Make his name my constant happy theme, Where'er I go, I'll always tell of him, Who gave his Life and bought me with his Blood To reinstate me in the arms of GOD. O Frederick, Jesus will shew you greater things than ever you have seen yet — when you feel your Soul drawing after him, don t fear to let it go freely, dont Stand to examin whither it be right; nor yet to Stop here, because you have got as far as ever you did before; but let your mind Soar away to the Blessed Shore

Remember me to your wife, O that she might find rest in the House of my Heavenly Father — I set out for Barrington tomorrow, if my Blessed Master permit.

I'll meet you again clothed with Eternal Light, in a Kingdon of Righteousness — If we never meet again in time

Your Brother   H. Harding

65. *H. Harding to Daniel Shaw*[245] *at Horton*

My Dear Brother

Yarmouth 17 Sep[r] 91

I have pass'd through many Scenes of Life since I saw you, & Enjoy'd many Happy Moments — Jesus my Blessed Master sends me where he himself would come, I left Barrington a few days ago, where Numbers were Groaning for Redemption, Some appeard under heavy distress and at Argyle the Spirit of God mov'd upon the Waters. I had only Two Meetings there — being Call'd to attend A Funeral yesterday in this place but shall return (with my Lords permission in a few days) and Visit both places before I set out for N. England — O my dear Brother I believe GOD Surely sent you to this Place to tell Saints and Sinners that Christ is Risen — O Let it encourage you my Brother wherever you go to hold up his Name & Witness for his Resurrection. Whether I may see you again is uncertain; But O I will soon meet Daniel in Immortality — Pray for your Brother in the Resurrection of Christ

H. Harding

66. *H. Harding to Dorcas Prentice at Horton*

My Dear Sister

Yarmouth 17 Sep[r] 91

I have Just heard of my Dear Grand-Mother entering the regions of Endless Glory which I doubt not Sometimes wrecks your mind, and Sinks your Soul in great distress — But O at other times Methinks I see you Joining her Eternal Songs Saying "Worthy is the Lamb that was slain" — I think I feel in some measure my Soul with you my Dear Sister and expect soon to reach the Immortal fields and strike the Endless Hallelujahs before the Throne

My Dear Grand father, I hope feels his Soul in the Kingdom and can say "Thy Grace is Sufficient for me" My Dear Sister Fally I see set by I think — Weeping for Joy that old Jacobs rod and Staff comfort her — But where is Jemmy, tell him his Grandmothers Groans for his Redemption is forever at an End — I only my Dear Sister snatch'd a moment to write you a few lines; I have wrote letters to the Christians from Shelburn, which I hope you have all receiv'd before these reach you — I Was a week at Barrington where was A great moving on Peoples minds — I left a Number there crying for Mercy, And some to appearance near the Kingdom — Had only two Meetings at Argyle, where A General Shaking appear'd among the Dry Bones And a Shouting among the Israelites I left there yesterday being call'd to attend a funeral in this place, and shall return to both Argyle and Barrington before I set out for the States, if my Master permit — Two or Three have been Converted of late in this place by the Means of Brother Daniel Shaw — My Soul is with the Church in your parts every day rejoicing in your Order in the Gospel

Yours in the Groans of a Dying Jesus

H. Harding

Yarmouth 29th Octo^r 1791

The Church of Christ at Falmouth

Dear Christians

The Ring-Straked & Speckled are my Hire Still —
And Ah' Blessed be God, I can say in A degree with Jacob, I
pass'd over with my Stake , and am become two Bands
The Lowing of the Milch-kine is heard in this Land —
The Angel of the Lord is riding on the White Horse thro
Barrington   Three are Converted, Numbers under great
distress Groaning for Mercy; and almost every Soul is Shock'd
thro the place — Jesus also spreads his Blessed Wings over
Argyle, his Kingdom is come into three Souls in that place of
Late, And Several were waiding   heavily under their Guilt. —
The Saints frequently in Meeting are Crying aloud "The Sword
of the Lord and of Gideon   And Righteousness breaks in like
an Overflowing flood into our Assemblies" — My Soul is A
Witness that you my Brothers & Sisters are Engaged with me in
the Everlasting Gospel; for I often feel your Groans,
I must bid you Adieu in great haste — The Vessel is
going off —

I Am yours Eternally in the Righteousness of GOD

H. Harding

VI

January, 1792

to

December, 1792.

68. *H. Harding to Joseph Dimock at Barrington*

Yarmouth 27th Jany 92

My Dear Brother

There is some Appearance of A reformation in this place, people flock in great Numbers to hear the Everlasting Gospel, Several seem moved by the Holy-Ghost, Doors are almost every where open'd for Meetings — And prejudices are Abundantly removed from peoples minds — Often and almost every time I speak I feel the Presence of my Blessed Master, there is I think A Little Cloud like the Bleeding hand of Jesus Arising in this part of the VinYard — The Christians have been several times on the Mount, & have Spoke with A Loud Voice of his Coming to them who look for redemption in Israel, so that I have Stopp'd Speaking once or twice — At Argyle I see the Goings of GOD in his Sanctuary. M^r —— I think is Savingly Born again — And I left Several Groaning for Redemption, & some to appearance near the Kingdom — O my Bro^r this I can truly Say is my Meat & Drink, to declare the Everlasting Righteousness of him in whom I am Eternally yours

H. Harding

69. *H. Harding to Thomas Bennett at Horton*

Argyle 14th Feby 1792

My Dear Dear Bro^r Bennett

It rejoic'd my Soul to receive your Letters, with the happy news of the Prosperity of Zion in that part of my Fathers Vinyard — All I Can say with regard to the Sepparation among the dear Children of my dying God is, I wish we may become all things to all, but let it be in the Spirit of the Gospel, and not in our own Conformity — I have often and almost Continually felt the Dear Saints with me in the Gospel since I came away — and many times have they handed me my Notes when Standing between the Living and the Dead

O my Dear Brother, I have seen the power of my GOD in A Wonderful manner since I came away — As many as Twenty Savingly United to GOD — Here will I raise my Ebeneazer, in the Presence of Hell, By the Name of my GOD, who answer'd me in the day of my Distress, And altho but A Child hath let none of my words hitherto fall to the Ground — O Lord my GOD, Thro' Thee I Shall Prevail, & my Soul tread down Strength, Ah' let it be recorded in the Records of Zion, that by the Boundless Grace of A Dying GOD, I ll wear out my waisting Lungs & totering frame proclaiming from the high places of Judah the Righteous Acts of my expiring Mediator

My Dear Brother I know from my own Experience your Soul shall advance into the Nature & Likness of God — Fear   lest you should Embrace Something wrong may Sometimes darken your mind, Grant it Liberty to act freely and it will bring to your Light the deep things of GOD — I want to write to all the Dear Christians but have not an opportunity now — Read these, and Remember me in the Name of my Master to my Dear Aunt D — Fally Bent Sally Hamilton & others

Write as soon as possible to Y^{rs} Unchagly

To Thos Bennett   Harris Harding

162

70. *H. Harding to Thomas Bennett at Horton*

Yarmouth 6th April 1792

My Dear Bro^r in Christ

      I have seen glorious days since I left you, truly the Lines have fallen to me in A Pleasant place, O the Goodness of God to me the Chief of Sinners — I pass'd over only with my Staff to this People, & Behold I am my Dear Brother thro Free-Grace, Become Two Bands. Never did I see the goings of my God in such A wonderful manner I think before — The Young Converts truly bear the Image of their dying Lord in A Heavenly manner

      We have Indeed my Bro^r happy happy Meetings — The Soul of your Unworthy Friend is an hundred fold rewarded — Blessed be God for ever putting me into the Ministry — O could I see you again how I tell you my Bro^r what great things my dying Lord has reveal'd to me since I saw you last — Near fifty in the last reformation are Savingly Born again, And can Lap with the Tongue — Very few that have been awaken'd turn back again to the World, but in Barrington, & Argyle we have been beset in A most devilish manner with Hypocritical Counterfeits — Yet the fire of God in his children has quite consum'd them, at least so far, as there is not One that I know of held A Christian, but Can say Shibboleth.

      Brother Bennett there was three young Men belonging to Barrington Shipp'd on Board A Vessel last fall bound for the West Indies in order to get clear of the Reformation; Two of them being greatly awaken'd by the Spirit of God — Last Saturday evening the Vessel return'd with the news of Two of them dying on their Passage-home with the Small-Pox, and the other Sick on board — Sabbath Morning as I was Praying in Meeting, it came to my mind to pray for him, I had no Sooner mention'd his name, than my Soul felt such A Union with him, I was sure the Lord has wash'd him in his Blood — I could hardly Speak, and as soon as I Concluded saw the Christians, and almost all the assembly in Tears. When Meeting was over we declar'd to the people what God had

163

reveald to us by his Spirit — On Thursday I went to A house where they had carried this Young Man the day before — As soon as I came to the door he Cry'd out "O Mr Harding!" then after recovering himself a Little, said "You can't tell what Sorrows Christ has carried me thro since I saw you Last. After we had gone to Sea, I began to think what means I had taken to wear my distress off my mind, & I grew afraid my Soul was Lost forever. It still follow'd me continually that I had Sold my Soul & Christ for about two Weeks. All this time I was curs'd by the Captain & all hands in a most dreadful manner as A dull Melancholy Fellow — One Night it being my Watch upon Deck, I was thinking in dreadful distress & Agony of mind that there was no Mercy for me; for I had rejected it, & it was gone forever. All at Once I know not how, I begin to think of the Mercy of God, And these words came into my mind, 'God will have Mercy, God will have Mercy,' and Still as my mind run upon them, my heart begin to burn within me, And God seem'd to come nearer & nearer till my Soul was fill'd with such unspeakable Joy as I never felt before, & remain'd so in A greater or Less degree for the most part of 2 or 3 Weeks, & by turns ever Since — My Soul felt such a Love for him while he Lay telling me of it that I Cannot express"

This my Dear Bro^r is some of the Spoils of the enemy that I have taken out of the Land of the Canaanite with my Sword since I saw you last, & my Bro^r do write by Capt Strickling about the Cause of God among you which I long to hear — I would write to more If I had time.

Adieu. Adieu. Adieu.

H. Harding

71. *H. Harding to Joseph Dimock at Horton*

Yarmouth 18th Ap^l 92

My Dear Brother in the Gospel

Still, Still Jesus is with me and the Arms of my hands are made Strong by the hands of the Mighty God of Jacob. There are above Twenty my Brother in Cape Forchu that Cry "The Sword of the Lord and of Gideon"— Opposition daily falls before the Gospel — O my Br^o   I have seen happy days & set in heavenly places with the Young Converts since I saw you — Several are very clear & are Indeed clothed with the Sun — Deane & his wife Betsy and Nabby Brown[247] are in the Everlasting Gospel — Yesterday a woman who lives at Salmon River that never has seen or heard anything about Conversion, till the Lord convicted & converted her about 5 Weeks ago, was at a Meeting truly Sick with Love, Crying out Repeatedly "O for Wings to fly to Glory" — The Young Converts Weeping for Joy all around falling on Each others Necks Rejoicing

O Josee! Josee! my Soul Rejoices that ever I was call'd to point my poor fellow Mortals to Behold the Ancient plan of Endless Life, & Declare the Everlasting Decrees of him, in whom Crucified

I am yours Eternally

H.H.

72. H. Harding to Thomas Bennett at Horton

Argyle 21st Ap^l 1792

My Dear Bro^r

The Blessings of him who was seperated from his Brethren are pour'd in upon my Soul from every Quarter, And O that name, let my Soul bear witness, that taught me Israel's Antient road has by his Eternal Spirit pointed out the Secrets of mens hearts of late in our assemblies, Bow'd Stubborn wills And caus'd rocky hearts to gush out Streams of Living Waters; Yes! my Dear Brother: Sometimes the power of the Holy Ghost rests upon my Soul, & I Can stand with one foot on Ebal and the other on Garazim in the name of the Lord, and deliver Eternal decrees and Messages to Saints and Sinners.

The Kingdom of God still advances at Cape Forchee I have great hopes for near Thirty I think they'l when try'd at the Waters, Lap with the Tongue. Some are Swallow'd up into Glory in A Wonderful manner; they have no Idea or Historical Knowledge of the operations of the Holy Ghost, until they have been brought thro, for the most past very soon; Some have been brought upon their knees Crying for Mercy and help, When the Lord Jesus brake into their Souls — When others in Meeting were groaning for redemption, would take hold and pull them down upon their knees, Crying that was the way to obtain Mercy — There are some so tender and Soften'd with redeeming Love that I Sometimes feel try'd, because I Stand no more in the Liberty of the Gospel to Stamp Jesus Image & truths upon their Souls — My Dear Brother God has not yet shew'd me, where I'm to go from this — In yours of the 27th February you desir'd me to let you know my mind concerning my Letters to the Christians being printed: I have no objection provided you and they think it beneficial to the Cause of my Blessed Master — Most of them are directed to Private Characters — you may Correct whatever you think Proper — I think I Can say with dear dear Bro^r Alline, "God forbid I should write or Speak anything but what I would publish (if possible) over the four quarters of the Globe-" Dr Bro^r I have not oppor^y to write to all my Dr Bro^{rs} & Sis^{rs} ; Read these & bid them rem^m

H. Harding

166

73. *H. Harding to Sally & Eunice Hamilton*[248] *at Horton*

Dear Sisters

Liverpool 5th July 92

I hope by this time, you can sy "The Lord is my Strength & Salvation: I will not fear what men or Devils can do unto me for he has become my Song & I will rejoice, Now my Redeemer Lives Ah lives in my Soul to Die no more" — O Girls, I Can Say this is my Theme & portion too, & in A few Days more my Soul will reach the land that flows with Milk & Honey; Blessed be GOD I in part possess it here — And O Lord my God, I feel that while I'm writing I Shall reign with you and the Dear Saints in Horton soon at his right hand. O for the Sake of him that has bought us with his Blood keep in sight of Canaan —

There are Several young People in this place (while others are Settled on A false hope) Singing that Song in Judah "We have A strong City Salvation has GOD appointed for her Walls" — I Expect to Leave this the first opportunity for Shelburn from there if GOD will to N. England And from there it may be to Glory — where if not before youl again meet

H. Harding

74.   *H. Harding To* M*rs*   *Edward D'Wolf*[249] *at Horton*

Liverpool 9th July 92

D^r   Sister in the Lord Jesus

I know you want to know how the Lords Cause prospers & how he deals with my Soul — The Christians in Chester seem'd to awake & Sinners mov'd in some degree — I found God with me almost every time I spoke, Stay'd but A few days, & then in the Name of my Master I think I can Say, I set out for Liverpool with high expectations of seeing the Place fill'd with the Glorious Presence of God.

While the Vessel was Sailing into the Harbour I was so overcome with A sense of the Gospel that I could hardly walk the Deck — As soon as we came to the Wharf (A Woman who I had known to be one of false hope before) Came running all in Tears telling that A Glorious Work there was among the People Seeing her former Spirit so much animated with and rejoicing in it — it began to raise some disagreeable fears in my mind And as the People were then Gathering for A Meeting, I soon had an opportunity of declaring my Masters Message to a Large Assembly. I think I had not spoke but A few Minutes, before numbers Rejoic'd & cry'd so loud my voice could not be heard — And while the most of the old Christians stood by Wondering, so Silently Weeping & looking On — These Young profess'd Converts were (Some of them Shouting for Joy; others in such distress seemingly for Sinners that one or two would be Employ'd in holding them, whilst others again would seem so overcome with the redeeming Love as to be almost as Motionless as if their breath was gone — I Soon found my Dear Lord had Something else for me to do in Liverpool than Speak and Rejoice with every One — And after I had insisted on their Saying Shibboleth before they pass'd over — Some were immediately offended, others without trouble quitted their Religion & turn'd to the world; I think there are Six or Seven among nearly Thirty who profess'd that are Savingly Converted — The Lord burns up all Sometimes when we meet. D^r   Sister I have often been with you rejoicing

168

in the Gospel since I left you
      I Am Your Ser^t & Bro^r   in the Dying Lamb

                           H. Harding

[written in margin:] To M^rs   Sally DeWolf, at Horton

75. *H. Harding to Hannah Potter*[250] *at Windsor*

My Dear Sister

                    Shelburn 31st Aug^t   92

      Although I omitted writing to you before (which was Occasion'd by the Vessels Sailing Sooner than I expected) Yet I have not forgot you, But many times feel you near my Soul in the despised Gospel

      But how do you live my Dear Sister, do you walk in the Holy-Ghost? does he often bring to you remembrance that Night when you left Egypt, and Eat the Gospel passover; when he lead you thro the Deep and you saw your Enemies Slain, Ah' when he Caus'd you to suck Honey out of the Rock, and your whole Soul Cried out "I pray thee let me go over and see that goodly Land, that holy Mountain & Lebanon" Then from the tops of the rocks you saw him, and from the Hills you beheld him, when you Eat of the Pomgranates, and tasted the clusters of Eshcol; when you saw the fields beyond Jordan white for Harvest; I hardly know how to stop rehearsing the Righteous[ness] of God towards you. I hope you can say my Soul has enter'd of late the promis' Land — He has roll'd off the reproach of Egypt from me, And I hear the Joyful Sound of the Hebrews release; O Hannah keep near, all the Good of the Land is before you.

      A am Dear Sister your Everlasting Friend

      In a Dying Jesus

           H. Harding

76. *H. Harding to Edward Manning at Falmouth*

My Dear Fellow Labourer in the Vinyard of God

Shelburn 1st Septr 1792

He that Separated me from my Fathers House & Mothers Womb to be A despised Messenger of his Gospel and A Witness of his Resurrection, many times fills me with the *New Wine*, and causes me to drink from the river of GOD

The Christians in Liverpool would be glad to see you in that Part of the Vinyard, O' Edward feed his Sheep & Lambs that he has bought with his Blood, and go where the Lamb would lead you; All thats Necessary in declaring the Gospel my Brother is the Holy Ghost; When we feel this we have Wisdom, matter & Subject — But methinks you have by this time try'd the Fleece born Wet & Dry — I'm going to Barrington (if GOD will Tomorrow) on my way to New England — Before we meet again here we may Strike Immortal Notes before the Throne

I am in haste — Adieu my Dear Bro^r

H. Harding

170

77. *H. Harding to the Revd Thos H. Chipman at Annapolis*

My Dear Dear Bro^r

Cornwallis 12th Decr 1792

I have waited a long time from writing You a Letter, because I should wish to inform you the present standing of the Christians here — And such alterations I never saw in any Place before in so short of time.

The Lord has been passing thro this Land in very deed, my Bro^r — And altho' many too many abuse their Liberty in the Blessed-Gospel; yet I have seen the Blood of Jesus sprinkled on the Door posts of many Hearts — And verily Believe as far as I can Judge the true Light now Shines Clearer than ever before, The last days of Glory is ushering in certainly upon Gods People.

We have had some Powerful Meetings since I came into the Country, The Voice of my dying GOD has (at times) shook our assemblies like the Wilderness of Kadish, Lavina Brown[251] and some Others have enter'd the Kingdom of GOD.

I expect GOD to pay Annapolis a visit shortly, O that I might be sent as Eleazer to Labans House; Lord lead me to my masters Brethren

I am my Dear Bro^r yours Unalterably

H. Harding

VII

February, 1793

to

October, 1793.

78. *H. Harding to Elphila Bent*[252] *at Horton*

My Dear Sis^r

Annapolis Feb^y   25, 1793

I can with Joy inform you that Jesus Reigns — Ah Fally! before you reach your Fathers Inheritance you shall see the Ancient Prophecies fulfilling amongst us As he has spoken by the Mouth of his Holy Prophets since the world began. And O I feel my Sister (at times) from the living GOD, that I shall live to see the latter days dawn in Zion, and Salvation come out of Israel — Yea, I have heard of late the Voice of the Bride and Bride-Groom ring thro the Ears of my Soul and saying "Now is Salvation Come down from the Lord and his Christ, for the accuser of our Brethren is cast down"

O my dear dear Sister the angel of the Lord is passing thro the Land — Sealing the Servants of GOD in their Foreheads — One or two has already come unto Mount Zion, And a great Cry my Soul has heard in the Land of Egypt.

I Suppose the Curtain will soon be Drawn and your Ransom'd Soul my Sister strike immortal notes — But O I can truly Say Fally, Altho invaded by Earth and Hell I will willingly travel thro Sin Death and Affliction since Omnipotence is my Strength and Everlasting support, for to ransom by the hand of Jesus my fellow men from the Grave Ah let his faithfulness to my Soul be recorded in the Annals of Eternity, and had in Everlasting remembrance before GOD

Keep Sight of Israel star, Its Almost Day brake with your Soul — When he the Dying Lamb shall beam all his Perfections into your ravish'd Soul forever.

I am Still Eternally yours in Christ

79.   *H. Harding to Thomas Bennett at Cornwallis*

Annapolis 25th March 1793

My Dear Bro^r

Heaven opens in Believers Souls, and Zions GOD appears amongst his people   The Sun beams of Glory are shining into our Assemblies in a most wonderful manner

Last Wednesday Evening God walk'd thro the midst of Israel and shook the Assembly like the wilderness — Truly my Dear Brother the coming of the Son of Man was like Lightening Shining down from One part of Heaven to the other — Some of the Christians ascending the Mount beheld the Counsels of Heaven reveal'd, whilst the resurrection of GODs Dear Son transported and fill'd every pow'r immortal in them when any speak with a loud voice of Redemption of Israel a Sinner it may be in the further part of the Room, would immediately scream out as if the Sword of the Lord pierc'd thro his very Soul —

Three or four are brought by the Blood of the Lamb to Mount Zion — Others brought into very clear Liberty that were out of Sight before — Several little Children are converted in a Powerful Manner, And every day almost, some come out as clear as the Sun.

The Christians are all converted into it, and all say they never saw such a Day of Gospel-Glory before — all opposition falls before it, and the Noise goes on and increses

I am your Happy, highly favour'd Bro^r   H. Harding

P.S. Two have come out into clear Liberty to Daye

Annapolis 25th March 1793

To Thos   Bennett

174

80. *Edward Manning to Thos Bennett at Horton*

Kingsclear New Brunswick   May 20 1793

Dear Bro^r

    I am surpris'd you have not wrote to me, If you knew how much it rejoic'd my Soul to hear from you, you would write to me every week, For I Suppose you have many things to relate to me respecting Gods marvelous work among you. If ever I knew what GOD could do its since I came to St. Johns, I want to see you to tell you my whole heart I could not tell you all in a Week — Near 70 Souls (if not more) has found GOD to be all and in all and truly lives in green pastures, and grows as the Calves in the Stall, Ah Blessed be the name of GOD I see a man with a drawn sword in his hand as Captain of the Lords-Host, he's come his voice is powerful and full of Majesty and divides the flaims of fire, and shakes the wilderness, Ah' I see his Star in the East my Brother — And I am come to worship him to Zion the City of the living GOD — O my Brother the Good of all the Land is before us And all behind is a barren wilderness

    The Lord-GOD is terrible befor his great Army
    "A Cowardly Crew they seem at first view
    "But led by their Captain great feats they will [do]"
O my Bro^r I can truly say by heart felt experience "Hitherto the Lord has helped me, I've seen the Stars in their courses fight for Zion" Blessed be GOD I see the Horse and his rider thrown into the Depths of the Sea. The Israelites come forth shining and travel three days Journey with incredible haste, which the Egyptians Essaying to do are drown'd in the Dragons flood

    My Dear Sister Fally[253] I hear is gone to inherit eternal Glory, my Soul in reading the Account found an Union with her in the realms of light —

    O my Brother we are to awake there in a few more revolving   moments. Tell Dorcas[254] to live in the enjoyment of Fallys GOD. I expect to come over about MidSummer —

    My Soul longs for the time to Come when I shall once more preach Jesus among that people who appears as stars of the First magnitude in the firmament of Gods power — Tell them I believe GOD is about to shake the Heavens and the Earth once more among them. Horton is yet to

NOTE: The bottom of the page is torn.

81. *H. Harding to Thomas Bennett at Liverpool*

Onslo 1st July 1793

My Dear Dear Bro^r

I have seen the goings of GOD in his blessed Sanctuary in this part of his Vin Yards, Some that were in darkness begin to feel the Heavenly Day dawn in their Souls again — Never did I see more openess in Christians minds than in this place to receive the Everlasting Gospel, One has already found Salvation to her Soul since I came here — But the opposition from opposers, exceeds all that you ever saw perhaps in your life, It really seems as tho Death & Hell were delivering up their Dead, But the House of Saul grows weaker and weaker continually and the House of David and his throne is establish'd more & more O my Bro^r By faith I obtain'd that promise arise and Speak to them all that I command thee for I have set thee saith my GOD as Brazen Walls against the whole Land Against the Princes thereof against the Priests there of & against the people of all the Land, they shall fight against thee but shall not prevail, for I am with thee saith the Lord God of Israel

And O I can assure you my Brother my Soul has often felt the eternal voice of the Lamb in them words

I long to have a Letter from you Pray write soon & direct your Letters to Horton. Remember me in the Bowels of Jesus to all my dear dear Bro^{rs} & Sis^{rs} at Liverpool

I am unchangably yours

Harris Harding

176

82. *M*ʳˢ *Sylvia Wright*[255] *to Tho*ˢ *Bennett at Liverpool*

Dear Bro r in the Lords Christ,

Annapolis 26th Sepʳ 93

I feel that arm that tumbles the Mountains about with words of eternal Silence, that glorious kingdom of eternal righteousness weighing the Mountains in a Balance and the Hills in scales. Yes my Brother I felt it pressing his way thro Legions of Devils And they will run violently down a steep place and be chok'd in the Sea. Ah it is pressing with the utmost Violence, he will not return back empty but be fill'd with the spoils of the slain — his glorious Kingdom will not break forth yet in his greatest glory, but when he comes the whole earth shall be fill'd with his glory, Devils, Hell and Death will be glad of some Dark Cavern to hide for Shelter, for your God is a consuming fire, burning All the Hay, Wood and Stubble.

God dwells in thick darkness and in tabernacles — And their are other tabernacles whose inhabitants will be cast out and each one center to his own Kingdom, And that Song shall be Sung, Now is come Salvation, and Glory and Power for the accuser of our Brethren is cast down forever down. My Broʳ be not cast down you know all things conspire to bring about his blessed decrees and eternal purposes, he will overturn overturn Overturn and reign a mighty Conqueror —

About our Dear Broʳ H —— g there has indeed my Broʳ been many cruel and false reports that he has not deserv'd, which has given great cause to the Enemies of the Lord Jesus to blaspheme — I know not how to reveal it, for it distresses my Soul to think that it is rais'd chiefly among our Neighbouring Christians, but this I know and am confident 'twas all done and transacted in the Kingdom of Darkness, and whoever spreads it is only doing the Devils drudgery, it has been told by some amongst us, and great pains has been taken to spread it by Sea and Land, but you are not a stranger to that Spirit of Darkness which reigns among Christians now a days, To give you my opinion from the best intelligence & most I can collect, he was not overcome with any indecent behavior but I

177

think the Young Woman had a great natural fondness for him and thought all his tender expressions for hers and other Souls was the effect of natural passion which she wish'd to be the case to her, and when she found herself mistaken she was fill'd with confusion and shame, Expressing herself in such words as would best Answer to clear herself, and tho she has told many stories which do not at all agree with each other,[256] Yet some have feasted themselves on reporting them, and M^r ⎯ has been foremost in it — But I can at times see the blessed hand of wisdom overturning Hell and calling each one by name, and Tho Harris may be hurld into the Lake he will come out as Gold tried Seven times — And all the Devil will gain by all his cunning ties and Hellish Crafts will be but the increase of his own chains Hellish Confusion and eternal Blackness, I care not what any says about me Christs name is good enough for us all to bear — O let me see his righteousness Shine — The morning Stars shout for Joy. These words "His ways are past finding out," has roll'd thro my Soul of late discovering such a depth and height of wisdom Love Strength and power, as will for ever ravish our Souls with silent astonishment. Dear Bro^r Manning will I dare say be with you soon and assist you in the Lord — We shall yet see the son of Man coming in the clouds of Heaven with pow'r & great Glory. You'l my Bro^r come this way when the Lord permits

Y^{rs} in the Bonds of Eternal Love

S.W.

178

83. *Edward Manning to Thomas Bennett*

Granville Octo^r 10th 1793

Dear Bennett

Since I've seen you Ive surely been (GOD Almighty only knows) where none but the followers of the Lamb whose wrestling Souls have felt the same, Can ever tell or ever know what different scenes I'm carried thro —
I've seen the foundations of the world discover'd, and O my Bro^r such Scenes of horor and Darkness as would make your very Soul Shudder to think of   Hell from beneath has been enlarg'd against the Strength of Israel, But it never fails, o my Brother nor never will — Underneath us is the Everlasting arms, and the Eternal GOD is our refuge. I've much to tell you about St. Johns but must omit at present. Certainly there has been the greatest reformation there I ever saw in my Life, And they thirst gloriously thirst for the Liberty of the Gospel, when I left them many were longing for the appearing of the Son of Man. James [Manning] Preaches and it seems as if nothing stands before him
The scene is much altered in Nova Scotia since I left it, Darkness, Darkness, Darkness. Good God you never saw such Darkness it may be felt. The Israelites have light in their dwellings, but some of them very Little and afraid to have more —

You'l hear many Stories flying from the powers of Hell. You may allow 31 points, for Hed Sea, Lee Way, Drift of Current, Variation of Compass & ^c ...²⁵⁷
I've travell'd through Grenvil, Horton, Cornwallis Falmouth & where there are Sentries appointed to keep out the Grand foe, I know from GOD I Shall yet see his cause revive, Certainly there will be an overturn, I feel Darkness removing, The Light Shining, The Voice Crying — The Bride Groom Approaching — The Bride Arising — The Sea roaring — The trumpet Sounding — The Heavens and the Earth Shaking — And all Nature grows to let the Opressed go free — You say you sometimes think Edward Manning is Coming to Liverpool to preach the Gospel there. I Sometimes think so too, but don't

know certain as yet. When I'm call'd I'll bend my course that way, Christ is my Pilot wise my compass in his word my Soul each Storm defies while I have such a Lord

Never did I see a greater need of being wholy taught of GOD — The Liverpool Christians are near to me as my own Soul, you must remember me to them, Tell them They are the ones that shall call the People to the Mountains, There they shall offer Sacrifices of righteousness, for they shall suck of the Abundance of the Seas and partake of the treasure hid in the Sands —

My mind turns, I'm surrounded with M — ds

So farewell   Yours in Christ

E. Manning

Section II
HYMNS
and
SPIRITUAL
SONGS

1.

Alline's Hymns
and
Spiritual Songs

1. A SINNER CONVINCED OF HIS DEATH AND BLINDNESS

1

Hard Heart of mine O that the Lord
Would this Hard Heart Subdue
O Come thou Blest Life giving Word
And form my Soul Anew.

2

I Hear the Heavenly pilgrims tell
Their Sins are all forgiven
And while on Earth their Bodies Dwell
Their Souls Enjoy a Heaven.

3

While I poor Wretch in Darkness Stand
With Guilt a Heavy Load
And Every Breath Expos'd to Land
Beyond the Grace of God.

4

The Christians Sing Redeeming Love
And talk of Joys Divine
And Soon they Say in Realms above
In Glory they Shall Shine.

5

But Ah Its all an unknown Tongue
I Never Knew that Love
I Cannot Sing that Heavenly Song
Nor Tell of Joys above.[258]

6

[I want, O God, I know not what!
I want what saints enjoy;
O let their portion be my lot,
Their work be my employ,

7

Fain world I know that Saviour mine
And taste his bleeding love,
With all the heav'nly pilgrims join,
While I this desert rove.

8

Then O to those transporting realms
My soul would soar away,
Where all the warriors wear their palms
In everlasting day.]

2. ON DEATH

1

I soon must hear the Solemn Call
Prepar'd or not to yield my Breath
And this poor mortal frame must fall
A Helpless prey to Cruel Death.

2

Then look my Soul, Look forward now
And Anchor Safe beyond the flood
But to the Saviours Footstool Bow
And get a life Secure in God.

3

Before these fleeting hours are gone
I'll bid this Mortal World adieu
And to the Lord I'll Now resign
My Life my Breath and Spirit too.

4

Then Welcome Death with all Its force.
No more Ill fear the gasping grave
Jesus my God my Last resource
We'll reach his arm my Soul to Save.

5

He will not hide his Smiling face
Nor Leave me in that trying Hour
I'll trust my Soul upon his grace
And Chearfull Leave this Mortal Shore.[259]

3. FREE SALVATION BY THE BIRTH OF CHRIST

1

Ye Sons of Adam Lift your Eyes
Behold how free the Saviour Dies
To Save Your Souls from Hell
Ther's your Creator and your friend
Believe And Soon your fears shall End
And you in Glory Dwell.

2

Doubt not his Word his grace is free
Believe he dies and calls for thee
And you poor Souls shall live
Can free Salvation be Deny'd
When in his Dying Groans he Cry'd
Father their Sins Forgive.[260]

3

[Believe and feel his boundless love;
It soon will bear your souls above,
To peaceful realms on high;
He swears as certain as he lives,
His hand a free salvation gives
"Why sinner will you die?"

4

Will you despite the vast renown,
And choose despair before a crown?
O have eternal joy!
Receive a kingdom in your heart,
Of life and joy that ne'er'll depart;
Nor earth or hell destroy.]

4. AN ADVICE TO A YOUNG CONVERT

1

Arise O youth, with all thy Soul
And Spread your redeemers Name
Nor Cease while fleeting moments roll
To Sound his well deserved fame.

2

Go in the Name of Christ your God
Shake off the world, and Bear the Cross
Jesus will be thy sure reward
Nor Shall your Labors e'er be Lost

3

He's Bought thee with his precious Blood
And wrote thy Name above the Skies
He'l be thy Father and thy God
When Suns and Stars Dissolves & Dies.

4

Then Every power and Every Thought
May Shout thro all the realms above
But then you never can Exhort
Poor Sinners to your Saviours Love.[261]

5. ON THE NAME OF JESUS

1

Jesus we love thy Name
And thee we will adore
And when we feel this Heavenly flame
We long to Love thee more.

2

Thy Name is all our trust
Thy Name is Solid peace
Thy Name is Everlasting rest
When other Names shall Cease.

3

There Ravish'd with thy Name
We never more shall rove
There Sound thine Everlasting fame
And Solace in thy Love.

4

Thy Name Shall be our praise
Thy Name Shall be our Joy
Thy Name thro Everlasting Days
Shall Countless throngs Employ.[262]

6. FREE GRACE
[Christ's death declares his grace is free]

1

Awake O Guilty World Awake
Behold the Earths foundation Shake
While the Redeemer Bleeds for you
His Death proclaims to all your race
Free Grace, Free Grace, Free Grace, Free Grace
To all the Jews and Gentiles too.

2

Come Guilty Mortals Come and See
The Saviour on the Cursed tree
For you all dressd in purple gore
His Weight of Woe has Veiled the Sun
Tis done: Tis done: Tis done: Tis done
That man might Live forever more.

3

See How the Wounded Lamb of God
Extends his Bleeding Arms abroad
To Save a fall'n world from Death
Behold him in his Agonies
He Dies. He Dies. He Dies. He Dies.
And Yields the last Expiring Breath.

4

He Dies and Triumphs O'er Death
To give the Dead immortal Birth
And Spread the Wonders of his Name
Shout Mortals Shout with Chearfull Voice
Rejoice, rejoice, rejoice, Rejoice
And give the Glory to the Lamb.[263]

7. WORTHY IS THE LAMB

1
Amazing Love Unbounded Grace
Through the Redeemers Name
Let mortal and immortal race
Cry *"Worthy is the Lamb.*

2
The Mighty Saviour from the Skies
Comes down to Bear our Shame
Beneath our Guilt he Bleeds and Dies
All Worthy is the Lamb.

3
Ten Thousand thousand thanks are due
O Jesus to thy Name
Let Saints above and angels too
Cry *"Worthy is the Lamb*

4
And we on these immortal plains
Inspir'd with Sacred flame
E'er Long Shall raise the highest Strains
Of *"Worthy is the Lamb.*[264]

8. INVITING SINNERS

The Christians inviting sinners

1

Sinners attend the Saviours Come
To Bring the Worst of Rebels home
O'er Dying Souls his Bowels move
His Grace is free his Name is Love.

2

We've Seen his face and heard his Voice
Enjoy'd his Love and must rejoice
And can but Court you to his Name
O Sinners Come Enjoy the Same.

3

Against the Rage of Earth and Hell
We have all Vow'd with Christ to dwell
He's gone before and we'l pursue
O Sinners follow Jesus too.

4

Our Names are with the Sons of God
Eternal Life is our reward
Christ Fights the Battle wins the race
While We Believe and Sing free Grace.

5

To gain the Crown Jehovah Dies
While we look on and Share the prize
The more we gaze the more we have
The more we get the more we love.

6

Come Sinners Share a Glorious Part
One View of Christ will melt your Heart
And you with all the Saints may rest
And Reign Eternal Ages Blest.

7

Soon by Our prince the field is Won
All fighting and our Sorrows done
And we Shall with archangels Share
O Sinners have a Mansion there.

8

There we shall Sail in Seas of Love
And Soar thro all the Realms above
Millions of Systems Joine as One
In One Eternal Song Amen.[265]

9. HAPPY YOUTH

1

While I am Blest with youthfull Bloom
I Will pursue that Sacred Lamb
That Bled and Died for me
If God inspires my Heart with Grace
And Lets me See his Smilimg face
A pilgrim I will be.

2

I'll Leave this World with all Its Toys
And Seek those far Superior Joys
That doth in Jesus Dwell
If Jesus be my God and King
Immortal Triumphs I will Sing
O'er all the powers of Hell.

3

A Frowning World I will Defy
And all Its Flattering charms deny
If Jesus Stands my friend
Not long I have the Storm to Stand
Of this Ensnarling Barren Land
My Conflict Soon will End.[266]

4

[With joy I'll spend my fleeting days,
To sound abroad my Saviour's praise,
And tell the world his love;
And when I quit this mortal stage
I shall in sacred strains engage,
With all the saints above.

5

There I shall with my Jesus dwell,
In joys beyond what tongue can tell,
On that immortal Shore;
Jesus my love shall be my joy,
His praises be my sweet employ,
And part from him no more.]

194

10. WONDERING AT GODS FREE GRACE

1

My Soul O wonder have I known
The Saviours Boundless Grace
And I So Blest O am I One
Of the redeem'd Race.

2

Shall I One Day be Call'd to reign
In the Bright realms above
Live with my God nor Sin again
But feast upon his Love.

3

O What a Wonder I Shall be
To all the Heaven Born race
Angels amaz'd may look on mc
A Miracle of Grace.

4

Inflam'd with Everlasting Love
My Jesus I'll adore
My Mansion in the Realms above
Where Death is known no more

5

O What a pleasing Thought is this
That Jesus is my friend
The Lord is mine And I am his
My Joys Shall Never End.[267]

11. LONGING TO BE WITH CHRIST

1

My Soul O God Aspires to be
From Interposing Darkness Free
Ravished with Scenes Divine
I Long to Swim in Boundless Grace
And See my Saviour face to face
And Know my God is mine.

2

I Long to find my Happy Seat
Where I might wash my Saviours feet
In Humble Tears of Love
To praise my God with all my Heart
And never from his love Desert
Till I Awake above.

3

Millions of years of Carnal Joy
With all their Crowns are Empty Toys
[With earthly Crowns, are empty Toys]
Compar'd with Christ my Friend
In him alone I Can be blest
'Tis he that gives me Solid Rest
And make my Sorrows End.

4

Shall I Shall I Ever be
Where I this Blessed Christ shall See
And Every Storm blow Over
On Wings of the Celestial Dove
I'd [I'll] Soar and Drink Immortal Love[268]
[And leave my friend no more.]

5

[There I shall bask in sacred beams,
And solace in celestial streams
Of sweet unmingled joy;
There I shall find my long abode
196

In perfect likeness of my god,
Where nothing can annoy.

6

A palm of honours I shall wear;
With all the heav'nly armies share,
In all their joys divine;
There I shall find eternal peace,
My songs of joy shall never cease,
And Jesus shall be mine.]

12. REDEEMING LOVE

1

Pilgrims Let us Join to Sing
Hallelujahs to our King
While as Pilgrims here we rove
Tell and Sing Redeeming Love.

2

Tell How Jesus on the tree
Gave his Life for you and me
Point to the incarnate dove
Show poor Souls Redeeming Love.

3

Sinners See the Saviour Dies
See him in his agonies
Can your Hearts forbear to move
Open to Redeeming Love.

4

Thus Expiring Bows his head
To The Caverns of the Dead
Then Triumphant Mounts above
Sounding his Redeeming Love.

5

Still he Labours on the Earth
Raising Wretched Souls from Death
He at every Heart doth move
Offering Redeeming Love.

6

Sinners Justly Doom'd to Hell
If they would in Heaven might Dwell
Room Enough in Realms above
Jesus Courts them to his Love.

7

Wretch'd Souls by Sin Astray
Owing Much with Nought to pay
Cease in Foreign Lands to Rove
Fly home to Redeeming Love.

8

Prodigals wipe off your Tears
Banish all your Slavish Fears
Jesus feels his Bowels move
Runs to Meet you with his Love.

9

Christ Extends his Bleeding hands
Courts you to the Sacred Band
Come and with the pilgrims Rove
Share and Sing Redeeming Love.

10

Wounded Hearts may Now Rejoice
Mourners hear the Saviours Voice
Hasten to the Courts Above
There to Sing Redeeming Love.

11

Soon from all the Storms of Night
We to Heaven will Take our flight
Winged on the Celestial Dove
Sailing in Redeeming Love.

12

Love Shall be our Lasting Theme
Love Shall Every Soul Inflame
Always Now in Realms Above
Ah, Amen, redeeming Love.[269]

XII

[With the countless throng we'll join
Each may say "This Christ is mine,"
Each enjoy a seat above,
Where there's nothing known but love.

XIII

Shining in immortal bloom;
Hail! all glory, this our home!
Shouts resounding all above,
Boundless is redeeming love.]

13. IN DEBT TO EVERLASTING LOVE

1
Down from the Glorious realms above
Descends the Saviour Cloth'd in [with] Love
Assumes a Body Can it be
To Bleed and Suffer Death for me.

2
Freely he Spilt his Life and Breath
To Save me from Eternal Death
And When no helper I Could See
Made known his Dying Love to me.

3
He took me from the Jaws of Hell
And told my Soul that all was well
His Love so great his grace so free
He Said he spilt his Blood for me.

4
O Love Amazing! Boundless grace
To me the worst of mortal race
How Could the Saviour Die so free
For Such a Worthless Wretch as me.

5
What Shall I do? What Shall I Say
What Can my Soul to him repay
Who Spilt his precious Blood so free
For Such a Guilty Wretch as me.[270]

6
[Lord all I have is double thine;
And I with pleasure will resign
My everlasting all to thee,
Who died for such a wretch as me.

7
This name shall dwell upon my tongue;
With joy I'll make his love my song;

I'll laud that name that stoop'd so free
To save a soul so vile as me.

8

Forever in the realms above,
Bound up in everlasting love,
I shall with joy and wonder see
That Christ who gave his life for me.

9

I'll sound with all the countless race
The wonders of redeeming grace;
And this shall be my lasting plea,
The highest note belongs to me.]

14. A CHRISTIAN'S TRAVEL

6

Sometimes I'm like a Wandering Jew
That Seeks a friend whom once he Knew
Nor Doth my Weary Footsteps end
Untill I find my Absent friend

7

Sometimes I'm like a Thirsty plain
Parch'd up with drought Thirsting for rain
And when I'm water'd from above
Chearfull I drink the Showers of Love.

8

O When Dear Jesus Shall I be
From all these Clouds and trials free
When Shall I reach the peacefull Shore
Where Storms of grief are Known no more.[271]

I

[None but the foll'wers of the Lamb
(Whose wrestling souls have felt the same)
Can ever tell, or ever know,
What diff'rent scenes I'm carry'd through.

II

Sometimes I drink of joys divine,
And Sing, *Ah! My Beloved is Mine:*
But unbelief returns again,
And loads my soul with fear and pain.

III

Some times I get a short release
From chains, and find a heav'nly peace;
I leap for joy, expecting soon
That all my sorrows will be gone.

IV

But soon, ah! soon my joys are fled,
And raging fears perplex my head;

202

Ten thousand beasts of prey return,
And cause my bleeding soul to mourn.

V

Then like a captive I complain
Till the blest star appears again,
Then heav'nly joys my fears control,
My God transports my wounded Soul.]

15.   THE CHRISTIAN SOON TO BE DELIVERED

1

Soon shall I quit this Mortal Shore
And Jesus Stand my friend
My Nights of Grief shall all be Oer
And all my Labors End.

2

Then I Shall reach the Realms of Bliss
Where my Beloved reigns
Then I Shall dwell where Jesus is
And Sing Immortal Strains.

3

There I Shall drink unmingled Joy
From Streams of Love Divine
No passing Clouds for to Annoy
Where God in Glory Shines.

4

O What Immortal Scenes of Bliss
Will Bear my Soul away
How Sweet the Realms of Joy & Peace
In Uncreated Day.[272]

16. PRAISE TO CHRIST
[A Song of Praise to Christ]

1

Jesus the Heavenly Lamb was Slain
A Rebel World to Save
Jesus the Sinners Life to gain
His Own a Ransom gave.

2

He Bleeds he dies beneath the Weight
Of Mans Enormous guilt
His Grace so free his Love so great
His Blood was freely Spilt.

3

Ten Thousand praises to thy Name
Thou Sinners Only friend
Let Every Tongue thy Love proclaim
Till Mortal Days Shall End.

4

Then Let Eternal Ages Sound
Thy Name in Realms above
Where Everlasting Joys abound
A Sea of Perfect Love.[273]

17. HAPPY STATE OF CHRISTIANS

1

Blest are the Souls that Know the Lord
And Humbly Walk before his face
They feed [feast] upon Immortal food
And Sing with Joy redeeming Grace.

2

Cheerful they t[h] read this Desert thro
Led by the blest redeemers hand
And when they bid the Earth adieu
With Joy will reach the Heavenly Land.

3

There from their Sorrows they shall rest
With Angels on the peacefull Shore
And with Immortal Glories blest
To Leave their Chief Delight no more.

4

O might it be my portion too
To have the Blessings they Enjoy
I'd bid all other Joys adieu
And Join in their divine Employ.[274]

18.   ON THE HAPPINESS OF SAINTS ABOVE

1

Great are the Joys of Saints above
Beyond What Tongues Can tell
Full they Enjoy their Saviours Love
And in his Bosom Dwell.

2

Now they have reach'd their happy home
The Sea of perfect Joy
Where Interposing Clouds ne'er Come
Nor Foes their peace annoy.

3

Their Joys are Now forever New
And all their Sorrows gone
All other Loves they've bid Adieu
And with the Lord are One.

4

Cheerfull they've run the Christian race
And reach'd the peacefull Shore
And See their Jesus face to face
Where Clouds Can Veil no more.

5

Arise my Soul the Crown pursue
And Taste redeeming Love
For I may Share the Glories too
With all the Saints Above.[275]

19. THE DOUBTING CHRISTIAN WRESTLING FOR A REAL KNOWLEDGE OF CHRIST

1

O Cutting Doubts When Shall I Know
That Jesus is my friend
When Shall I Leave these floods of Woe
When will these Conflicts End.

2

Sometimes I think I feel his Love
And taste of Joys Divine
But Ah too Soon in Doubts I rove
And Cannot Say he's Mine.

3

But still I must presume to Know
Since all I have's at Stake
Tell me, Dear God, O stoop so low
For the Redeemers Sake.

4

Tis for the Glory of thy Name
And my Eternal Joy
That I Should Know and Love the Lamb
Then Lord these Doubts Destroy.

5

I never Shall with peace be blest
While Doubting this I rove
Nor Dare I Sleep Nor Dare I rest
Till I have known thy Love.

6

O Come Dear Jesus, come, I pray
And Speak the Word of peace
Take all my Doubts and fears away
And make my Sorrows Cease.

7

O might I see the Happy Day
When I Could all resign;
These Doubts and foes be fled away
And Know that Christ is mine.[276]

20. THE DOUBTING CHRISTIAN

1

When will the blest Immortal Dove
These Heavy Doubts and Clouds remove
And let me know my Standing Sure
O will his Love O'er on me Shine
That I may say my God is mine
And Doubt this Love to me no more.

2

Dark State of Mine to live so far
From Christ the Bright the Morning Star
And Wander in these Shades of Night
My Faith is Weak my Joys are Low
Long Nights I Wade thro Seas of Woe
O Jesus Bless me with thy Lights.

3

Lord Take me by the hand I pray
And lead me to Eternal Day
Where Every Fear & Doubt Shall Cease
There shall I Drink of living Streams
And bask in thine Immortal Beams
Where all the Glorious Realms are peace.[277]

21. THE VANITY OF THE WORLD

1

This World with all Its Charms
Are Vain and Poison too
O Let me fly to Jesus' Arms
I'd bid them all Adieu —

2

Methinks my Soul Can Say
I find no pleasure here
The more for Earthly Joys I stray
The Greater is my Fear —

3

Too Long I've Sought for Joy
Where it was never found
Why Should I Still my Life Employ
To Search a Desert Round —

4

My Hungry Soul Aspires
To Bid them all Adieu
My Heart Awakes with Strong Desires
The Saviour to pursue —

5

Lord Help me to Arise
From Every Earthly Toy
Give me a Life that Never Dies
And be my Only Joy — [278]

22. THIRSTING AFTER JESUS

1
As Pilgrims wish their rest to find
So Doth my poor Distress'd mind
Long to Enjoy a place of Rest
Among the Saints forever Blest.

2
I cannot live contented here
Unless my Jesus does appear
His presence brings a Heavenly feast
And makes me in his Goodness Boast.

3
Lord Speak and set my Spirit free
And Cause me to rejoice in thee
Let all my Life and Strength be thine
Till I awake in Realms Divine.

4
Immortal Love Shall then inflame
My Soul to Sound thy lasting fame
And blest Beyond What Tongue can Tell
For There I shall with Jesus Dwell.[279]

23. THE DOUBTING CHRISTIAN, LONGING TO KNOW THAT HIS REDEEMER LIVETH

1

Without a Doubt O Could I Know
Dear Jesus That I was in thee
My Soul would Soon forget her Woe
And O How Happy I Should be.

2

Ah if I felt that Christ was mine
With Joy I'd Sing his Boundless Love
My Tongue Should Dwell on themes divine
Till I Should Soar to realms above.

3

But if in Doubts I spend my Days
No Happy Moments Shall I See
But wander in these Dismal Ways
Distress'd and poor wherer I be.

4

This Would be a Scene of Woe
And life Itself a Burden prove
And must I Still a mourner go
Without my friend my Life my Love.

5

O Thou that came to help the poor
Make bare thine arm and set me free
Thy Goodness Knows no Bound nor Shore
Then Lord Extend thy Love to me.[280]

24. THE CHRISTIAN'S WONDER AND JOY

1

Hail ye Dark Tennants of the Earth
Hear the glad News thy Saviours birth
Jehovah Breaks thy Shades of Night
Brings Immortality to Light.

2

A God Descends becomes a Man
My God An Infant of a Span
What the Eternal bear my Woe
My Soul, And Can he Stoop So Low.

3

Steal pleasing Scene into my Heart
And Ravish Every power of Thought
O Let me leave Created Good
And Nothing Know but Christ my God.

4

O Bear my Panting Soul Away
To Realms of Everlasting Day
There There with Rapture Shall I Gaze
To [On] God in his Meridian Blaze —

5

Good God and are Such Glories mine
Yes Lord I feel the Life Divine
But would Enjoy the Perfect Scene
Without One passing Shade Between.[281]

25. THE CHRISTIANS TRIUMPH OVER DEATH

1

Mount my Soul on Wings Triumphant
Jesus Bids the Dauntless Rise
One Sweet Ray of Life Immortal
Conquers Death and Never Dies
O my Jesus. O my Jesus
Bear my Soul above the Skies.

2

Let me feel the pleasing Rapture
Rising in Immortal Bloom [birth]
I Shall have no Grave to Enter
Never feel Expiring Death [breath]
Life Eternal Life Eternal
Swallows up the Grave and Death.

3

Fear and Grief and Empty Story
While I feel that Jesus Reigns
Raptures of Immortal Glory
Loses all the Sense of Pain[s]
Draws the Curtain, Draws the Curtain
Let me t[h] read the Blissfull plains.

4

While in time my Soul does enter
Realms of Everlasting Day
Thus to God my Life I'd Center
Till my Soul was Stole away
Live for Ever. Live forever
In my Soul O God my Stay.

5

O Pleasing Scene I Can but Wonder
While I On Jehovah Gaze
And I O thought partake the Splendor
Of his most Meridian blaze
Lost in Glory Lost in Glory
Forever Join Angelic Lays.[282](a)

213

26. THE SOARING MIND

1

Break Sacred Morn with beams of Light
And from My Soul Expel the Night
And Sweetly Steal my heart away
With raptures of immortal day —

2

I feel a mind that fain would Soar
For far Beyond this Mortal Shore
Nor Earth Nor Hell Shall ever Confine
While I'm Blest with Wings Divine.

3

Come then O thou Immortal Dove
And bear me to the Realms above
There I might Soar and Still find room
And make that Sea of Love my home.

4

There Shall I find my Joys Compleat
These little Worlds beneath my feet —
While Thought remains I Still Shall be
Lost in my God that Boundless Sea.[282(b)]

27. REJOICING IN THE CROSS OF CHRIST

1

My Soul Embrace the Saviour's Cross
And Count all other gains but Loss
Through Losses, Crosses, Grief and pain
Yea Lose thy Life, and Count it gain.

2

To Share thy Sufferings Lord I'm blest
And Count more than Earthly rest
And the reproaches of thy Name
Far more than Earths Exalted fame.

3

And O my Trials are but Small
For Christ my Captain bears them all
His power Subdues my greatest Foes
Thus I Surmount a World of Woes.

4

Lord God increase my Life Divine
I'd Know no other Life but thine
All Earthly Glories I'd adieu
The King of Glory I'll pursue

5

And O the Happy Hour Shall Come
When all the pilgrims reach their home
And I with the blest Band Shall rise
To Share the Everlasting prize.[283]

28. PANTING FOR THE SPIRIT OF GOD TO BEAR THE MIND AWAY

1

Breathe on my Heart O Sacred Dove
And let me Feel Immortal Love
Inspired with One all Conquering Ray
Would bear my Cheerfull Soul away.

2

with joy I'd Stretch Lifes Active Strings
To Mount on thy Celestial Wings
And Gladly Leave these Dismal Coasts
To Reach and Join the heavenly hosts.

3

O Peacefull realms! O happy home.
Where no intruding thought shall come
O let me Enter the full Scene
Without a Cloud to Intervene.[284]

29. THE CHRISTIAN TRIUMPHING IN GOD

1

O Jesus Shall I Ever Dwell
At thy blest feet then all is well
There Shall I find my Realms of Peace
Where Warr And Death forever Cease.

2

There is my portion there my Choice
To See thy face and hear thy Voice
And there forever would I Sing
Sweet Anthems to my God and King.

3

Plead with my Seat and my Employ
Increasing in Immortal Joy
Till all my powers were Stole Away
In raptures of Immortal Day.

4

O What A thought And Shall I be
With God to all Eternity
Brought from the Jaws of Death & Hell
With [To] Perfect Bliss With God to Dwell.[285]

30. FOR THE MORNING

1

Hail Happy Morn I Gladly rise
Wish thee to Soar above the Skies
With Jesus I'll begin my Race
Run On And Sing redeeming Grace.

2

And Hail A Brighter Morning near
When Heavens great Sun Shall once appear
All Suns and Stars Shall Cease to Shine
But this Eternal Sun of Mine.

3

Far, Far, from interposing Night
Awake in Uncreated Light
My raptured Soul with all the throng
Shall Join in Heavens immortal Song.[286]

31. SOARING AWAY WITH LIFE DIVINE

1
One Spark O God of Heavenly fire
Awakes my heart with warm Desire
To reach the Realms above
Immortal Glories round me Shine
I drink the Streams of Joys Divine
And Sing redeeming Love.

2
O could I Wing my Way in haste
Soon with Arch Angels I would feast
And Join their Sweet Employ
I'd glide along the heavenly Stream
And Join their most Exalted theme
In Everlasting Joy.

3
Too mean this Little Globe for me
Nor will I E'er Contended be
To feed on things so Vain
Its Greatest Treasures are but Dross
Its Grandeurs Short, its pleasures Curst
Its Joys all mist with pain.

4
But resting in my Saviours Arms
My Soul Employs Transporting Charms
And Everlasting Love
Theres Life Theres Joy Theres Solid peace
Theres friendship that can never Cease
A Rock that Cannot move.

5
Soar then my Soul Stretch Every thought
To Reach within the Heavenly Court
Above this Mortal Orb
There let me with Archangels rise
And find my feet above the Skies
Where Sins no more Disturb.

6

There with an Everlasting Band
Of Kindred Saints of Gods right hand
My happy Lot shall be
To Soar, to Shout, to reign, to rest
Forever and Forever Blest
With thee O God with thee.[287]

32.   ON THE BIRTH OF CHRIST

1

Rouse all ye tenants of the Earth
Attend your great redeemers Birth
The God an Infant doth appear
Rejoice ye Gentiles with the Jews
Good News, G.N. G.N. Good News
To Every Nation far and near.

2

Hark Hark Methinks the Angels Sing
The praises of their Newborn King
And tell the Great Redeemers Name
Fear not O Shepherds hear the Voice
Rejoice, R. R. Rejoice

3

Go to the Manger there you'l find
The Saviour Dwells with Brutal kind
The Long Expected day is Come
Glad Tidings to the World is Brought
Fear not..Fear not..Fear not..Fear not
O Shepherds make your Saviour Room.

4

Mortals attend the prince of peace
Let all your hopefull Sorrows Cease
Redeeming Love is at your Door
Come Mourning Souls his grace receive
Believe..Believe..Believe..Believe
And you Shall live forever more.[288]

33. GOD ALL IN ALL

1

Think O my Soul thou art to Land
Ere Long in heaven at Gods right hand
Where Love Shall Every Thought Employ
And Nothing reign but perfect Joy.

2

Mount up and Count thy Trials Small
And Let all Earthly Grandeur fall
As Dust and Chaff and Empty Dross
And Count all things but Jesus Loss.

3

His Love redeems from Death and Woe
And makes my Heaven begin below
But Vastly more his Love Displays
Where they Behold him face to face.

4

There Every Soul Drinks Deep in Love
While Soaring thro the Courts above
Their Happy home is that pure Sea
Of Vast Ah Vast Eternity.

5

Gazing with pleasure there they Sail
Where perfect Bliss Can never fail
Wrapt in the Nature of the Lamb
They Shout the Wonders of his Name.

6

Attraction glows to Every Heart
With Burning Love that Cannot part
While all as One the Armies move
Attracted to the Source of Love.

7

Shouting they Soar with Sweet Surprize
Their Anthems shake the arched Skies
Echoes resound thro all the plain
In One harmonious Lofty strain.

8

And there I trust to bear my part
Wrapp'd up in the Redeemers heart
There Ravish'd with immortal Flame
Resound my Saviours Lasting fame.[289]

34. A MINISTER LEAVING HIS PEOPLE TO GO ABOARD WITH THE GOSPEL

6

If I never more return
Do not my Long Absence mourn
If I am but near my God
All is well tho far abroad.

7

God is every where the Same
Let us part and Spread his Fame
Soon we'l end this Mortal race
Then all meet him face to face.

8

There where Christ our Lover Reigns
We Shall Join immortal Strains
Bask in Everlasting Joy
Nothing Shall our peace annoy.

9

Halle[lu] jahs then our Song
Sounding thro the Countless throng
Christ our God that Lovely Name
Be our Everlasting Theme.[290]

I

[Ye that do in Jesus dwell,
Christian brethren now farewel;
Part in peace, and part in love,
Sing and pray where e'er ye rove.

II

Wipe your tears and leave your pains;
Why lament when Jesus reigns?
Tho' in body we may part,
We are still as near in heart.

III
Walk with Jesus while below,
Spread his name where e'er ye go;
Fight the battles of the Lord,
Present is your blest reward.

IV
If to distant lands I go,
'Tis the jubilee trump to blow;
May my Jesus be with thee,
When you're well remember me.

V
When I near my Master get
I shall find you near my heart;
We shall often meet as one
Pleading at our Father's throne.]

35. THE [GREAT] LOVE OF CHRIST — DISPLAY'D IN HIS DEATH

1

As near to Calvary I pass
Methinks I See a Bloody Cross
Where a poor Victim hangs
His Flesh with Ragg'd Irons Tore
His Limbs all dress'd with purple Gore
Gasping in Dying pangs —

2

Surpriz'd the Spectacle to See
I Ask'd who Can this Victim be
In Such E[x]quisite pain
Why thus Consign'd to Woes I Cry'd
'Tis I the Bleeding God reply'd
To Save a World From Sin.

3

A God for Rebel Mortal Dies
O Can it be My Soul replies
What! Jesus Die for me
Yes Saith the Suffering Son of God
I Give my Life I Spill my Blood
For thee poor Soul for thee.

4

Lord Since thy Life thoust freely given
To bring my Wretch'd Soul to Heaven
And Bless me with thy Love
Then to thy feet O God I'll fall
Give thee my Life my Soul my all
To reign with thee above.

5

All Other Lovers Ill adieu
My dying Lover Ill pursue
And Bless the Slaughterd Lamb
My Life my Strength my Voice And Days

I will Devote in Wisdoms Ways
And Sound his Bleeding Fame.

6

And when this tottering Life shall Cease
I'll Leave these Mortal Climes in peace
And Soar to realms of Light
There Where my Heavenly Lover reigns
I'll Join to Raise immortal Strains
All Ravish'd with Delight.[299]

36. SOARING AFTER JOYS DIVINE

1

Lord I can live On Husks no more
I pant for Joys Divine
My Soul to Worlds [realms] of Bliss would Soar
And Drink of living Wine.

2

O for thy Wings Immortal Dove
To Reach those Climes of Bliss
Soon would I Solace in thy Love
And Dwell Where Jesus is.

3

There would I Drink immortal Joy
And in full Glory blaze
Transporting Themes to my Employ
While on my God I Gaze.[292]

37. THE BELIEVING HEBREWS

1

Shout Brethren for the Lord hath broke
The fatal bands of Pharohs yoke —
Our Souls have left the Slavish Ground
And now to Canaans Land are bound.

2

God has Destroy'd by his high hand
Both Horse and Rider in the Sand
And we with Miriam will Sing
All Glory to the Hebrews King.

3

He Still will make our foes to fall
He'll be our Captain Strength and all
Our Jesus Leads us by his hand
For to possess the promis'd Land.

4

Then Let us Thread the Desert thro
Bid all our Loves and fears adieu —
A Fire by Night Shall Lead our way
And a Blest Cloud of Love by Day.

5

Christ is the Stream shall us pursue
And cheer us all the Desert thro
We are Surrounded by his Love
And feed on manna from above.

6

Let Unbelief no more be Known
And Every Murmuring Thought be gone
If we the God of truth Believe
We Shall go in the Crown receive.

7

O Thou Immortal *Hebrews* King
Thy Name with Joy we gladly Sing
Thou Bought thy Tribes with Blood Divine
And now we are forever thine.[293]

227

38. THE WONDERS IN CHRIST'S DEATH

1

How Vast Moriah is thy Lord
Enormous Guilt a Bleeding God
See Heaven and Hell upon the Tree
A Saviour Dies and lives for me.

2

A God in Agonies of Death
And for his foes resigns his Breath
Behold him Crush'd beneath my Guilt
Untill his Vital Blood is Split.

3

But O I'm lost how can it be
Jehovah Suffers this for me
O Yes so Boundless was his Love
He dies to Bear my Soul above.

4

Away all other Lovers away
And mount my Soul to the Bright day
Where Love immortal shall inflame
My ravish'd Heart to praise the Lamb.[294]

39. LONGING TO BE MORE IN LOVE WITH CHRIST

1

Jesus, My Lord I thirst for thee
Wrapp'd in thy Love my Soul would be
Descend O tho Immortal Dove
And fill me with the Saviours Love —

2

With Zeal I would my Christ Pursue
And bid Created Joys Adieu
Nor Can I Give my Spirit Rest
Till fully in his Love I'm blest —

3

O Jesus Lead me on my Way
'Till I Shall reach Eternal Day
Let the Attraction of thy Love
Bear me Away to Realms Above —

4

There in those Seas of Joys Divine
My Soul Shall in full Glories Shine
Gaze on thy Beauty and Adore
My God my all forever more.[295]

40. MOUNT PISGAH

1

Now on the borders of our land
We'll raise A cheerful voice;
And while our souls thus gazing stand,
Let every heart rejoice.

2

We'll trim our lamps with grace divine,
And wait our bridegroom's call;
He shall with him in glory shine,
Where he is all in all.

3

We are his bride redeem'd with blood,
And seal'd upon his breast;
And soon he'll take us home to God,
To be for ever blest.

4

And when we hear our Master Call,
We will with joy obey;
For Jesus is our all in all,
Then why should we delay?

5

O what transporting scenes of Joy
Shall open to our view!
Eternal anthems our employ,
In joys forever new.

6

Think fellow pilgrims what delight
Shall ravish ev'ry heart!
With Jesus in the realms of light,
Where we shall never part.[296]

41. GOD'S BOUNDLESS LOVE

[Surprised at God's Love]

1

For me Dear Saviour hast thou bled
Ah! Lord I feel thy Blood Divine
Yea thou hast rais'd me from the Dead
And gave my Soul a life [with thine] Divine.

2

O What a Thought Surprised I be
That God Should Stoop from realms above
And Die to give a Wretch like me
A Mansion in his Boundless Love.

3

Impress O Thou Eternal King
These Truths of Love on all my Soul
Thy Name I will with wonder Sing
When mortal Worlds Shall cease to roll.

4

O How Transported I Shall be
When I am quit from all but Love
My God and Shall I reign with thee
In thine Eternal realms above.

5

Ah! it was goodness like thyself
To Stoop and take my guilt away
To pluck me from the Dismal Gulph
And Seat me in Eternal Day.[297]

42. CHRIST WORTHY OF ALL LOVE AND ADORATION

1

Worthy art thou immortal Lamb
To be tho whole Creations Theme
My Heart all Ravish'd Longs to rise
My Notes of Love in Heavenly Lays.

2

I feel my Soul in Love with thee
And with thee pants and Longs to be
Where no intruding thought Shall move
To Interrupt my Charms of Love.

3

Thy Charms Dear Christ attract my Soul
And shall my Strongest power Controul
I'll praise thee while this Earth I rove
And In Eternal Realms above.[298]

43. A HEAVENLY RAPTURE

1

Methinks I feel a Warm Desire
Enlivened with Immortal fire
In this Imprison'd Heart of mine
And longs to Wing Itself away
To Realms of Everlasting Day
To Lofty Scenes [themes] and Themes [scenes] Divine.

2

In Records of Eternal fame
There is my Portion, there is my Name
And there methinks my God I See
Where angels Sail with Lofty Wing
And Seraphs Tune the Immortal Strings
There, There my Spirit longs to be.

3

Those Boundless Realms of Joys Divine
Those Saints and Angels all are mine
Jesus my Saviour makes them so
And soon he'l call me home to rest
At his right hand forever blest
With all that Saints or angels know.

4

There I shall t[h]read above the Stars
And Laugh at Hells Intestine Jars
The Sun and Moon beneath my feet
There I shall t[h] read the Blissful shore
And Mourn my Distant friend no more
Where Jesus reigns there is my Seat.

5

Unbounded Love will Shine on me
The Mighty fiat I shall See
Shine forth in his Meridian Blaze
Perfection in Transparent light
Shining Beyond Conception Bright
Calls Every power aloft to Gaze.

6

Thus Gazing with Delight I Stand
Surprising Scenes on Either Hand
To Suck me in their Joyful Tide
The more I See, The More I Love
My raptured Soul Still Sours above
From Pole to Pole In Wonders Glide.[299]

7

[Thus burning in the sacred flame,
Lost to the state from whence I came
Nor room to ask how, where, or when;
The present scenes engage my soul
And every pow'r of thought controul,
I'm lost with joy in God, Amen.]

44. WITH THOUGHTS ON HIS OWN DEPARTURE

6

How will the Heaven Transporting blaze
The power of all my Soul Employ
I Soaring Still aloft Shall gaze
On that Eternal Source of Joy

7

Though Millions are the hosts above
They now in God are all but one
And all so ravish'd with his Love
They nothing know but God alone

8

My Soul so ravish'd in that Sea
I've lost myself and Wondering Gaze
This God is all I feel or See
I'm lost in his Meridian Blaze

9

I Drink I Soar I gaze I rove
O'er the transparent Scenes of Bliss
Still Lost with Wonder in his Love
My Soul and what a God is this

10

Ten Thousand Blazing realms of Light
Proclaim their God and Say Amen
My Soul still Soaring in her flight
My God is all, I drop my Pen.[300]

I

[Now to the pilgrims born of God
In Jesus' name these lines I hand,
To cheer you on your christian road,
And point you to the heav'nly land.

II

When I am gone and ye survive
Make the Redeemer's name your theme;
And while these mortal climes ye rove,
The wonders of his love proclaim.

III

Soon I shall end this rapid race,
And tread your immortal climes no more;
But through Jehovah's boundless grace,
Safe shall I reach the heav'nly shore.

IV

No distant space to take my flight,
When I shall close these mortal eyes,
But in eternal realms of light
Awake with pleasure and surprise.

V

O what transporting seas of bliss!
I then shall sail with sweet delight!
These God my lasting portion is,
Shining beyond conception bright.]

236

2.

New Light
Spiritual Songs

J. DIMOCK

1
Once more the Dear Redeemers Name[301]
His Endless love his dying fame
Awakes my Soul with chearful voice
To invite you to the Heavenly Choice.

2
Let those that once have known his Name
Leave all their doubts and own the Same
O Tell his Goodness And his Love
Wherer you rest, Wherer you rove.

3
O Brethren let your Souls Rejoice
Redeeming Loves your Happy Choice
O Let your Heart rejoice and Sing
For Jesus is your Heavenly King.

4
O Never Never Cease to tell
The Love that in your Christ doth dwell
O Sound his Name from pole to pole
Till fleeting Moments Cease to Roll

5
And they your never Ceasing Strain
Will Sound thro all the Heavenly plain
And there I trust thro' Boundless grace
To meet you there all face to face.

6
And O poor Sinners Come and Share
And you shall have a Mission there
There you Shall have a Glorious port
Wrapt in the Dear Redeemers Heart.

7
O come and Share a Glorious prize
Of perfect Bliss that never dies
To triumph in Redeeming Grace
And See this Jesus face to face.

J. DIMOCK

1

Tho Gloomy Hours and Happy Days
Tho Sore Distress, Tho pleasant Ways
My Soul hath travelled in
A Miracle indeed I think
Sometimes I rise Sometimes I Sink
But Jesus is my hope

2

Sometimes I feel a Glimmering Ray
Of the Bright Sun from Endless Day
And Sing this Christ is mine
Then I can Soar to realms above
Can shout and Sing redeeming Love
With Saints and Angels Join.

3

Then Can I tell my friends around
The Happy pearl my Soul hath found
For Jesus is my friend
I Charge you when you soar above
You tell my Christ I'm Sick of Love
My Soul for him doth pant.

4

Then I am like a soaring Lark
I think I ne'er Shall see the Dark
Nor mourn an absent friend
But Soon I left my Heavenly friend
The pleasing Scene was at an End
And I in Sorrows t[h]read.

5

And then my Soul by Sin Opprest
Goes Mouring for my wonted rest
My Christ is all my Cry
If Ere I meet my Blessed Christ
I'll hold him fast in my Embrace
And tell him all my Woe.

H. HARDING

Awake my Soul Come View the Happy Day
That hastens on to wipe thy Tears away
One shinning Ray of that immortal Sun
I shall fill my Soul with Heavens Eternal One
Then shall I bow before the great I AM
And heavenly Armies Shout "All worthy to the Lamb."

H. HARDING

Hark I Hear the Angels heavenly Voices rise,
 And sound immortal Anthems thro the upper Skies
Your Heart, your soul, your Voice stammering tongue
Imploy   Join the Sacred heavenly song.

H. HARDING

Soon freed from Sorrow shall you See
That Friend who Died on Calvary
Who there Shall be your lasting Song
Amen all Glory to the LAMB.

T. BENNETT

In Chariots of Fire, we'll soon Soar Away
Soon we'l awake in Heavens pure Day
Eternity, Rolling shall one thought Employ
Ravished and Soaring in One Scene of Joy.

240

EDWARD MANNING

1

I've found my Soul Deliver'd
My Joys are from on high
By God I'm highly favour'd
I feel his coming nigh
He's brought me from destruction
And undertook my Cause
From Sin Death and Affliction
My ransom'd Soul he draws.

2

Ah' draws me where or whether
I feel a warm desire
My Soul Aspires tither
Up in the Car of Fire
I see my Foes A Falling
My God he goes before
I hear his Spirit calling
Come thread the peacefull Shore.

3

I see all Heaven engag'd
And God within me Reigns
Which makes my Foes enraged
That I have left my Chains
I've left your Dismal world
And call my God my All
While your in Darkness hur'd
Upon this Earthly Ball.

4

Within one theres A fire
That burns with Rapid flame
And with A Pure Desire
Cries Worthy is the Lamb —
Yea Worthy Thou art forever
For thou wast slain for me
And I obtain the favour
To know thy Love is free.

B. CLEVELAND

THE WORK OF GRACE

1

I'd tell the wonders of my God
But O too great for Tongues to tell
How Rich, how free, that Gracious Word
That Sav'd my Guilty Soul from Hell.

2

Amaz'd to think where I have been
In the Dark paths of Slippery Death
Bearing A Dreadful Load of Sin
Expos'd to Sink at every Breath.

3

The Burden'd Earth groaned under me
The Vilest of the Sinfull Race
Th' Astonish'd Rocks and every Tree
Rose up and Curs'd me to my face.

4

All Heaven Look'd frowning from Above
And Hell was gaping wide Below
My Prayers and Tears Abortive proved
To Save my Soul from Endless Woe.

5

How Dreadfull was my Enmity
Against the Eternal King of Heaven
My Heart so full of Blasphemy
I Could not ask to be forgiven.

6

Justice pursu'd me close Behind
And upon the Brink of Hell
My Strength all faild and I Resignd
And Jesus took me as I fell.

7

I'll Sing thy Goodness O my God
But O! How far my Language fails
To Speak the Mercies of that Blood
Which did for my poor Soul prevail.

8

For me A Rebel to his Throne
A Traitor to his Dignity
Its pity Brought a Pardon down
For me A Wretch condemn'd to Die.

9

A Different Aspect I Beheld
The Hills and Rocks all Smiling Stood
And all the Verdant groves and fields
Spoke forth the piaises of my God.

10

I Long'd to praise my Saviour too,
But thought he Scarcely Could be mine
O Can he, Can he, Stoop so low
Could Christ for me his life resign.

11

Praise Shall Employ my future Breath
Till I Shall End this mortal race
Then Shall I triumph over Death
And praise my Saviour face to face.

B. CLEVELAND

LONGING FOR CHRIST

Tho Undeserving of thy grace
I Long O Lord to see thy face
And bow Before thy feet.
I beg for food as for my Life
I cannot live without relief
Thou Didst the thirst Beget.

2

My panting Soul Aspires to be
Wrapt up in that unbounded Sea
Of my Dear Saviours Love
Then I Should Scorn all mortal things
Disdain A Share with Earthly Kings
My portion far above.

4

I know my Journey soon will End
And I Shall See my Bleeding Friend
Ah See him face to face
Where all my Sorrows Shall be O'er
And Storms of Death shall Beat no more
But Everlasting Love —

5

There to possess the free reward
Fill'd with the fulness of my God
And tho the Vessels Small
Ill Stretch to grasp the Boundless Sea
Enlarging to Eternity
Yet never fathom all.

244

B. CLEVELAND

1

Come to the Glorious Gospel feast
Ho every One that will
O Come ye Starving Souls and Taste
Those Joys that none Can tell

2

Arise Ye Mortals that are Sad
And Bordering on Despair
Lo there is Balm in Gilead
And a Physician there.

3

Look to the Saviours Bleeding Side
Behold the purple Gore
It was for wounded Souls he Dy'd
The Sin Sick to Restore.

4

Behold him on the Cursed Tree
With arms Extended wide
For Sinners Such as you and me
The Bleeding Saviour Dy'de.

5

'Tis finished said his Dying Breath
And Conquer'd Death and Hell
That Rebels doom'd to Endless Death
Might in his Bosom Dwell.

6

Come then receive his grace and tell
The Wonders of his Love
Till we arise with him to Dwell
In the Bright worlds above.

7

No Sin nor foe Shall there Annoy
Or Wound your peacfull Breast
But Boundless Love un mingled Joy
And Ever lasting Rest.

[ANONYMOUS]³⁰²

Mercy O Thou Son of David
Thus Blind Bartimeus pray'd
Others by thy Grace are Saved
Now to me Vouchsafe Thine Aide

As he Cried Many Chid him
But he Cry'd the Louder Still
'Till the Gracious Saviour bid him
Come and Ask me What you will

Mony was not what he wanted
Tho by Beging Used to Live
Lo he asked and Jesus Granted
Alms what none but he Could give

Lord Relieve this Grievous Blinding
Let mine Eyes Behold the Day
Lo he Saw and won by kindness
Followd Jesus in the way.

Now methinks I hear him praising
Publishing to all around
O is not my Care amazing
What A saviour I have found.

Now I freely Leave my Garments
Follow Jesus in the way
He will Lead me by his Counsel
Bring me to Eternal Day.

There I shall Behold the Saviour
Spotless innocent and pure
Sure he Reigns with him forever
For he has promised me sure

246

Section III

ALLINE'S

POETRY and

JOURNAL

1.

From the

Anti-Traditionalist

O Lord my God, and yet the World Asleep!
Will Nothing pass the Impenetrable Crowd [Shrow'd]
Or Call them to the Scene Unparalel!
O Send an arrow by my Willing pen,
A Message to my fellow men in chains
To Loose with Joy their twice Ten Thousand Bands
Lead them to See what made Archangels Gaze,
And woke Surprize in all the Realms of Bliss;
When from Eternal Grandeur Stoop'd a God
And Stoop'd the great I AM to fallen Earth,
Enters the manger Cloth'd in Mortal flesh,
O Thought! with Beast the Visitant first Seen.
Ah 'Worse than Beast, our Vilest Selves we See,
Before our Hearts will find this Infant room!
But O is God a Bethlem's Babe in Clay!
Witness ye Brutes that gave your manger up,
And ancient Sages, that Beheld the Star,
Say was Jehovah there; But small your gifts:
But O Enough since ye pour'd out your all.
Say O ye Countless Millions that unseen
To Mortal eyes thick round the manger flew,
How Burn'd your Breasts & straind your Eyes when on
The Scene ye Gaz'd; Strange Scene to all your hosts,
But O and Say, is this your God; Ah this
O Adamant, my heart! not melted still.
Hear lies thy friend, nor passive long remains
How Soon he's Call'd to Walk the fields of Blood,
And Waste his Life to gain the prize for me.

Witness ye Stars, that Forty Nights Beheld
This Jesus Wandering thro the Desert Wiles
With but the Sable Canopy, or the
Cold Mists to Screen the Innocent Divine;
Or while Beneath the Bending Shrubs he lays,
Witness ye howling Monsters of the Wood
Have you not roaming cross'd his Labouring paths,
Or seen your exile maker pass your kin —
Without the Common food, his hand so oft,
When you were Howling throw'd around your Den:
While Hell Loose Augmenting Still his grief,

With Rage and Lyes deride him with a Stone
And Court him with the Shadows of the World
To prostrate Heaven in homage to their Gulf,
O Heaven Stand amaz'd! Rouse Earth, and feel
Such Love: what pains   Sustain, O Wretch'd men
What pangs of Woe, and all for you and me;
And now emerging in the Raging World
A mark for all the arrows of the Vile;
Yet all his Life one Constant Liberal Act
A Heart Exhausted; Inexhausted fund.
But O How fast the floods of Sorrow pour
Like rapid Torrents on his Spotless Soul!
Witness that Night (Angels can ne'r forget)
When Peter and his Mate so Dead with Sleep
Left him to Sink in Agonies and Death!
O Gethsemane how couldst thou bear the Shock!
And Witness Every garland to perfumes
More Rich (tho all in Blood) than all your Banks.
Nor was you wet with Dew Divine till now,
O had those tears (too rich for you) but reach'd
One Dropt the Barren garden of my Heart
Nor Tears alone your greens are tinged with Blood,
Keep near my reader See his Vesture Stain'd
From Every pore of his Disolving Heart.
Mingled with Tears, my Soul! O What a Garb!
With Bended Knees and lifted Eyes Behold
His gesture all an interceding Look!
Hark my Soul! The Bitter Cup he says,
For who, for me! Ah me, O Break my Heart!
For who are those Methinks I hear a Mob,
Yes, See the Wretch'd Band as Black as Hell
Ah! Lantherns! Torches! but you'l need eer Long
A Light Divine Unlike your Hellish Lamp
Or Midnight roam and never find the Mane [Man]
Is Judas there! O flee my Soul Deceit!
Dragged without pity to the Bar Unjust
With Verdicts Brought from all the Courts of Hell
And he Consign'd to all they can inflict;
Mangled with Thorns; O the reproachfull Crowne

And Yet he Crowns poor Sinners with his Love
At the Expense of his own Vital flood.
But See their rage! O how the Scour[g]ing Thongs
Plow Deep their furrows thro his Mangl'd Back
O agonizing Scenes; And pains Accute!
My Bones, saith he, all thro my Skin [I] Tell
Now on he goes Crush'd with the Massy Wood
(Gauling it grates) And all his Bleeding Soul
(Pressd like a Cart) with more Enormous Weight
Thus up to Calvary (place of a Scull) he wades
Without the Camp indeed; reproach and pain
O Peter! Why desert! fear not; Step up:
Thy Saviours Weary Steps are marked with Blood
Think on that Hour "I Sink"! well the same hand
Is nigh (tho Bleeds) can save from Sinking Still!
[But O I'm lost! Is this the Lord of all?
Graze O my Reader, stand amaz'd and say]
But O my reader, stand amaz'd and Say
Why this? for what? O how! for me! Ah my
Desertion, Guilt and Woe hath Crush'd him [Thus]
Thus [Now] on the Cross the Helpless Victim Stretch'd
(Tho power to Call twelve Legions to Assist)
His Limbs Extended, to the last extent,
Then thro his nerves, O how the Irons grate!
Till pains accute rack'd all his torterd frame,
What! Where! O! Yes! Good Lord how can I write:
Feel, Feel my Soul! O Break my Heart with Love
While Floods I weep with Sorrow and with Joy,
Nor wonder that I weep; greater wonder
My writing not Immense in Tears of Blood,
While I record the Scene Unparallel
But O! Impress! [ah] Thou whose Name I speak
The record on my Heart with marks Divine,
To Stand and Shine when other Suns shall Cease,
And Tower as Monuments appraise [of praise] to Thee,
But let me turn And with my Reader Gaze
Once more with wonder on the Bloody Scene;
Rais'd with the Cross they give the Sudden plunge
To rack his frame Lay on the ragged Nails,
252

O How! Good God how canst thou yet Survive
And why my Soul, why all this Rack of Woe,
Is it for me the God of Nature Growns
How can I write! or dear forbear, I gaze
I'm lost! believe, then doubt; the Scene so Strange
My Faith is Stagger'd by the Stoop so great;
And yet again I feel, and must Believe;
It must be true; Its like the God I own.
And Near your Hearts, O Reader waits the Same
Knocking with his endearing charms of Love
O hear, receive, and feel the Sacred truths!
Give him thy Sins receive his grace then Shall
This Christ the Conquest and the Crown, be thine.
And then Eternal Ages speak his worth,
But hark! Methinks I hear him Cry whats that,
"Eli Eli Lama Sabaathame [ani] ?"
Has he n God! why then without a Friend?
Ah that he might befriend the abandon'd World
But O what poor Relief! Ah oft I hearde
The tender Mercies of the Wickeds cruel
See the vile Wretch with Vinegar & Spunge
Reproach and Gaul for an Expiring prince!
Ah Deep he drinks in more Malignant Gaul
While pains accute like Daggers thro his heart
His Torturd Soul is Sorrow Full to Death
Ah See the Sun well may he veil his face
While the Great Sun in Midnight Darkness clad
And rocks of Flint can feel his Dying Groans
While O this heart an Adamant remains!
O when Dear Lord shall it dissolve with Love
And all my Soul feel that Bled for me?
But O he hangs yet on the Bloody Cross
And groans methinks, I hear but groans for who
For you and me, O reader, see him Die,
And in his Death makes sure Eternal life:
And from his Groans immortal Songs of Joy,
And O my Jesus, thou inspire my Soul,
And point my pen to reach the readers heart
To Teach them more than angels can Express

But hark "I Yield" methinks I hear him Say
Into thy land O God my Bleeding Soul
And Dying pray my God their sins forgiven
O pity them that pity not themselves
And Show Mercy tho for Him they none
[And Show them Mercy tho' For Me they've None]
But am I not deceiv'd! and does he pray!
What pray for those who Brue their hands in Bloode,
Yes, Tis the truth, it is I hear him pray:
Listen. O Heavens: & Hear ye Sons of men
Father forgive them cries the Dying Lamb
The Bleeding Victim in the pangs of Death
Say O my reader, dost thou hear the Cry
Or Canst tho stand against such Melting Love
And O he Dies! But no my Saviour Lives
Ah lives for me, And lives to Die no more
Rejoice ye Dying Sons of men, he lives
And Crowd with all your Sins ye mourner crowd
Ye Sinking Millions to his Courts of grace
His Grace is free, and all is done for you
Youve Seen him wade thro all your guilt & Wo
In Seas of Blood thro all his Life or Death
A Lingering Death thro' all his Servile Walk
From the Course manger to the Bloody Cross.
There won the field in Death, then Towr'd aloft
With Scars of Honours to the Realms of Light,
To Spread for you the gates of Endless Day
And Court you to the Mansions of Delight
O what displays of Everlasting Love!
Free Grace the News, Free Grace the Lasting Song
Free Grace to Jews and to the Gentile throng
Free Grace shall be the Everlasting theme
Jehovahs product — And Jehovahs fame
Boundless his Nature Boundless Love his Name[303]
                    Finis Mr. Allin

O Dreadfull Scene what Heart of Stone but Bleed
To See those Countless Millions plunge Ah plunge
In Death and Loss, Whatever Child [could] be lost?
Down, Down they Sink with rapid force to the
Unfathomable Gulf of pain and Woe —
Where all the Racks of fall'n Nature Crowd
But O as yet there is a who can tell
Tho none but God hath power to Interpose
Hark, hark, glad News, Jehovah looks with Love
Assumes their Guilt, bears their Enormous Load
And bleeds and Dies to lift a Dying World
While Love Doth graft them on the tree of Life
O Jesus ride Victoriously to Spread
They Love thro' all these Mortal Regions Now
Bring Countless Millions from the Jaws of Hell
[To thy dear Heart with me among the Crowd] 304

What God the great the good first cause Self mov'd
Steps in the Sinfull region! Dark abode!
Assumes our Guilt And Wades thro all our shame
With Pains Equisite and Expiring Groans
By Loss of Life and Streams of Blood Divine
Treads out the Torters of the Rebells Hell,
To Turn their Choice Regain ther Sinking Will,
Restore them back to his Immortal Charms;
And Reinstate them in Consummate Bliss,
Makes them again Sons of the Deity!
And yet! O must I Say the World Asleep;
Ah Sleeping Oer the Wretch'd Gulf of Hell,
[Expos'd to plunge where hope is known no more]
Persuing Shades, as if they toiled for Life,
While Rapid Time hurls off the Mortal stage
Till Instantaneous Sunk in Endless Night.305

2.

From the
Liverpool Sermon

And is my God Nail'd to the fatal Tree
Good god and are those Cutting pangs for me
O melt my heart! My Senseless soul arise
And fountains flow from both my Wishful Eyes
Then Soar my Soul in grateful Songs of Love
To Reach My Jesus in the Realms above.[306]

Mr. Alline's Preface To his Sermon O That Men would praise the Lord for his Goodness And for his wonderfull works to the Children of Men.

May he whose love call'd forth the Angelic Train
To Sing with Joy thro Heavens Immortal plain
And from the Blaze of uncreated Day
Has deignd to Bleed in Clods of Sin and Clay
That he might his own Boundless love display
Hand this abroad by his own Sacred dove.
To Teach immortal Souls redeeming Love!
Read Meek enquirer with a thirst divine!
Ill be thy waiter, and the Blessing thine;
And while you read may Heavens own balmy wing
Awake with Joy the Deathless mind to sing
A theme like this My Jesus is my King
And great thy Love; how Bright thy Glories Shine
From thy own Womb display'd such floods Divine
To Make thyself and all thy glories mine
Fain would I Sing the Merits of that Blood
I see the wounds, away Created Good
My Heart, awakes my Jesus is my God
And Still Descend, O thou Immortal Dove
Abstract my panting Soul to realms above
And wrap me in the mantle of thy Love
There where thy Glories in Meridian Blaze
My Ravish'd Soul would ever on thee Gaze
And Humble Anthems to Jehovah raise
Ah this with all the Universal throng
Shall be my Joy my Glory & my Song
Jesus my all to him doth praise belong.[307]

259

3.

From the

Journal

What days [to come] kind Heaven intends for me
My Chearful Soul O God devotes to thee
And every power of Life and Soul Engage
By grace divine while on this mortal Stage
Then in the last declines of Mortal Breath
Help me with Joy to Triumph over Death
And in my Dying Groans let me proclaim
The wonders of my Dear Redeemers Name
O let me tell to the Surviving Race
Redeeming Love and his unbounded grace
Then from the Changing Scenes of Day & Night
Let me with Sacred ardor take my flight
Leaning my Soul upon my Heavenly friend
Find all my Labours and my Sorrows End
My Soul Redeem'd from Death & Endless Woe
Will bid Farewell to all these Scenes Below
Chearfull I'll reach the Blest the Blissfull Shore
Where Storms of Sin & Death are known no more
[Where sin and death shall plague me never more]
Here, Here, [There, there,] with all the Glorious hosts above
My Soul shall feast on Everlasting Love
And Live with Jesus on those peaceful plains
Where all the Saints [every saint] in Love immortal reign
O Blessed Jesus shall my portion be
Forever found bound up with Joy in thee
O Shall I once hear my Redeemer Say
Come happy happy Spirit come away
Come home into the Saints eternal rest —
And Lean upon your dear Redeemers breast
O shall I shall I Blessed Jesus Reign
Where I shall never never sin again
There Endless ages on the Blessed Shore
Let me be found thy Goodness to adore
Near thy Dear Feet to Sing Redeeming Grace
There let me Sound thine Everlg fame
And give the Glory to the Slaughtered Lamb.[308]

4.

Alline's Death

An Act of Mr. Allen's Death.

In a Letter from————at Newbury Port

The following Extracts from some minets which I kept of your Sons Sickness & Death I now send you Concluding it will be Satisfactory to his beraved parents to know the particulars of the last Days of so pious a Son. Jan 22nd He arriv'd at my house accompanid by the Revd Mr. McClintock Very feeble, to appearance in the last Stages of a Hectic, and much Oppress'd with the Asthma. 25th he rode to meeting preach'd from Luke 19:5. 26 to day had a faint Sinking turn oppress'd at his Stomach too weak to proceed On his intended Journey to Boston 27th Confined to his Bed, 28th Last Night an Abcess which had been forming Some Days broke and Discharg'd a Quantity of peutrid Blood & Water which has lessen'd his pains and is able to set up. 29th Still worse his feet Swelt and his Cough Severe Expecting Death approaching he committ'd to my Care his papers with directions to be particularly Carefull of a Number of Hymns which he had prepar'd for the press with Directions also to Write to his friends in Nova Scotia concluding his Brother would come to take Care of them. 30th this Morning worse had no sleep last Night kept awake by the Asthma Cough and fever. Told me he found himself going the Sympthom of Death upon him and Said *None but Christ None but Christ.* yesterday the Doctor who attended him from the time of his arrival ask'd him; how he did, he answering, I have Nothing I have Nothing to promise myself respecting this Life, I am going and Willing to go, not because I must die but Because I have a friend who will Support me in· Death. Saturday 31st he told me he had a Wearisome Night with his Bodily pains One asked him how he did, I am Says he in terrible distress But yet I'm well — He would often Say he had Such Views of divine things as made him almost forget his pains, to Day restless and without Sleep the nurses constantly holding him up in the Bed, his Strength decays very rapidly he desir'd me to set down and write some things he should tell me respecting his life Having a desire he said that poor Sinners Should be made Acquainted with Some remarkable providences of God towards him but he was too

263

weak to converse with and must put it off. It seems he preach'd every Sabbath from the time he left Nova Scotia. Told me it had pleas'd God so far to bless his Labours particularly among the young people at Harrisacket that he had no reason to be Sorry that he had undertaken the Journey tho in much weakness frequently Express'd in his prayers and conversation most benevalent wishes for the Spiritual welfare of his friends in Nova Scotia And the Churches with which he was Concerned. He was about to Send For Some of his friends in Boston but Concluded It Was too late — He chose to Converse on no Subjects but Christ and the Love of God in our redemption. Sabbath Morning no Sleep the last Night his fever by the Asthma increasing he Said he had Some Sweet hours. O What should I do without Christ, but Jesus is with me. At Noon there was a Sudden Alteration in him [he had] his reason well, Distress'd for breath and patient [in his] Distress and resign'd to the Will of God — I Said he was fast approaching to his entarance on a Glorious rest, he said with great Earnestness *I long for it, I long for it.* I observ'd to him the promises of the Gospel were a divine support to all who love Our *Lord Jesus Christ.* O yes said he the promiser is greater and he is with me. Going to Meeting he desir'd a remembrance in our prayers And Said O tell my friends that the Bless'd Gospel Which I have preach'd to them is true in which they must live in the Belief of And in which they will be Safe in Death. O Preach that Bless'd Gospel. By reason of his great Bodily pains and longing to be with Christ he would Sometimes check himself fearing he was too Impatient to be gone. I wish says he to wait Gods time. He said he begg'd God not to outlive his usefullness. O I long said he that poor Sinners [should have such views of the Lord Jesus, as I have], He would frequently Exhort the Spectaters to get an interest in Christ Assuring them that none but Christ [would] Answer for them when they Came to Die. In the afternoon he told me he was afraid he should Lose his reason, but hop'd that God would Continue to him that Blessing; In the Evening I observ'd to him that Christ was now his only help, he Said: O I need not be told that, he is now my Only desire; His Distress increas'd and he long'd to depart. I Observ'd to him that I [trusted] that
264

he would soon Obtain the Glorious fulfilmint of the promises, I have no Doubt says he, not One, any more than I was now there. He Lay groaning and in great distress, till Midnight reaching for Breath. He said his thoughts began [to be] Confus'd that he was not in a Condition to Pray desir'd us to go to prayer — and at the close pronounced a Joyfull *Amen*. It was Evident Soon after that his reason began to fail his Broken Sentences were the Breathings of a Soul Swallow'd up in Christ. In this State he remaind Two hours the Last Sentence he Spoke was — Now I Rejoice in the Lord Jesus and Breathd his Soul into the Arms of Jesus with whom he Long'd to be.[309]

265

Appendix I

"FORETASTE of HEAVEN"

Alline's Letter to the
Gospel Church
at Argyle,
January 20, 1783.

To the Gospel Church at Argyle.

O that these few lines from your Brother & Servant might find you alive to God, blesst with the presence of the blessed Jesus, filled with love to his Name, & strengthened by his word to stand as living witnesses from his kingdom of grace among men.

I know dear Brethern & Sisters, you have many enemies without & many more within and therefore need divine strength, light, & incouragement to run the Christian race.

O watch against every enemy, & especially those of your own household that are most in disguise. be sure to keep up that divine converse with your Lord & Master as will naturally warm you with love to God, & your poor fellow man.

O think on the heart of Strangers, remembering that you were once strangers in a land of slavery & have still the wormwood & the gaul in remembrance, & can you but glow with gratitude to the lovely Jesus (who spread his mantle of love over you) & long for the Salvation of poor sinners? O that you may ever bear in your mind the love of God, & in your body the dying of the Lord Jesus.

And as you have lately come out to witness for God, O remember that the eyes of God, Angels & men are upon you! yea, & men & devils watching for your halting.

& should you stumble, others may fall. O therefore live unspoted to the world, which will be not only good to others, but unspeakably to your own happiness both here & hereafter.

& O how it would grive my soul to hear any one had turned aside to folly and caused the world to blaspheme! but I hope I shall have joy & rejoiceing to hear of your welfare & success in the Lord.

My heart is often with you, long to see you & have much to say, but my hands are continually full. therefore after intreating you to incourage every gift of prayer & exhortation (especially Ebenezer Hobbs,[310] who I think may be of growing benifit if he follows the Pillar of Cloud) in there proper place & station for the groath & welfare of the whole Body; I leave you in the hands of my kind Master, who I trust, will stand by,

270

support & bless you & bring you off more than conquerors, to the peacefull realms of immortal glory, where thro boundless grace I hope one day to meet you & part no more,

Adieu

Henry Alline

N.B. In the praise of God & for your Joy I will inform you that your Masters cause is greatly reviving in this part of the Vinyard. Many souls have been born to God since I left you, & many more now groaning under their sins & enquiring of the despised Nazarene. I preach every day & the houses are filled with hungry hearers; & many of the young men who have been delivered are so strong & bold in the cause of Christ that often after I have preached some one will arise & speak by exhortation as long as the sermon & many of their exhortations have been greatly blesst & some times three or four speak one after another.

O rejoice with me my dear Br & Sr give God the Glory, & pary for the continuence of his goodness displayd.

I have been at Halifax, preached there every evening about Ten days, found great attention to the gospel, & I have some seeds of grace sowen that will not be lost.

I have much to say to you my dear dear fellow Pilgrims but my hands are so full I can scarecely get time some times to write my Journal.

2.

Charlotte Prescott Letters 1789-1790

Charlotte Prescott[311] to Elizabeth Prescott

December, 1789, Chester.

My Dear Sister,

Yes doubly so, I trust, for the blessed Jesus has had compassion on you, notwithstanding all your fears; O! hear him say,

Arise and bid your doubts to o'er,
Soon you shall reach the peaceful shore,
Where you shall in my bosom dwell
Far from the snares of earth and hell.

Dear Betsy, cast your burden on the Lord who has promised to sustain you. Does he not say "He that cometh to me I will in no wise cast him out." "His blood cleanseth from all sin." How impressive and endearing is his language. "Open to me my love, my dove, my undefiled, for my head is filled with dew and my locks with the drops of the night." My dear Sister, view him in the garden groaning under the enormous load of our guilt, until he sweat great drops of blood. When I think of his extreme suffering, and of the complete salvation he wrought out of his own people, I am constrained to cry with Mr. Alline, "My soul, and what a God is this."

Charlotte Prescott to Elizabeth Prescott

[1789], Chester.

Dear Sister, what a reason have we to bless and praise our Gracious Redeemer who beheld us in mercy, when we were cast out in the open field of ruin, to the loathing of our persons. He then did cast the skirt of his love over us: and did say to us live. This was a time of love indeed! may this fill our hearts with love to Jesus, may we remember what he has done for our souls, which will incline us to cleave to him and live near to him — then and then alone can we be happy.

I have been much depressed since I saw you, but blessed

273

be Gôd he says "Though sorrow continue for a night, joy cometh in the morning. He has this day afforded me the light of his countenance. He has this day fed me with the bread of life. I can praise his blessed and holy name. O that Jesus would behold in mercy those that are on the road to destruction. My heart feels for them who are out of the ark of safety. May you, my dear Sister, be much engaged in prayer. They that wait on the Lord shall renew their strength." When you are near your heavenly friend, remember your unworthy sister,

Charlotte Prescott

Charlotte Prescott to Mrs. Sarah Brown

1790, Chester.

Dear Sister in Christ,

Although we are strangers in person, I trust we are joined in the everlasting love of Jesus. That Saviour will, I trust, soon bear my soul beyond death and the grave, to the mansions of eternal glory, prepared for all that love the Saviour. O that I may evince my love to him, by living to his glory. I have now desires to follow my blessed Jesus through evil as well as good report: and though my heart wanders from him, he like a tender parent brings me back, and causes me to rejoice in his unchanging love. How rich, my dear Sister, are those who have Jesus for their portion. Well might the Poet say

There's life, there's joy, there's solid peace,
There's friendship that can never cease,
A rock that cannot move.

I am not in so happy a frame as I have been, but he is faithful who hath said "I will never leave thee nor forsake thee."

Your Unworthy Sister in Christ

Charlotte Prescott

3.

Nancy Lawrence

Letters

1789-1792

Nancy Lawrence[312] *to Mrs. Sally Bass*[313]

Lincoln, Mass. Aug. 29, 1789.

My dear Dear Sister,

Your Julia[314] is return'd and she will have reason to bless God not only through Time but through an endless Eternity that ever she went to Nova Scotia. I was sure I was guided by infinite goodness and led by the providence of God; not that their is any thing in Local situation; no God is every where the same unchangeable being and can rool [rule] on his undisturbed affairs with equal ease in one place as another; but he chooses these ways which his infinite wisdom sees best

My dear Sally I knew nothing of the power of religion when I left this place no more than the vessel I sailed in [to Nova Scotia] and had I then lost my life Eternal death would have been my portion, my just and inevitable doom, my dear sister we partake of the fallen nature which renders us enimies to God — the scriptures saith the natural man is emnity against God — and while we remain in that State we are subjects of wrath fitted for destruction, we must be reinstated in that Image of God which we lost by the fall. We must have our nature our hearts changed by regenerating Grace by the opperations of the spirit of God with our Spirits or never enter the Kingdom of Heaven, for our saviour saith except ye be converted and become as little children ye shall in no wise enter the kingdom of God, and again except ye be born again ye shall never enter the kingdom of heaven — I dont mean that the animal nature must be changed; but that all our desires, inclinations and pursuits must be turned on another way — or wills & affections renewed, and the chief end and aim of all our actions be to Glorify God and enjoy him, by this change we are brought to delight in holyness and conformity to the will of God and have a foretaste of Heaven while on earth which must be or we never shall behold his face in love in an unregenerate state. Heaven would not be a seat of happiness to us — but the reverse for we would not have all the faculties of our souls engaged & delighted in praising God and beholding the spotless purity and holyness of his nature in admiring the

276

Glorious plan of salvation, the wonders of redeeming love and the riches of free grace

Now my dear sister permit me to intreat, to consider, search and look into these things and may the spirit of God assist you, it is of [unintelligible] importance for what is time in comparison of eternity, a mere sipher, a point & perhaps at the close of a day, an hour, it will be at an end with us and our doom inevitably fixt. We must not only seek but strive for an interest in Christ, and after all depend on the Grace of God — I am well aware this will be stiled inthusiasm perhaps hypocricy or insanity, but I can bear reproach for Jesus sake, my treasure is not here and tis of little consequence how I fare in this Inn of human life I only wish to conduct so as not to injure the cause of religion and approve myself to God through Jesus Christ — but I hope you will not think it madness but seriously examine & may God be with you — believe me —

Your affectionate sister

Nancy Lawrence.

Our Dear Brother & his wife desire their best love to you.

Nancy Lawrence De Wolf to her brother and sister[315]

Horton, Jan. 29, 1792

....The work of God is going on in this place there are some souls brought to the knowledge of the truth, others growning for redimption. O that you might have a sense of your real situation, where you stand, if you once see it you could not rest one moment — for ten thousand worlds I would not be in an unconverted state one hour, nay moment, but that might decide my case for a whole Eternity, so uncertain is life & I should be shut out from the Presence of God, gone forever beyond the reach of hope — but blessed be His name He has of His free grace given me a portion that earth nor Hell can never deprive me of.

> And now I'm in care
> My neighbours may share

I cant bear that *one* soul should be shut out from the presence of God, reject His grace and never know His love and when I think of you — nature opperates with Grace

> And fain my pity would reclaim
> and snach the firebrand from the flame

farewell my dear, dear friend — O that we may be united together in Christ; then if our bodies are separated we shall be one spirit with Him and neither life nor death can separate us from the love of God in Christ Jesus...time is flying, Eternity advancing.

4.

Joseph Dimock

Journal

1791

Part I

I spent the summer of 1791, being then 23 years of age, in Annapolis county, and was labouring in connection with the late Rev. Handley Chipman. He enjoyed a blessed revival of religion, which extended from Digby Gut up to Aylesford. A great number of persons professed faith in the Redeemer, and in some instances the opposition was very great.

Some time in the month of September, my mind being much exercised about visiting the South shore of Nova Scotia, I crossed over from Granville to Digby, and proceeded on to Sissiboo, where I spent the Lord's day and preached at the house of a Mr. Sabine.[317] Both Mr. S. and his wife appeared to be pious; two of their children, a son and daughter, were, I hope, savingly converted, and many others appeared deeply affected. In my prayer during the forenoon service, the Lord I believe put it into my heart to pray for the leading man of the settlement, (whom I then supposed to be at home a mile from our meeting,) that he might be blessed in his person and his family, and that his influence might be used for the promotion of piety and good order in society. I afterwards learned that he was present at the time, and that in going out of the house he was heard to say He makes a pretty good prayer, but I don't want to encourage any such renegades to come here. He then addressed several young fellows, who had assembled at the door to play some trick upon me of which he knew, on my going out, saying — "He is a simple, good kind of fellow enough, perhaps it is not worth while to take any notice of him" — when they dispersed with others who have come to see the sport, without offering me any injury.

The next day I was set across at the mouth of Sissiboo river, and travelled to Montagan. I was without food until night, when I stopped at the house of a Frenchman, by whose hospitality I was fed and lodged comfortably. I proceeded the next morning on my journey and at 11 o'clock I passed the last house on the road, and after walking about two miles, I found the place where I had been directed to cross to Cape St. Mary's, by marked trees. Leaving the bay I came to Salmon River, and crossed just before sunset, and was disappointed in finding only two French huts on the river. I went to the door of the only one on the south side of the river, and knocked for entrance. A female opened the door, and on my asking for liberty to stop the night, she said she was fearful I had been in some house where the small-pox was, as they heard it was in that part of the country, and that I could not come in. I then asked her if she could give me a piece of bread, as I had had no dinner; she told me the man had gone to the mill, and that she had none, nor flour to bake with. I then asked for a little fire, and added that I would go into the woods near by and remain all night — this she refused, lest I should set the woods on fire. I then went into an hovel near the house, where I found some salt hay, and determined to make myself as comfortable as possible for the night. After a little time the woman came to the door and said, if I were sure I had not been where the small-pox was, I might go into the house; I told her I had not — but still, rather than excite any alarm in her mind, as she had nothing to give me to eat, if she would allow me I would rather sleep in the hay. She went back to the house, but soon returned, and taking me by the hand, said she could not rest and leave me there — that, if I would come in, she would boil some potatoes and do the best she could for me. I went in and, after partaking of the potatoes with some milk, retired to rest.

The next morning I arose before day, and crossed what was called the New River before the tide made into it. The persons I met could furnish me with nothing to eat, and informed me it was 12 miles to the next house. There was nothing left for me to do but to proceed onwards, which I did by walking part of the way on a sand beach, and the remainder by crawling through the woods and bushes; the only direction I had was, to keep the roar of the surf on my right hand, as the bushes were so thickly matted that I could not keep in sight of the water until I came to Cranberry Head. After I had travelled about four miles, it began to rain heavily. The only relief I found from the gnawings of hunger was by pulling and eating twigs of yellow birch as I walked through the forest, and indeed these afforded me no small relief.

I arrived at last at the house of Mr. Foot,[318] whose kind companion prepared me supper — consisting of Indian cake, butter, cheese, milk, &c — and never did I partake of so sweet a meal, having been nearly two days with but little to eat, and my clothing being thoroughly wet through. I felt thankful to this hospitable woman and her husband for the kindness shown to me, and, I trust, grateful to the God of all my mercies. How welcome to a hungry and weary traveller to obtain a quiet shelter and resting place! Never shall I forget my feelings when I took my pack from my back to rest my weary limbs, and partake of the bounty of heaven prepared for me by hospitable friends.

5.

Joseph Dimock

Journal

1791

Part II

The work prospered. People thronged to meeting, sometimes from fifteen or twenty miles distant. Often have I known young females to come twelve miles on foot on Lord's day morning before we had had our breakfast.

One very sultry day in July, about noon, I walked up to a door. The good lady standing in the door, I bid her the time. 'And here you come,' said she, 'trudging along, almost melted with heat! and what if after all you should be mistaken? What if you are spending your youthful and best days in those fatigues, and the Lord has not sent you or called you to it?' I replied, 'It is an important question, and one that I ought to have decided on long ago; but if I have, it is no harm to ask it over again, as to my call and my motives — whether my eye is single — whether it is my sole aim that God may be glorified and sinners saved.'

I crossed to Digby and preached to some Scotch people, who appeared much gratified and wished me to come again. They had no preaching, but used to meet on Lord's-days and read a sermon &c, I promised to come again in a fortnight. In the interim they had heard that I was not a Collegiate, and so had not come into the ministry at the door. They appointed a Committee to ask of me as to the truth of the statement. After the morning service I was asked into a private room to take some refreshment. They the Committee of inquiry began, a Mr. Thompson[320] being spokesman. 'Sir,' said he, 'there is a report in circulation which we could not believe, but we wished to be satisfied about it. We have been appointed to wait on you and respectfully to inquire as to the truth of the report, which is that you was not educated at the College.' I answered, 'The report is true.' He then said, 'We would then ask you, by what authority you do these things? that is by what authority do you preach?' I replied — 'I will gladly tell you. When first I was brought to an experimental knowledge of the truth I felt much concerned for those around me that appeared thoughtless and ignorant of salvation, as I had formerly been myself; and I often made some attempt to warn sinners to flee from the wrath to come, both in private and publicly.' I then related the exercises of my mind on the subject, from the year 1785 unto the year 1790, when I began to preach. When I had done, he

284

rose, took me by the hand, and bade me God-speed, saying, 'Sir, the state of the country calls loudly for teachers, which, with your exercises on the subject, is a sufficient warrant, in my opinion, for you to preach. I should be sorry to discourage you. And now we shall be glad to hear you again this afternoon. Our society is now waiting for our report; but as you have fifteen minutes more, and you began your narration by saying "When first I was brought to the knowledge of the truth" — will you give us a short account of it?' — Here I gave a short account of my experience, which was heard with much affection. They retired, made their report, and then requested me to proceed in the afternoon worship. I know of nothing that ever disturbed my harmony with those good folks afterwards.

I suppose this was the first Baptist preaching in Digby (I am not sure that was the case). What was the fruit, or whether any, I know not but on the other side of the Gut there was a gracious work among coloured and white people. Perhaps ten or fifteen were brought to hope in the Saviour; among them was a Mr. Towner,[321] who was a churchwarden, and who afterwards was a Baptist elder on Digby Neck, Sissiboo, &c.

Those days were among the pleasantest of my life. If ever I had no care but for the glory of God and the salvation of sinners, it was then. The opposition was great in some persons — husbands forbidding their wives, and parents their children, to attend meetings. But the word of God prospered more abundantly.

285

6.

Edward Manning's
Conversion
1789

Edward Manning's conversion
1789[322]

My first awakening was when I was about ten years of age, in the year of our Lord 1776, by hearing that man of God, the late Henry Alline, pray at my father's house. I well remember his addressing me, though but a child, and the tears dropping from his face upon mine, while he exhorted me to flee from the wrath to come. But though much affected at the time, I soon, to my shame, shook it off, and continued very thoughtless till the age of twenty-two. Though at seasons during that period convictions would return and I would feel unhappy in view of death, judgment, and eternity. But I lived a wicked life I may say with truth

'Jesus sought me when a stranger
Wandering from the fold of God.'

In the year 1789 there was an awakening in Falmouth, where I was brought up. On the 26th of April, in hearing the late Rev. John Payzant preach, and several young converts confessing their Lord and Master, with much sympathy of soul for poor sinners, and for me in particular, my heart was broken. I could not contain myself, but wept aloud, and came to a decision to seek the Lord; and to use my own expression at the time, 'I am determined, if I am lost at last — I am determined to go to hell begging for mercy.' — I endured much horror of mind until the evening of the 29th of the same month, when I attended a prayer meeting where I thought the Lord was present to heal, but that there was no hope for me. I was in a most awful state, and thought I was literally sinking into hell. Then I saw the Justice of the Almighty in my eternal condemnation, a most astonishing change having taken place in my views of that justice. If I ever loved any object, either then or since, it was the eternal justice of God. It appeared to me that I could not but love it, even though it proved my eternal condemnation. The view was overwhelming. I was lost for a season to time-things, and when I came to my recollection, God, and all creatures appeared different to me from what they ever did before. An indescribable glory appeared in every thing[323]

The next day being the 25th day of May 1789, was to be a thanksgiving day for the recovery of his Majesty's health, and I with a number of christian friends was to go to Horton in order to keep the day. In the morning I felt a great solemnity on my spirits. I had a great discovery of the vanity of the things to come and sense. I felt a sense of what a miserable state the world was in, and what it was to die out of Christ. I saw a number of young people. I could not help weeping over them, entreating them to turn and live, and many were very much affected, so as to cry aloud for mercy. We set out on our way. I was in amazement. I would sometimes feel my heart to leap for joy. But I was mostly taken up in meditations upon the stupidity of the world of mankind, when their eternal all was at stake. I discovered the whole world sinking down into eternal misery — and they know it — blindfolded by the God of this world. In this exercise I continued until we got within two miles of where the meeting was to be held, when my mind turned upon Mr. Harris Harding, a gospel minister who had preached very often where I lived, and who was frequently made, an instrument in the hands of God of alarming my mind, but had been gone to Annapolis for several weeks. I expected to see him that day. As soon as my mind turned upon him, I immediately burst into a flood of tears, and cried aloud. I thought of an old christian man that I had been acquainted with before: — I felt the same nearness, if not greater, to him that I did to the other and cried out louder still. My mind now turned upon the christians in general, and love kept increasing. My mind turned upon God: — an inquiry arose in my breast, whether it could be possible that God would be infinitely condescending, or could be possessed of such a nature as to have mercy upon me. I immediately discovered, that it was possible. At this discovery my whole soul was set on fire. I cried out, how loud I cannot tell. I do not recollect what expressions came to my mind, or whether there were any or not. But this I know, my soul was wrapt up in God's eternal love. I felt nothing but that glory. The people that were with me were some distance behind; they heard me cry out, and said to each other that I was rejoicing. Joseph Baily, an eminent

288

christian, was in the company, and he came up, and said, 'Edward, what is the matter?' I cried out and said, 'O, Mr. Baily, my soul is melted with love to God.' I had not strength to sit up, but leaned upon my horse's neck, and he (Mr. B.) was in the same position, rejoicing and praising the Lord. Then I could call heaven and earth, yea, God, angels and men to witness that I knew my Redeemer lived, and I should live also. Then I could cry, "Holy, holy, holy, Lord God Almighty, the whole earth is full of thy glory!'

*** I was intensely filled with supreme love to God. I saw his glory in every thing around me. It was not a confidence of my own safety, nor merely a certainty of my own individual interest in his love that caused me to rejoice; but the glory and harmony of his perfections overcame me, and a satisfactory belief of my personal interest in his mercy followed as a consequence. Thus I obtained liberty to my poor imprisoned soul. My happiness was unspeakable, and I may say, full of glory.

Soon after this memorable day I united with the Congregational church in Cornwallis, under the pastoral care of the Rev. J. Payzant. I enjoyed many happy seasons among the professors of religion in that communion. My happiness was however greatly interrupted by an almost continual impression that I must engage in preaching the gospel. I began to pray and exhort, in Falmouth, Windsor, Newport, Horton and Cornwallis; but the impression to preach the gospel continually followed and oppressed me; so much so, that in the month of September I left home in company with the late Rev. T.H. Chipman and one or two young men, and travelled through the wilderness to Chester without any road, and directed only by marked trees. We arrived at Chester the same night, and lodged at the house of the late pious deacon, John Bradshaw.[324]

7.

Edward Manning's

Letters

1791-1793

Edward Manning to Thomas Bennet[325]
Onslow, April 19, 1791

Dear Bennet

After many trying scenes, outward and inward, I am permitted to come to Onslow, where I behold the outpouring of God's Spirit upon the inhabitants thereof. Some, I verily believe, have found the Lord to be their everlasting portion: others have taken up with something short, and I fear will eternally perish; some are groaning for liberty. The angel still continues to trouble the waters, so that it may be said indeed that Onslow is a place highly favoured of the God of heaven. His tabernacle certainly appears, and O he dwells in them, walks with them and has become their God in an everlasting covenant. We have blessed meetings. The christians seem to grow, and are willing to have their names cast out as evil for the cause of their God. It is a blessed sight to see the young christians leaning upon their dear Jesus, going hand in hand to glory. It would do you good to see them; I don't doubt but it will to hear of it. I hope you have seen happy times, and that your soul is brought into that liberty which you long for so much; O, dear friend, that God who has brought you so far will bring you and your unworthy friend, to those regions of unspeakable joy, where we shall doubt his goodness no more.

Edward Manning to James Manning[326]
Kingsclear, New Brunswick, May 20 1793

Dear Brother

I am surprised you have not written to me. If you knew how much it rejoiced my soul to hear from you, you would write to me every week; for I suppose you have many things to relate to me respecting God's marvellous work among you. — If ever I knew what God could do it is since I came to St. John's. I want to see you, to tell you my whole heart. I could not tell you all in a week. Nearly seventy souls (if not more) have found God to be all in all and truly live in green pastures, and grow as the calves in the stall. Ah! blessed be the name of God, I see a man with a drawn sword in his hand, as Captain of the

291

Lord's host. He is come, his voice is powerful and full of majesty, and divides the flames of fire, and shakes the wilderness. Ah! I see his star in the East, my brother and I am come to worship him, to Mount Zion, the city of the living God. O my brother, the good of all the land is before us, and all behind is a barren wilderness. The Lord God is terrible before his great army.

> 'A cowardly crew they seem at first view,
> but led by their Captain great feat they will do.'

O my brother, I can truly say by heartfelt experience, 'Hitherto the Lord hath helped me.' I have seen the stars in their courses fight for Zion. Blessed be God, I see the horse and his rider thrown into the depths of the sea. The Israelites come forth shining, and travel three days' journey with incredible haste, which the Egyptians essaying to do are drowned in the dragon's flood.[327]

My soul longs for the time to come when I shall once more preach Jesus among that people who appear as stars of the first magnitude in the firmament of God's power. Tell them I believe God is about to shake the heavens and the earth once more among them. Horton is yet to blossom as the rose.

Appendix II
THE CRITICS

1.

William Black

"Real Lovers of

Jesus."

1787

William Black to the Reverend F. Garrettson in Horton
Halifax, Feb 14, 1787

Rev. and Dear Brother,

According to your desire and my promise, I now send you my thoughts on the propositions you mention. You justly observe, as they are so zealously propagated through the province, they must certainly do much harm.

1. It is affirmed, that 'man has nothing at all to do; that if he lift a hand towards his own salvation, he will be damned?' But is not this contrary to the words of St. Paul, — 'Work out your own salvation, with fear and trembling.' If indeed by 'towards salvation,' they meant, towards *purchasing* it, they would affirm nothing but the truth; but if they refer to our obtaining salvation, the assertion is utterly false. For though Christ has died for us, he has neither repented nor believed for us; still, therefore, if we repent not, we shall perish — if we believe not, we shall be damned. The Scriptures urge us to *turn, seek, knock, strive, wrestle, run*, &c. And is this, I would ask, doing nothing? absolutely *nothing*? Is it not for *salvation* that we are to seek, ask wrestle and run? Does the sinner repent that he may perish, or believe that he may be damned? or rather does he not do both in order to salvation? Is not believing itself called a work? — 'This is the work of God that ye believe;' and St. Paul says, 'We have believed that we might be justified,' that is plainly, in order to justification, and of course, to salvation. Shall we then be damned for attempting to stretch forth the withered hand, and touch the hem of his garment? Does not the Gospel call upon us to renounce our self-righteousness, to fly to Christ, and to lay hold on the hope set before us? And can any soul be saved without doing this? Does not Christ command us, if we would be his disciples to deny ourselves? Is the man in his proper senses who would affirm that all this is nothing?

2. It is vehemently contended that 'neither repentance nor payer precedes the new birth.' This also is contrary to the Scriptures. — With regard to *repentance*, John the Baptist thus opens his mission, 'Repent ye, for the kingdom of heaven is at hand;' and our Lord began to preach in the same words.

296

Matt. iv:17. The apostles proclaim the same doctrine — 'Repent and be converted that your sins may be blotted out.' — Now here repentance is put before forgiveness. Simon Magus was exhorted to repent. Acts viii:20. 'God commandeth all men every where to repent.' Acts xvii:30. Paul showed to both Jews and Gentiles that they should repent, and do works meet for repentance. Acts. xxi:20. But enough of this. — In relation to *prayer*, it may be observed, — some well-meaning people, apprehensive lest sinners should put prayer in the place of the Saviour, have gone very unscriptural lengths; and sometimes from the pulpit have said more against praying than against swearing. 'No unconverted man,' say they, 'ought to pray; it keeps him from Christ, and he will never be converted till he leaves off praying.' I am really of opinion that many of those who speak thus, wish well to the cause of religion; and seeing many rest in the bare form of prayer, and building on their self-righteousness, were, in order to avoid this rock, before they were aware, led into serious error; and instead of opposing the *abuse*, have inveighed against the *use* of a precious ordinance of God. This clearly appears *from the nature of prayer*. Prayer is the desire of the heart made known to God, either mentally or by words. Having offered this short definition of prayer, I ask, can a man who sees himself under the curse of a broken law, and feels the wrath of God abiding on him, can he help groaning, 'Who shall deliver me? Lord save or I perish!' Would it be his duty to suppress such prayers — to stifle such desires after the favour of God — the pardon of sin — the conversion of his soul, lest he should not come to Christ so soon, or lest he should make a Saviour of prayer. Is there not another and a more excellent way of speaking against self-righteousness, than by opposing prayer? Heartless forms, I am aware, are an abomination unto the Lord, but not the earnest groans of the broken and contrite heart. *From the obligations to pray.* — Seek ye the Lord while he may be found, call upon him while he is near — Call upon me in the day of trouble — If any man lack wisdom, let him ask of God — Is any afflicted, let him pray. — To mention only one passage more — the apostle exhorts Simon Magus to repent, and *pray* God, if perhaps, the thoughts of his heart might be forgiven him. Can there be a stronger demonstration of the propriety and necessity of prayer in an unregenerate sinner than this? That he was an unconverted man, none can deny; and yet the apostle exhorts him both to *repent* and *pray*. This, surely, is a sufficient precedent for any minister. *From the promises made to prayer*, — as, 'Seek, and ye shall find,' 'Knock, and it shall be opened unto you." *From the answers to prayer recorded in Scripture.* — Jacob wrestled until he obtained the blessing. Manasseh prayed, and was delivered, though such a monster of wickedness before. The publican's prayer was heard; and he went down to his house justified. Bartimeus did not cry in vain, 'Jesus thou Son of David, have mercy upon me!' Saul arose and washed away his sins, *'calling on the name* of the Lord Jesus.' Cornelius' prayers as well as his alms came up in memorial before God. These, among many other considerations, evince that it is the duty of all who desire to be found of God in peace, by prayer and supplication, with thanksgiving to make known their requests unto him.

3. An extremely dangerous notion has of late been received by many, respecting sin in believers. Those born of God are said to be *dead unto sin* and *alive unto God.* They are no longer slaves unto sin that they should obey it in the lusts thereof, but *new creatures* in Christ Jesus. But we are told that true faith may not only exist *without good* works, but that it may consist *with the most diabolical* works of *darkness* — that a man may be a drunkard, an adulterer, and even a murderer, without forfeiting his title to the favour of God. One told me, the other day, that if he were to live in the forementioned vices, from that day till the day of his death, his title to heaven would remain secure, nor would he be a whit the less a child of God, than when walking in the obedience of love. 'It is true,' said he, 'I do not wish to do so. If I were, it would becloud my evidences.' Yes, replied I, and forefeit your title too; for 'faith without works is dead,' and 'when the righteous man turneth away from his righteousness, and committeth iniquity, and dieth in them; for his iniquity that he hath done shall he die. All his righteousness that he hath done shall not be mentioned; in his trespass that he hath trespassed, and in his sin that he hath sinned, in them shall he die.' But it is vain to reason with such

298

persons. Press them with the *Law*, and they cry 'Moses is dead — we have nothing to do with the law.' Have they forgotten what our Lord Says, or do they think him as blind and legal as a Methodist. — 'Think not' says he, 'that I am come to destroy the Law or the Prophets: I am not come to destroy, but to fulfil. For verily, I say unto you, till heaven and earth pass, one jot or one tittle shall in no wise pass from the Law, till all be fulfilled. Whosoever, therefore, shall break one of these least commandments, and shall teach men so, he shall be called the least in the kingdom of heaven: but whosoever shall do and teach them, the same shall be called great in the kingdom of Heaven.' Do they imagine St. Paul was mistaken when he said, 'We are not without law to God, but under the law to Christ?' — Press them with the *Gospel*, tell them with the apostle that 'they that do such things shall not inherit the kingdom of God,' another subterfuge is at hand. 'Oh, 'tis only the body that sins — the soul cannot sin.' By this absurd distinction they open the flood-gates of iniquity, and by a single stroke, make void both the Law, and the Gospel. According to this view, the body can act without the soul; Christ may command the soul, and the devil the body; grace may reign in the soul, and sin in the body. But the apostle declares, — 'Sin shall not reign in your mortal bodies, that ye should obey it in the lusts thereof: sin shall not have dominion over you.'

One of their teachers on a certain occasion illustrated his sentiment by this (beautiful?) simile — 'A believer,' said he, 'is like a nut; it may fall into the mud, but the kernel will not be in the least defiled.' What a dreadful insinuation is here; for mark the explication: — 'Though we sin with the body, the soul remains pure and undefiled.'

I also heard another of their teachers affirm that, 'a man might live in adultery and murder ten months together, and yet be a child of God — a man after God's own heart — that his soul might never sin all that time.' To prove this, he produced the case of David. That noble testimony concerning David, they forget, was not given when he was covered with the guilt of uncleanness and blood. Nor can they ever prove that David was 'a man after God's own heart' when he perpetrated those evil deeds, unless they can make it appear that the holy God delights in murder and adultery; that he forbad David to do the thing he willed he should do; that he reproved him for fulfilling his will; and that he punished him severely, inwardly and outwardly, in his person and in his family, for accomplishing his will and pleasure.

After all, I cannot but form a favourable judgment of many who hold these unscriptural tenets. I believe many of them would shudder at the thought of reducing them to practice. Many of them, I doubt not, are real lovers of Jesus. I desire always to distinguish between a man and his opinions. You may make of this letter what use you think proper.[328]

Yours, &c.

William Black.

2.

Jacob Bailey

"Verse Against the

New Lights"

c. 1784

"Verse Against the New Lights",[329] by Jacob Bailey[330]

Behold the gifted teacher rise
And roll to heaven his half-shut eyes;
In every feature of his face
See stiffness sanctity and grace
Like whipping post erect he stands
And stretches out his wavering hands
Then with a slow and gentle voice
Begins to make a languid noise
Strives with a thousand airs to move
To melt and thaw your hearts to love
But when he fails by soft'ning arts
To mollify your frozen hearts
Observe him spring with eager jump
And on the table fiercely thump
With double fist he beats the air
Pours out his soul in wrathful prayer
Then seized with furious agitation
Screams forth a frightful exhortation
And with a sharp and hideous yell
Sends all your carnal folks to hell
Now to excite your fear and wonder
Tries the big jarring voice of thunder
Like wounded serpent in the vale
He writhes his body and his tail
Strives by each motion to express
The Agonies of deep distress
Then groans and scolds and roars aloud
Till dread and frenzy fire the crowd
The madness spreads with rapid power
Confusion reigns and wild uproar
A concert grand of joyful tones
Mingled with sighs and rueful moans
Some heaven extol with rapturous air
While others rave in black despair
A blended group of different voices
Confound and stun us with their noises
Thus in some far and lonely site
Amidst the deepest glooms of night

Where roll the slow and sullen floods
O'er hung with rocks and dusky woods
I've heard the wolves terrific howl
The doleful music of the owl
The frogs in hoarser murmurs croak
While from the top of some tall oak
With notes more piercing soft and shrill
Resounds the spritely whip-poor-will
These give the ears a wonderous greeting
Not much unlike a pious meeting
Here blue-eyed Jenny plays her part
Inured to every saint-like art
She works and heaves from head to heel
With pangs of puritanic zeal
Now in a fit of deep distress
The holy maid turns prophetess
And to her light and knowledge brings
A multitude of secret things
And as Enthusiasm advances
Falls into ecstasies and trances
Her self with decency resigns
To these impulses and inclines
On Jemmy Trim a favourite youth
A chosen vessel of the truth
Who as she sinks into his arms
Feels through his veins her powerful charms
Grown warm with throbs of strong devotion
He finds his blood in high commotion
And fired with love of this dear sister
Is now unable to resist her

3.

Bishop Charles

Inglis

"A Charge to the Clergy on

Evils of

Enthusiasm"

1791

A Charge delivered to the Clergy of Nova-Scotia, at the Triennial Visitation holden in the Town of Halifax, in the month of June 1791 (Halifax, 1792)[331]

....The evils attending lukewarmness, are numerous. A decay of piety, a neglect of religious duties and ordinances, a disregard to the divine laws, of the great end for which we were sent into the world, will ever be its inseparable concomitants; and to fill up the measure of its inconsistency, it is accompanied with pride, security and self-exaltation; — of all which, a prevalence of vice and immorality will be the sure consequence. Hence appears how incumbent it is on the Clergy to counteract these evils, which are subversive of man's happiness here and hereafter.

Extremes are apt to produce each other; and in other matters, so also we find it to be the case in religion. When a general indifference about it prevails, men of an enthusiastic cast are hereby encouraged to transgress the rules of Order, and disseminate their wild notions; to the injury of society, and rational piety. These men run when they are not sent; they cry — thus saith the Lord God, when the Lord hath not spoken.[332] And in all this, they think themselves justifiable by the lukewarmness that surrounds them.

On the other hand, such conduct, whilst it misleads the weak and ignorant, serves to confirm the lukewarm still more in their supine neglect, and prejudice them against religion. They think themselves safe and right, if they can but guard against such extravagance; and the farther they recede from it, the better. Even some Clergymen, though otherwise respectable, yet fearful to incur the imputation of being actuated by Enthusiasm, may be induced to slacken their exertions, and suffer their ardour to be checked...

Enthusiasm, when applied to religion, signifies a vain belief in private revelations, calls, or some commission, from the Deity. An Enthusiast therefore is one who vainly and without grounds, believes that he has such revelations, calls or commission. In general, this proceeds from a heated or disordered imagination; the suggestions of which are mistaken for luminous communications from God. Now, I am credibly informed that there are several persons in the Diocese, who, from a persuasion that they are favoured with extraordinary revelations and commissions from heaven, undertake to Preach, and administer the Christian Sacraments; regardless, not only of all literary qualifications for the office, but also of those stated methods which our Saviour and his Apostles have appointed to supply the ministry of the Church; and are in some degree observed by almost all regular Societies of Christians. Nay, I am assured that some lay claim to immediate and divine inspiration, equal to that of the Apostles themselves.[333]

It is far from my design or inclination to speak harshly, or even unkindly of these people; however it may be my duty to warn You against their errors and proceedings. That they are under delusion, will admit of no doubt; but how far that delusion is involuntary, or their ignorance invincible, or otherwise, is only known to the Searcher of hearts. Charity induces me to suppose that they think themselves right; and this sincerity is what distinguishes an Enthusiast from an Impostor. To me they appear to be objects of compassion, rather than of resentment; and were they convinced of their delusion, and brought to see and know the truth, which can only be effected by gentleness and humane treatment, they would probably become regular devout Christians. What I mean to offer here concerning them, shall be delivered in the spirit of brotherly love; and thrown into the form of a few brief observations —

1. I would observe that the Almighty has always condescended to treat men as rational beings; thereby making our faith and worship a reasonable service. Whenever, for wise and great purposes, he hath given an extraordinary revelation or commission to any person; he hath, at the same time, furnished that person with proper credentials to gain the assent of mankind....

God is as able to work miracles at this day, as he was in the days of Moses, or of the Apostles. His hand is not shortened; his regard to truth, and to the preservation of his rational creatures from error, is not withdrawn. It is therefore a duty which we owe to ourselves, to truth, and to God, to be

306

on our guard against pretensions to a divine revelation or commission, if not accompanied with the credentials which the Almighty hath been pleased to afford in all such extraordinary cases. Hence the Apostle's admonition — "Beloved, believe not every spirit; but try the spirits, (both with regard to their doctrine and powers) whether they be of God: Because many false Prophets are gone out into the World."[334] And whoever receives any person as coming with an extraordinary revelation or commission from God, without such trial according to the rules of holy Scriptures; or when not attended with miracles, which only can prove the authenticity of such extraordinary missions — whoever does so, I say, is liable to deception in things of the greatest moment, and dishonours the Almighty; for what can be more derogatory to his honour, than to attribute the crude effusions of ignorance to his blessed Spirit? Our Saviour equally blames the Jews for not receiving him, who came in his Father's name, with proper credentials; and for receiving others who only came in their own name, without credentials.[335] There has been no age since the Gospel was first preached, but has produced pretenders to extraordinary revelations, visions, and particular commissions from heaven; and these are not only inconsistent with, but contradictory to, Holy Scripture, and each other. Judge then what confusion must be introduced among mankind, and how subversive it would be of the Gospel, and of all rational religion, were those pretensions to be admitted.[336]

2. I would observe in the next place, that the Church of Christ, which is his spouse and body, is not a tumultuous, disorderly, and unorganized multitude, as these people seem to suppose. It is a regular, well-formed Society, to which our blessed Saviour, who is its Spiritual head, has given laws for its government; Sacraments, and other Ordinances, as means of grace and edification; and has also appointed ministers to preach his Gospel, execute his laws, and administer his ordinances....

But as in the natural body, where each member has its proper place and office, if any member were to desert its place, and usurp the office of another, the oeconomy of the whole would be interrupted, and danger of dissolution ensue: trust so

307

in the spiritual body — a departure from the ordinances established by our Lord, and the members of his Church usurping each other's functions, must be productive of the greatest evils — error, delusion, contention, and the reverse of every thing that is decent or edifying. This passage strongly represents the necessity of order in the Christian Church, and the irregularity of those self-appointed Teachers who disturbed the Church of Ephesus, when St. Paul wrote this Epistle. In a word, to suppose that any man may usurp the ministerial office, without any other warrant or authority than his own good opinion of his own sufficiency, is an error fraught with consequences destructive to Christianity, and subversive of its influence; and implies a disposition very inconsistent with the meek and humble spirit of the Gospel, in him who reduces it to practice.

3. I would observe, that supposing, not granting, there is an extraordinary call or revelation to a person; yet even this would not supercede, or set aside the positive Institutions of Jesus Christ. The uniform tenor of Scripture clearly decides this point. We are not left to mere conjecture upon it. No one who takes the word of God for his rule, can be at a loss how to form his judgment....

No mental accomplishments, no advances in piety, however great — no station, however exalted, could justify an intrusion into the Sacerdotal office, or an interference with its peculiar duties....

If it be alleged, that the state of the Jews was different from ours — that we are under the Gospel Dispensation — and that similar transgressions are not now visited with punishment: I grant there is a difference, but with respect to the case before us, it does not consist in this, that a less degree of guilt is incurred now than formerly by a violation of order, and divine Institutions....

Finally. It is worthy of observation, that most of the Epistles in the new Testament were written to counteract the designs, rectify the errors, and heal the disorders which were occasioned by self-appointed Teachers in the days of the Apostles....

To such an height of irregularity had those self

constituted Teachers risen at this early period, that some preached Christ even of envy and strife; and with the design of mortifying the Apostles, and adding to their afflictions.[337] St. Paul, who relates these and many other matters of the same kind, manifests the utmost mildness, how much soever he disapproved of them....

Let us imitate this great and amiable Apostle in a similar case; opposing gentleness to rage, brotherly love to hatred, and a regard for peace and order to strife and confusion. Let us pray the father of light that he would guide all to a knowledge of the truth. Let us earnestly beseech the Lord of the harvest, that he would send many faithful and regular labourers into this harvest, which is so plenteous.

4.

"New Light
Fanaticism"
1799

Bishop Charles Inglis to the
Reverend Mr. Bailey, April 3, 1799

Reverend Sir:

By the last post from Annapolis I was favoured with your letter of the 23^d March, containing an account of the disorderly proceedings of the New Lights & Methodists at Annapolis & its vicinity; for which I return you my thanks.

You ask for my advice & directions at this critical season & indeed you seemed to have acted with much propriety on the occasion. You were perfectly right in not suffering any of your family to go near them. I wish you could prevail on all the members of your Congregation to follow your example in this particular.   Nothing could more effectually defeat the sinister views of those disturbers of Society, as neglect would be a full antidote to their phrenzy.

With respect to a direct opposition to their measures, the expediency of it depends much on circumstances. At Clements, where a Clergyman only visits occasionally, it may be proper, & have a good effect. But where a Clergyman is settled, & regularly opens his Church, perhaps the best method is, indirectly to shew the best tendency & unscriptural nature of their principles & proceedings.   For instance — St. Paul assures us, that the fruits of the Spirit are *peace, charity, gentleness,* & we have no account in the Bible that the true Spirit of God in his sanctifying influences has attended with convulsions, violent agitations, screamings etc.   The Spirit therefore that is contrary to peace, charity & gentleness, cannot be the Spirit of God. But we find that Demoniacs were violently convulsed & *wallowed foaming*; & these resembled the agitations that are exhibited by the deluded creatures you mention.

Their proceedings are too violent, I conceive, to be lasting.   Mental tempests, like those of the atmosphere, must soon spend & exhaust themselves.   In the meantime, it is melancholly to see our fellow creatures thus deluded; & we cannot, without deep regret, reflect on the probable injury to real religion that is likely to arise from it.   For experience has uniformly evinced that fanaticism leads directly to infidelity; &

that it has a malignant influence on the principles of even those who have not been drawn into its vortex. For many are hereby led to consider all religion as a mere illusion. The fanaticism in the time of Charles I, was one principal cause of the dissoluteness that prevailed in the reign of Charles II; & from what the nation has not yet perfectly recovered. Superadded to this evil, society is threatened with danger. Fanatics are impatient under civil restraint & run into the democratic system. They are for Leveling every thing both sacred & civil; & this is peculiarly the case of our New Lights, who are, as far as I can learn, Democrats to a man — the Methodists will probably fall into the same plan.

You tell me that atheistical Books, such as that of Volney, & others highly democratic, are distributed by those people. By Volney's book I suppose you mean his *Ruins: Or Survey of the Revolutions of Empires* — a wild, romantic, frothy, impious performance, without solidity or argument. I wish you could ascertain who they are that circulated that book; & that you could procure some of those you call democratic. There cannot be a clearer indication or proof of the views & purposes of those who circulate such books. This was one of the methods practised in France to bring about the horrid revolution in that country. It was also practised in Ireland, & contributed not a little to the rebellion in that Island. You would therefore do well to make particular inquiry on this point.

I cannot forbear repeating again my wish that you could dissuade your people from attending the meetings of those deluded creatures. Many go to hear them out of an idle curiosity, & this serves to buoy them up, & feed their fanaticism. I would neither persecute nor attend them. Either would serve to enflame them more; but neglect extinguishes the flame of enthusiasm. It is therefore a duty which parents owe to their children, to Society & to God, to exert their authority, & keep their children out of the way of mischief. I can scarcely believe that Black would have the audacity to reprove you for not letting your family attend him, or even to desire it. But if he should be so void of decency & common

312

sense as to attempt either, you would be justified in shewing a spirited behaviour & reprimanding him severely for his irregular & preposterous conduct.

In the year 1791, the New Lights made a prodigious stir, so that I thought it my duty to advent to them in the Charge that I delivered at my Triennial Visitation that year. If you have that Charge, You can see in it my sentiments on those points where they appear to be most irregular & vulnerable. This will save the trouble of now writing what is contained in that Charge — if you have it not, I shall look for a copy among my papers & send it to you.

The times, My Good Sir, call for diligence & exertion in the Clergy to prevent their flocks from being led astray by ignorant & mistaken zealots. In charity we must suppose that they think themselves right; but their errors are not the less pernicious, either to the souls of Individuals, or to Society. We must therefore guard against them with earnestness & Christian temper. I trust & firmly believe the great Shepherd of Souls will not abandon the Church he hath founded, nor suffer error to prevail over his truths. The Gates of Hell will never prevail against it, nor shake its foundation that was cemented with his precious blood. In every age of his Church similar events have occurred. Ignorant & enthusiastic men have disturbed its peace; but they have passed away like a morning cloud; whilst this church has remained the same; & will so remain till the Kingdoms of this earth shall become the Kingdoms of the Lord, & his Christ.

I pray God to prosper Your endeavours in the cause of true religion & Order; I am

> Reverend Sir
> Your affectionate Brother
> & humble servant
> Charles Nova Scotia[338]

314

Footnotes to Chapter I
The Historical Background

Footnotes to Chapter 1

THE HISTORICAL BACKGROUND

1. See, for example, M. Armstrong, "Neutrality and Religion in Revolutionary Nova Scotia," in G.A. Rawlyk (ed.), *Historical Essays on the Atlantic Provinces* (Toronto, 1967), p. 40.

2. J.M. Bumsted, *Henry Alline* (Toronto, 1971), p. 78.

3. G. Stewart and G.A. Rawlyk, *A People Highly Favoured of God* (Toronto, 1972).

4. J. More, *The History of Queens County, Nova Scotia* (Halifax, 1973), p. 162.

5. See J. Davis, *Life and Times of the Late Rev. Harris Harding, Yarmouth, N.S.* (Charlottetown, 1866), p. 178.

6. (New York, 1916), pp. 159, 217.

7. H. Alline, *Life and Journal* (Boston, 1806), pp. 26-27.

8. *Ibid.*, pp. 27, 34.

9. *Ibid.*, pp. 34-35.

10. *Ibid.*, p. 35.

11. The centrality of the "New Birth" in the New Light experience in New England's "First" Great Awakening is argued persuasively by A. Heimert, *Religion and the American Mind, from the Great Awakening to the Revolution* (Cambridge, 1966).

12. The following discussion of Alline's theology is largely based upon his two theological works, *Two Mites* and *The Anti-Traditionalist* (Halifax, 1783). Unlike some other scholars interested in Alline, I have placed more stress on *The Anti-Traditionalist* since I regard this work as Alline's final and brave attempt to develop, in a creative way, many of the ideas first put forward in a tentative and often opaque manner in *Two Mites.* In addition, it should be pointed out that Alline's disciples regarded *The Anti-Traditionalist* as being his most important theological statement.

13. See *The Anti-Traditionalist*, pp. 24-25.

14. *Ibid.*, p. 40.

15. *Ibid.*, pp. 62-63.

16. *Two Mites,* p. 20-21.

17. See for example, *The Anti-Traditionalist*, p. 65.

18. *Two Mites*, pp. 121-135.

19. *Ibid.*, pp. 124-125.

20. *Ibid.*, p. 126.

21. Quoted in a letter fragment in the Manning Papers, Acadia University Archives (A.U.A.)

22. *Two Mites*, pp. 128-129.

23. *Ibid.*, pp. 132-133.

24. *Ibid.*, pp. 150-151.

25. *The Anti-Traditionalist*, pp. 53-54.

26. S.A. Marini, "New England Folk Religions 1770-1815: The Sectarian Impulse in Revolutionary Society" (Unpublished Ph.D. Dissertation, Harvard University, 1978), p. 2. Professor Marini's thesis, in revised form, has been recently published under the title *Radical Sects of Revolutionary New England* (Cambridge, 1982) I have learned a great deal from Marini's fine thesis and book. Some of my criticism of Marini's work as well as my praise is to be found in my unpublished paper "Alline, Randall and the Free Will Baptists", written a few months before the publication of his book.

27. M. Richey, *A Memoir of the Late Rev. William Black* (Halifax, 1839), p 45.

28. Quoted in Marini, "New England Folk Religions," pp. 453-454.

29. *Ibid.*, p. 479.

30. This theme is developed in D.D. Bruce Jr., *And They All Sang Hallelujah, Plain-Folk Camp Meeting Religion, 1800-1845* (Knoxville, 1975), p. 95. See also Marini, *Radical Sects*, pp. 156-171. This chapter concerning the evolution of hymnody is aptly entitled "The Language of the Soul". There is much useful background material in an often neglected Ph.D. dissertation, A. Beuchner, "Yankee Singing Schools and the Golden Age of Choral Music in New England, 1760-1800," (Unpublished Ph.D. Dissertation, Harvard University, 1960).

31. M.W. Armstrong, *The Great Awakening in Nova Scotia 1776-1809* (Hartford, 1948), p. 91. See also Armstrong, "Henry Alline's Spiritual Hymns and Songs," *Dalhousie Review*, Vol. XXXIV, (1954-5), pp. 418-425 and Marini, *Radical Sects*, pp 158-162. Armstrong unfairly, I feel, described Alline's hymns as

being "mostly doggerel."

32. H. Alline, *Hymns and Spiritual Songs* (Boston, 1786), pp. i-ii.
33. *Ibid.*, pp. 51-52.
34. *Ibid.*, p. 131.
35. *Ibid.*, pp. 153-154.
36. *Ibid.*, p. 162.
37. *Ibid.*, pp. 182-183.
38. *Ibid.*, pp. 348-349.
39. *Ibid.*, pp. 380-381.
40. I have attended a Sunday service conducted by Frederick Burnett, near Hartland, New Brunswick, where this oral tradition is still an important feature of religious worship. Mr. Burnett, a Free Christian Baptist preacher, has provided me with a great deal of valuable information about the continuing impact of the Allinite tradition and I continue to learn a great deal from him about the region's Evangelical religious culture.
41. p. lxiv.
42. *Ibid.*, p. lxiv-lxv.
43. *Ibid.*, p. lxv.
44. *Ibid.*
45. P. Miller, *Errand into the Wilderness*, (Cambridge, 1964), p. 167.
46. Alline, *Life and Journal*, p. 180, David McLure to William Alline, Aug. 3, 1784.
47. *Ibid.*
48. Noth Hampton Congregational Church book, New Hampshire Historical Society, Concord, N.H. I originally learned of this fascinating document from Professor David Bell, of the University of New Brunswick Law School. Professor Bell has taught me more than he probably realized about the evolution of the anti-Calvinist Baptists in Nova Scotia and New Brunswick in the Post-Revolutionary period.
49. See for example, "Henry Alline", *Christian Instructor and Missionary Register of the Presbyterian Church of Nova Scotia* (March, 1859), p. 74. Ms. Laurie Stanley provided me with this valuable source.

50. Davis, *Harris Harding*, p. 187.

51. *Ibid.*

52. Quoted in Armstrong, *The Great Awakening in Nova Scotia*, p. 86.

53. This quotation, from an "old Yankee Nova Scotian" is to be found in the Public Archives of Nova Scotia (P.A.N.S.), "Mather Byles III Journal," MG 1 Vol. 163.

54. This theme is developed at much greater length in Stewart and Rawlyk, *A People Highly Favoured of God*, pp. 94-120. See also P.A.N.S. "Records of the Church of Jebogue in Yarmouth," p. 138.

55. P.A.N.S. "Records of the Church of Jebogue in Yarmouth," p. 140.

56. D.C. Harvey (ed.), *Diary of Simeon Perkins, 1780-1789* (Toronto, 1958), p. 177.

57. See, for example, *The Anti-Traditionalist*, p. 36.

58. H. Alline, *A Sermon Preached at Liverpool, 20 November, 1782* (Halifax, n.d.) p. 23.

59. See *The Anti-Traditionalist*, p. 24.

60. *Ibid.*, p. 48. See also p. 12 and also the many hymns composed by Alline which are preoccupied with the "ravishing process."

61. (Chicago, 1977), pp. 105-110.

62. See, for example, Mary P. Ryan "A Women's Awakening: Evangelical Religion and the Families of Utica, New York, 1800-1840," J.W. James (ed.), *Women in American Religion* (Philadelphia, 1980), p. 110.

63. *Ibid.*

64. Mathews, *Religion in the Old South*, p. 110.

65. *The Anti-Traditionalist*, p. 40.

66. See T.W. Smith, *History of the Methodist Church ... of Eastern British America* (Halifax, 1877) pp. 150-151; G. French, *Parsons and Politics* (Toronto, 1962), pp. 33-39; N. Bangs, *The Life of the Rev. Freeborn Garrettson* (New York, 1830), pp. 150-188; W.C. Barclay, *Early American Methodism, 1769-1844*, Vol. I (New York, 1949), pp. 166-171.

67. Barclay, *Early American Methodism*, Vol. I, p. 171.

68. J.M. Buckley, *A History of Methodism in the United States,* Vol. I (New York, 1897), p. 369.

69. Quoted in Smith, *History of the Methodist Church,* pp. 193-194.

70. Quoted in Bangs, *The Life of the Rev. Freeborn Garrettson,* p. 154.

71. Buckley, *A History of Methodism in the United States,* Vol. I, p. 171.

72. Smith, *History of the Methodist Church,* p. 152.

73. *Ibid.*

74. Garrettson to F. Asbury, 1786, quoted in Bangs, *The Life of the Rev. Freeborn Garrettson,* p. 177.

75. *Ibid.,* p. 179.

76. *Methodist Magazine* (1827), p. 672.

77. United Church Archives, Toronto (U.C.A.), "The Freeborn Garrettson Journal."

78. *Ibid.*

79. *Ibid.*

80. Quoted in Smith, *History of the Methodist Church,* p. 166.

81. U.C.A. "The Freeborn Garrettson Journal."

82. *Ibid.*

83. Quoted in Bangs, *The Life of the Rev. Freeborn Garrettson,* p. 171.

84. Quoted in Barclay, *Early American Methodism, 1769-1844,* Vol. I, p. 171.

85. See Smith, *History of the Methodist Church,* pp. 200-209.

86. *Ibid.,* p. 197.

87. *Ibid.,* p. 99.

88. This material is taken from D. Stratas, "A Study of the Historical Demography of the Maritime Provinces, 1763-1901," (Unpublished paper, Queen's University, 1981) Pt. II, pp. 15-16.

89. The Methodist-New Light struggle has not received the scholarly attention it obviously merits. It is noteworthy that in those areas of Nova Scotia where Garrettson and other

American Methodists had a considerable impact in the 1780s, the Free Will Baptists received their greatest support as the nineteenth century unfolded.

90. See, for example, N. MacKinnon, "The Loyalist Experience in Nova Scotia 1783 to 1791," (Unpublished Ph.D. Dissertation, Queen's University, 1974).

91. G. Wood, "Evangelical American and Early Mormonism," (Paper presented to the Fifteenth Annual Meeting of the Mormon History Association, May, 1980), p. 2.

92. Quoted in J.M. Cramp "History of the Maritime Baptists," p. 26. This very important source is to be found in the Acadia University Archives.

93. Wood, "Evangelical American," p. 7.

94. *Ibid.,* p. 10.

95. *Ibid.,* p. 12.

96. *Ibid.,* p. 20.

97. This description of Manning's conversion is based upon Manning's manuscript "Reminiscences of his conversion" to be found in the Manning Papers, A.U.A. All the quotations are from Manning's description of his conversion. Professor Barry Moody, of the Department of History, Acadia University, presented a paper on Manning's long and distinguished career at the annual meeting of Canadian Society of Church History in Halifax in June 1981.

98. Manning's conversion is dealt with at considerable length in Cramp, "History of the Maritime Baptists", pp. 52-54.

99. See Alline's detailed description of the New Birth process in *Two Mites*, pp. 121-135.

100. *Ibid.,* p. 94.

101. Armstrong, *The Great Awakening in Nova Scotia*, p. 101.

102. *Ibid.*

103. *Two Mites*, p. 93.

104. *The Anti-Traditionalist*, p. 42.

105. See Alline's *Life and Journal*, p. 174.

106. "Account of Mr. Black" *Arminian Magazine* (1791), p. 178.

107. *Ibid.,* p. 234.

108. *Ibid.*, p. 298.

109. U.C.A., "Freeborn Garrettson Journal".

110. Quoted in Bangs, *The Life of the Rev. Freeborn Garrettson*, p. 167.

111. See the Reverend J. Bailey to the Reverend Samuel Peters, April 29, 1785, in W.S. Bartlet (ed.), *The Frontier Missionary: A Memoir of the Life of the Rev. Jacob Bailey* (New York, 1853), pp. 222-223.

112. Quoted in Armstrong, *The Great Awakening in Nova Scotia*, p. 124.

113. J. Marsden, *The Narrative of a Mission* (Plymouth-Dock, 1816), p. 49.

114. B.C. Cuthbertson (ed.), *The Journal of John Payzant* (Hantsport, 1981), pp. 43-48.

115. U.C.A. "Freeborn Garrettson Journal."

116. Cuthbertson, *The Journal of John Payzant*, p. 44.

117. For a more detailed discussion of Harding's career see G.A. Rawlyk, "From Newlight to Baptist: the Second Great Awakening in Nova Scotia," in B. Moody (ed.), *Repent and Believe* (Hantsport, 1980), pp. 1-26 and Davis, *Life and Times of the Late Rev. Harris Harding*.

118. Davis, *Life and Times of the Late Rev. Harris Harding*, p. 5.

119. *Ibid.*, pp. 7-8.

120. *Ibid.*, p. 10.

121. *Ibid.*, p. 178.

122. Cramp, "History of the Maritime Baptists," p. 35.

123. H. Harding, "Account of the Rise and Progress of the First Baptist Church in Yarmouth, Nova Scotia," in Davis, *Life and Times of the Late Rev. Harris Harding*, p. 206.

124. Cuthbertson, *The Journal of John Payzant*, pp. 37-38.

125. *Ibid.*, p. 38.

126. Davis, *Life and Times of the Late Rev. Harris Harding*, p. 143.

127. *Ibid.*

128. A.U.A., Manning Letters, Alexander Crawford to Edward Manning, Oct. 2, 1813.

129. C.B. Fergusson (ed.), *The Diary of Simeon Perkins, 1790-1796,* p. 174.

130. *Ibid.,* p. 177.

131. A.U.A. "Personal Letters of Henry Alline, Joseph Dimock, Harris Harding, Edward Manning and others, dated from 1778 to 1793," hereafter referred to as the "New Light Letters," Harding to Thaddeus Harris, May 14, 1789.

132. *Ibid.,* Harding to the Reverend John Payzant, Aug. 23, 1791.

133. *Ibid.,* Harding to Thomas Bennett, April 6, 1792.

134. *Ibid.*

135. *Ibid.,* Harding to Dorcas Prentice, Aug. 27, 1791.

136. For biographical information about Dimock see Cramp, "History of the Maritime Baptists," pp. 37-52 and G.E. Levy (ed.), *The Diary of Joseph Dimock* (Hantsport, 1979), pp. 7-17.

137. Cramp, "History of the Maritime Baptists," p. 376.

138. *Ibid.,* p. 299.

139. *Ibid.,* p. 299.

140. *Ibid.,* pp. 299-300.

141. A.U.A., "New Light Letters," Dimock to Thomas Bennett Dec. 18, 1790. This version of the letter is to be found in Cramp, "History of the Maritime Baptists," p. 39.

142. Dimock to Bennett, Aug. 20, 1791 in Cramp, "History of the Maritime Baptists", p. 40.

143. *Ibid.,* p. 43.

144. Quoted in *ibid.,* p. 301.

145. *Ibid.,* p. 59.

146. See "A Brief Memoir of the Rev. James Manning," in *The Baptist Missionary Magazine,* Vol. 2 No. 5 (Sept, 1835), pp. 174-175.

147. Cramp, "History of the Maritime Baptists," p. 135.

148. A.U.A., "James Innis Diary."

149. See Cuthbertson, *The Journal of John Payzant,* p. 47.

150. C.B. Fergusson (ed.), *The Diary of Simeon Perkins, 1797-1803,* p. 214.

151. Cuthbertson, *The Journal of John Payzant*, p. 44.
152. *Ibid.*
153. *Ibid.*, p. 47.
154. *Ibid.*, p. 45.
155. *Ibid.*
156. *Ibid.*, p. 46.
157. *Ibid.*, p. 47.
158. *Ibid.*
159. *Ibid.*
160. *Ibid.*
161. *Ibid.*
162. *Ibid.*
163. *Ibid.*, p. 47.
164. *Ibid.*, pp. 47-48.
165. *Ibid.*, p. 48.
166. *Ibid.*, p. 49.
167. *Ibid.*, p. 52.
168. *Ibid.*, p. 53. See also the Cornwallis Church Records, A.U.A., for a far less detailed account of these developments.
169. Cuthbertson, *The Journal of John Payzant*, p. 55.
170. Fergusson, *Perkin's Diary, 1797-1803*, p. 45.
171. Quoted in Cramp, "History of the Maritime Baptists," p. 24.
172. Similar religious movements were quite common in Northern New England at precisely the same time. See Marini, *Radical Sects of Revolutionary New England* for a good description of the fragmenting Evangelical ethos.
173. See Davis, *Life and Times of the Late Rev. Harris Harding*, p. 184, for a letter about the New Lights written, sometime in the 1830s, by the Reverend David Nutter.
174. *Ibid.*
175. *Ibid.*, p. 185.
176. *Ibid.*, p. 184.
177. By the 1820s, Edward Manning had certainly come to the

conclusion that Scott's view of Christianity was superior to that of Alline. See A.U.A., "The Manning Journal" for the 1820s, in particular, for a fascinating introspective account of one man's spiritual and intellectual journey from Alline's Free-Will New Lightism to Scott's Calvinist Orthodoxy.

178. See E.C. Wright, "Without Intervention of Prophet, Priest or King," in Moody, *Repent and Believe*, p. 70.

179. See Marini, *Radical Sects of Revolutionary New England*. My most recent work on Nova Scotia revivalism in the 1770 to 1820 period would support the conclusion of Professor Jon Butler who has argued that "eighteenth-century revivals of religion in America" were basically "erratic, heterogeneous, and politically benign." See his extremely important article "Enthusiasm Described and Decried: The Great Awakening as Interpretative Fiction," *Journal of American History*, Vol. 69. No. 2 (Sept., 1982), p. 325.

Footnotes to Chapter II
The New Light Letters and
Spiritual Songs

180. David McLure to William Alline Sr., North-Hampton, N.H., Aug. 23, 1784, in H. Alline, *The Life and Journal of the Rev. Mr. Henry Alline* (Boston, 1806), p. 180.

181. *Ibid.*

182. See the Handley Chipman 1789 manuscript version of Alline's Journal, A.U.A.

183. C. Inglis, *A Charge delivered to the Clergy of Nova-Scotia, at The Triennial Visitation holden in the Town of Halifax, in the month of June 1791* (Halifax, 1792), p. 23.

184. J. Davis, *Life and Times of the Late Rev. Harris Harding, Yarmouth, N.S.* (Charlottetown, 1866), p. 179.

185. See for example the most valuable manuscript volume of "Spiritual Songs that were sung in Yarmouth County, Nova Scotia and in Victoria, Carleton and Northern York Counties, New Brunswick. Chiefly by the Free, Free Christian and Primitive Baptist People," collected by Frederick Burnett. I have a copy of this manuscript and my contention concerning the continuing popularity of these hymns and spiritual songs is supported not only by this document but also by Mr. Burnett, the foremost authority on the Allinite oral tradition in the Maritime Provinces.

186. See Davis, *Harris Harding*, p. iii.

187. (Halifax, 1902), p. 30.

188. *Ibid.*, p. 30-34.

189. Davis, *Harris Harding*, p. 223-235.

190. See Victor Turner, *The Ritual Process: Structure and Anti-Structure (Ithaca, 1979), p. 139.*

191. *Ibid.*, p. 139-140.

Footnotes to Alline's Letters

192. In this letter, Alline was emphasizing a point he consistently stressed throughout his preaching career — that conversion was of primary importance and that the sacraments and church polity were — as he once put it — "non-essentials." "O may the time come," he once noted in his *Journal* "when Ephraim shall no longer vex Judah, nor Judah envy Ephraim, and there might never more be any disputes about such non-essentials as water-baptism: the Sprinkling of infants or baptizing of adults by immersion: but everyone enjoy liberty of conscience." (*Journal*, p. 67.)

193. Thomas Handley Chipman.

194. Cornelius Rogers had immigrated to Nova Scotia in 1762. A son of Benjamin and Phoebe (Harding) Rogers, he had been born at Kingston, Mass., on August 26, 1739. He married Abigail Holmes of Kingston, on December 16, 1763. It seems clear that the conversion of Abigail Rogers and her daughter, in October, 1782, helped significantly to consolidate Alline's position in the Yarmouth region.

195. The Reverend Jonathan Scott (1744-1819) was Alline's most vociferous Nova Scotia critic. Born in Lunenburg, Massachusetts on October 12, 1744, Scott, in 1758 moved to Roxbury where he was apprenticed as a shoemaker. Then in 1765 he decided to settle permanently in the Yarmouth area of Nova Scotia where on March 14, 1768 he married Lucy Ring who died on December 20, 1777. He married Elizabeth Boss, of Cornwallis on December 8, 1783. Scott farmed and fished and became increasingly involved in the activities of the Congregational Church at Chebogue and was ordained minister of this church on April 28, 1772. An orthodox Calvinist Congregationalist, Scott opposed what he considered to be Alline's divisive revivalism and because of this policy, he alienated most of his congregation during Nova Scotia's Great Awakening. After a protracted and acrimonious controversy with his Church, Scott finally left Chebogue in 1795 for Minot, Maine where he became minister of the Congregational Church located there. Scott died at the age of seventy-five on October 15, 1819 at Minot Maine; his second wife did not die until May 14, 1843. Scott was regarded by his Maine congregation as "a worthy pastor." On his grave stone is to be found the following apt inscription:

My flesh shall slumber in the ground
Till the last trumpet's joyful sound
Then burst the chains with sweet suprise
And in my Saviour's image rise.

There is much valuable information about Scott in C.B. Fergusson (ed.), "The Life of Jonathan Scott," *Bulletin of the Public Archives of Nova Scotia*, No. 15 (Halifax, 1960) and H.E. Scott (ed.), *The Journal of the Reverend Jonathan Scott* (Boston, 1980) as well as G. Stewart and G. Rawlyk, *A People Highly Favoured of God* (Toronto, 1972).

196. Jacob Brown was one of the original New England settlers of Horton, having been granted his land in 1759. He was unmarried and an ardent supporter of Henry Alline and his New Light disciples.

197. William Wells, a native of Yorkshire, had emigrated to the Cumberland region in the early 1770s. An ardent Methodist, he played a key role in the conversion of William Black. Wells was a successful merchant and farmer who had business contacts in Halifax where he was well known as a supporter of the Evangelical cause.

198. Henry Fergusson, like Wells, was sympathetic to all Evangelical preachers who visited Halifax in the early 1780s. Fergusson probably originally settled in Halifax in 1752 but there is virtually no biographical material available concerning this friend of Alline and also of William Black.

Footnotes to
The New Light Letters

199. Probably, William Bennett.

200. Captain Thomas Young (1735-1833), a native of Salem, Massachusetts, who, on January 31, 1771, married Priscilla Alline, sister of Henry and eldest daughter of William and Rebecca Clark Alline.

201. Sarah Brown, of Falmouth, was the wife of Samuel Brown who had received his grant of land in 1761.

202. Charlotte Prescott was born in Halifax in October, 1764; the daughter of Dr. Jonathan Prescott, and Ann Blagden. With her family she moved to Chester where in 1786, at the age of twenty-two "the Lord was pleased to enlighten her understanding in the mysteries of redemption." Through the preaching of Thomas Handley Chipman and John Payzant, she first experienced intense conviction "My heart," she once observed "sunk within me under a load of guilt. I knew that God would be just if I were sent to hell; but how he could save me consistently with the claims of justice I knew not. Thus black despair brooded over my spirit. I thought if any person was an object of pity, I required it more than all, but none deserved it less. Often did I use these words of the poet,

Shew pity Lord, O Lord forgive,

Let a repenting rebel live."

Charlotte Prescott could, "neither report, believe, nor pray: my heart in rebellion refused the mercy I had sought, until those words came with power to my mind, 'By grace ye are saved through faith, and not of yourselves, it is the gift of God.' This calmed my troubled mind. All was peace; I beheld by faith the bleeding suffering Saviour, bearing my sins on the cross. I was delighted with the suitableness of the provision made in the gospel." Regeneration had finally come to an exhausted yet exhilarated Charlotte Prescott. In 1788, Charlotte was baptised by the Reverend Thomas Handley Chipman and she was, during these years, an unusually active and energetic New Light and a close confident of Harris Harding and Joseph Dimock, in particular. She married George Boyle a member of the Cornwallis New Light Church by whom she had three children, one son and two daughters. They lived for a brief time in Windsor and then at Horton and in 1796 moved to Liverpool where by 1808 they had become bitter critics of Payzant and staunch Baptists. After the death of her husband, Charlotte moved to Chester where she died in March, 1833. She asked her close friend Joseph Dimock to preach her funeral sermon from the text "By grace are ye saved" a verse she declared which had "been sweet to her through all her pilgrimage." Much valuable information about Charlotte Boyle is to be found in Dimock's "Memoir of Mrs. Charlotte Boyle," to be found in the *Baptist Missionary Magazine* (Jan. 1835), p. 1-8.

203. Phebe Fox Lockwood, was the second wife of Moses Lockwood, having married him in 1786.

204. Thaddeus Harris was a son of Lebbeus Harris (1713-1792) a native of Connecticut who served as a member of the Nova Scotia Assembly from 1761-1765. Two sons of Thaddeus "were sprinkled" by Henry Alline. Thaddeus, born on February 29, 1748, and died in 1836, was a member of the Cornwallis New Light Church and was chosen a deacon of this church on January 30, 1783. In 1792, during the New Dispensation crisis, he first supported Payzant's opponents and then modified his stance by declaring that "he held to all the Articles of the Church except that of the Sacraments and desires to walk with us as a Member of this Church still." A decade later, in June, 1802, however, Thaddeus was still surprisingly ambivalent, regarding the importance of the "ordinances of God's House." He had found it extremely difficult to abandon what to him was the Allinite legacy. (See the Cornwallis Church Records, B.H.C., A.U.A.)

205. "Col D'Lancys Daughter" was probably Elizabeth, the daughter of the New York Loyalist Stephen De Lancey. Elizabeth married her cousin William on October 2, 1808. In all likelihood Elizabeth quickly abandoned her New Light "enthusiasm."

1790

206. There appears to be no readily available biographical material about Helen Grant.

207. Hannah Webber was the daughter of James and Sarah Webber of Chester. James Webber first settled in Chester in 1760.

208. Elizabeth Prescott was born on April 12, 1769, daughter of Dr.

Jonathan Prescott and Ann Bladgen and sister of Charlotte. Elizabeth married Ashael Wells of Cornwallis in 1792. Wells was an active New Light as was his father, Judah Wells (1738-1779).

209. Joseph Bailey was the fifth and youngest child of Joseph Bailey and Hannah who had been married in Rhode Island on May 26, 1749. Joseph Bailey, the younger, was related to the Dimocks and was in fact, Joseph Dimock's uncle. Bailey was probably one of Alline's first converts and he became one of the Falmouth preacher's most committed disciples. He often accompanied Alline on his preaching tours and, moreover, even before Alline's death Bailey had begun to itinerate on his own. It has been observed that he, in fact, "stirred up the people" more than Alline did in the Barrington region.

A member of the Cornwallis New Light Church, Bailey was a powerful, enthusiastic exhorter. In 1784, Simeon Perkins spitefully referred to him as "the Preacher or Pretended Preacher" (Perkins, *Diary, 1780-1789,* p. 232). According to Perkins, Bailey played a key role in splitting the Liverpool Congregational church into New Light and Old Light factions. He frequently preached in Liverpool in 1785 showing great concern about the growing significance of the Methodists. By the following year, however, the New Light position in Liverpool was being defended instead by Chipman, Payzant and Harris Harding for Bailey had sailed on August 2, 1786 in the sloop *Nancy* for Rhode Island. He returned to Nova Scotia and contributed in a major way to the conversion of Edward Manning as well as to the New Light extension of the Garrettson Revival. Bailey died sometime during the last decade of the eighteenth century, possibly in 1791.

210. William Blair of Onslow was born in 1716 and died on August 4, 1791. He was a leading New Light in the Onslow region of Nova Scotia.

211. Betsy or Elizabeth Blair was born in 1768 in Onslow and died in 1848. In 1793 she married Shelomith Woodworth another New Light. Contemporaries frequently commented on the fact that most of the nine Blair children possessed unusual spiritual gifts.

212. Thomas Lynds (1747-1839) of Onslow was the son of Jacob Lynds, an emigrant from Ireland. Thomas married Rebecca

Blair. He, together with his brother John, were among those who laid hands on Edward Manning at his ordination in October, 1795 as minister of the Cornwallis New Light Church. The Lynds brothers later became Baptists.

213. Charlotte Lusby must have been a young New Light convert.

214. Betsy Lusby, sister of Charlotte, was an integral part of the New Light web connecting Onslow, Amherst and the Cornwallis-Horton region of the colony.

215. Susy Lynds (1776-1862) was the daughter of Thomas and Rebecca Lynds of Onslow. In 1790, she was a little older than twelve — but not by much. She married Robert McCurdy in 1794.

216. George Boyles or Boyle, a native of Ireland, was a member of the Cornwallis New Light Church and a schoolmaster and he was a particularly close friend of Thomas Bennett and Harris Harding. After marrying Charlotte Prescott of Chester, he eventually made his way to Liverpool where in the summer of 1796 he established a school. Simeon Perkins was not particularly impressed with Boyle's teaching ability. When Harris Harding was charged in the autumn of 1796 with having sexual relations with Mahitable Harrington, Boyle and Bennett, among others, accompanied Harding as "he made a publick Confession, (of his Faulty conduct of Late)" (Harvey, *Perkins' Diary 1790-1796*, p. 429). By 1799, Boyle was operating a tavern in Liverpool and was, moreover, involved in the fishery and in trade and was an active New Light Baptist. In 1808, for example, he tried to force the Reverend John Payzant to permit Thomas Handley Chipman to preach in the Congregational "Meeting-House." Two years later in September 1810, George Boyle was charged and then acquitted "for an Assault on the Body of Ann Lesslie Junr attempting Rape." (Fergusson, *Perkins' Diary, 1804-1812*, p. 245).
Boyle died sometime after 1812, his wife Charlotte, with her two surviving children, moved to Chester where she died in 1833.

January to July
1791

Mary Freeze was the daughter of Samuel Freeze of Amherst

335

and later of Upper Sussex, New Brunswick. Married three times, the first ten of Freeze's twenty-two children were daughters. His huge family became the core of the Free Will Baptist Church in the Upper Sussex area.

218. Dorcas Prentice, a resident of Horton, was an aunt of Harris Harding; she lived with Harding's grandparents Lebbeus and Fally Harris. A member of the Cornwallis New Light Church, her name was removed sometime before 1799 from the Church's membership roll.

219. Keturah Whipple lived in Horton and was a member of the Cornwallis New Light Church. She was probably the daughter of Daniel Whipple, a cordwainer, and Christiana Murray, his wife. Her name, like that of her close friend Dorcas Prentice, was removed sometime before 1799 from her Church's roll.

220. William Freeman, a native of New England, resided in the Amherst area where he and his family remained active, for decades, in the New Light movement.

221. Nancy Brown may have been the daughter of Darius Brown of Horton.

222. Benjamin Cleveland, a disciple of Henry Alline, was a gifted hymn writer and an active member of the Cornwallis New Light Church. Born on August 30, 1733 in Windham, Connecticut, he died in Horton, in March 1811. He married twice: on February 20, 1754 to Mary Elderkin who died on April 24, 1783, and on March 25, 1784, to Sarah Hibbard. Benjamin Cleveland fathered twelve children. A key leader of the Cornwallis New Light Church, Cleveland attacked those who advocated what he considered to be "corrupt principles and practices;" he also vociferously opposed Edward Manning's decision to become a close-communion Baptist. Cleveland's considerable talent as a hymn writer has not received the attention that it merits. Only three of his hymns are included in this volume because only three were to be found in the Bennett volume. But there are other of his hymns which are still sung in some Baptists Churches in Nova Scotia and New Brunswick. Perhaps the best known of these has as it first line "O could I find from day to day a nearness to my God."

August 1791

223. Lavinia DeWolf was the eldest daughter of Edward DeWolfe and Sarah Brown who had been married on November 26, 1773. Lavinia was born on September 5, 1774, and married a Robert Dickson in 1798. When Harding's letter was written Lavina was not yet seventeen nor was she a member of the Cornwallis New Light Church.

224. Nothing is known about these two women or about their families. They were probably a part of the important teen-age segment of the Horton-Cornwallis New Light population.

225. It is noteworthy that this letter and others addressed to the Reverend John Payzant were really sent to the members of the Cornwallis New Light Church to be "Communicated" to them. This letter it should be stressed, was received at the height of the New Dispensation crisis. Yet no implicit or explicit mention of New Dispensationalism is to be found in the letter. It may have been that for a variety of complex reasons Payzant and his supporters exaggerated the "heretical features" of the movement especially when its most effective leaders were some distance away.

226. Daniel Welsh was a member and a Deacon of the Cornwallis New Light Church. Sometime before 1799 his name was apparently removed from the Church rolls.

227. Amasa Bigelow (1755-1799) was a shipwright and a member of the Cornwallis New Light Church. Amasa was the son of Isaac Bigelow, born in Colchester Connecticut on May 4, 1713 and Abigail Skinner who were married on March 14, 1734. Isaac Bigelow was in 1777 one of the seven founders of the Cornwallis church and his son Amesa, in 1795, with Thaddaeus Harris "laid their hands on Mr. Manning's head at his ordination in 1795." (A.W.H. Eaton, *The History of Kings County Nova Scotia* (Salem 1912), p. 317).

228. Lebbeus Harris (1741-1827) was the son of Major Lebbeus Harris (1713-1792?) who immigrated to Horton from Connecticut in 1761 and who served in the Nova Scotia Assembly from 1761-1765. Lebbeus, the younger, was an uncle of Harris Harding and was chosen a deacon of the Cornwallis New Light Church in March 1786. Until his death in 1827 he, like his brother Thaddeus, remained a staunch supporter of Henry Alline and Harris Harding.

337

229. Judah Wells was the son of Judah Wells, the senior (1738-1779), and Anne Bigelow who were married on January 31, 1760 in Connecticut and who immigrated to the Cornwallis area in the early 1760s. Judah Wells, the younger, who was born on January 5, 1763 and died on June 13, 1791, was an immersed member of the Cornwallis New Light Church. His wife was Eleanor Simpson.

230. Moses Lockwood, of Greenwich, Connecticut, came to Cornwallis after the American Revolution. In 1786 he married, as his second wife, Phebe, daughter of James and Grace Fox.

231. Asa Dewey was the son of Moses Dewey (1718-1800) and Mary English who were married on May 12, 1744 in Connecticut. The Dewey family immigrated to Cornwallis in 1764. Asa, who was born in 1748, was a member of the Cornwallis New Light Church and was also, in all likelihood, one of Alline's converts.

232. Taking into consideration the horrendous problems confronting Payzant, many of them created by Harding, this is a remarkable letter.

233. Julia Ann Swigard was a member of the Cornwallis New Light Church and also, the evidence suggests, active in the New Dispensation movement. In August 1792, she was suspended from the Church "on account of her levity, singing songs, and has no desire to lay the least restraint upon herself." (Cornwallis Church Records, B.H.C., A.U.A.)

234. Susanna Eaton, born on June 24, 1769 was a daughter of David Eaton (1729-1803) and Deborah White who were married on October 30, 1751, in Massachusetts and who immigrated to Nova Scotia in 1761. A member of the Cornwallis New Light Church, she was criticized in August 1792, for "her levity, dancing and etc." She responded by stressing her continuing desire "to walk with the Church except in the Sacrament." (Cornwallis Church Records, B.H.C., A.U.A.). Like her friend Julia Ann Swigard, Susanna Eaton was very much involved in the New Dispensation movement. She married Captain Harry Cox on december 19, 1793.

235. Marvin Beckwith was born in 1768, the son of Captain Samuel Beckwith and Rebecca Chipman. Samuel Beckwith had come to Nova Scotia from Connecticut in the early 1760s. Marvin

was a member of the Cornwallis New Light Church and his controversial preaching led to his "suspension" from the congregation in August, 1792. After a regular Sunday service conducted by the Reverend John Payzant, Marvin delivered an impromtu "indecent" sermon to a number of young friends which, "in an unbecoming manner," he used "The term of God damned devil and such like expressions in a way not becoming the gospel and justifying himself in it." (Cornwallis Church Records, B.H.C., A.U.A.) Little else is known about Marvin Beckwith — a key New Dispensation leader.

236. Elphila Bent was possibly related to Harris Harding. Nothing is known of her; she may have also been related to David Bent from Annapolis County.

237. There is, unfortunately, no readily available information about this Horton resident.

238. Lydia Randall, daughter of Caleb and Mary Rand, was, without question, one of the principal actors in the New Dispensation movement. On April 25, 1779 she married Green Randall, who was also a member of the Cornwallis New Light Church, and by him had seven children. Green Randall died in Havana, Cuba sometime after 1822 and after having endured an extraordinary marriage.

The Reverend John Payzant noted in his *Journal* in May, 1791:

> The Second Sabbath of May it was the turn to have the Church meeting and the Sacrament at Horton. Mrs. R: rose against all the orders of the Church, and that they were but outward forms and Contrary to the Spirit of God. These novelties in the Church caused many to follow the same examples, which made much trouble in the Church. Some time I conversed with Mrs. R: on the subject. She told me that she had seen by the Spirit of God, that Baptism and the Lord Supper, with all the Disciples [Discipline?], of the Church, was contrary to the Spirit of God and his Gospel, and that Marriage was from the Divel. That she was determined to live sapate [separate] from her Husband, for it was as much sin for her to have children by him as by any other man and she saith that there [were] many that would follow her in it, that there were many young women that were converted, which she had as soon see them have children by any

339

man; to Marry. I told her that she was involving herself in an abstruse that she would find much defeculty to get out, likewise I begged of her not to advance such sentiments for she had not well considered them for she would make herself an object of Redecule. She answered that I new nothing of them therefore that I would not be a proper Judge, for her mind had gone farther in these things, than mine. I told her that there were not one of those sentiments, but what I had — seriously examined, and found them far from what God in his word had Revealed, so that I looked on them as eroneous. (Cutherbertson, *The Journal of John Payzant*, p. 44)

Despite her heretical views, and despite the fact that Lydia Randall energetically propogated them throughout the Horton and Cornwallis area, she was never disciplined at this time by her church. Was it because she was too powerful and too influential? Or was it because she made a clear distinction between word and actions? In other words, she continued, throughout the 1790s, despite her radical rhetoric, to accept the basic tenets of orthodox Christian morality. Yet it is clear that Lydia Randall never jettisoned her so-called New Dispensation views. In April 1803, her former New Dispensationalist friend, the Reverend Edward Manning, Payzant's successor, felt the time was propitious to drive her from his church. On April 9, a committee was named, headed by Manning, to visit Mrs. Randall "a member of this Church suppos'd to have entertain'd erronious sentiments etc. such as denying the Scriptures, the Coming of the Messiah or crucifiction of the Lord Jesus Christ etc. also conducting with the greatest impropriety towards her Husband etc." On September 10, 1803, Manning, assisted by Benjamin Cleveland, presented his Committee's report concerning Mrs. Randall to the Church. It was stressed that:

Mrs. Randal was in grand errors — She affirm'd that a part of the Bible was priestcraft etc & the other part was no more that what one Christian would write to another when rightly influenc'd — the Marriage covenant she deny'd & treated her Husband with every degree of disrespect, disbeliev'd the divinity of our Lord & imbib'd many other Sentiments and also absented from the Church, would not receive any admonition etc.

340

It was therefore recommended and the Church accepted the recommendation, that "she should be suspended in a public manner on the ensuing day." She was suspended on September 11, 1803, and it was according to the Church Records, "a solom thing." (Cornwallis Church Records, BHC, AUA)

Manning evidently felt compelled to suspend Mrs. Randall for one major reason. She and men like Daniel Shaw and John Pineo, who were also suspended, posed a serious threat to Manning's position in the Church. They represented an Allinite past he desperately wished to forget and, moreover, their form of religious anarchy threatened not only the ideological underpinnings of his recently accepted Calvinism but also his ministerial authority and power. It should be kept in mind that as late as 1797, Manning, who was then minister of the Cornwallis New Light Church, was still overtly extremely sympathetic to all New Lights — radicals like Shaw, Pineo and Lydia Randall as well as more conservative Allinites like Thomas Handley Chipman and Joseph Dimock. By 1803, Manning had turned his back on his earlier flexible, almost open-minded New Light approach to doctrinal and church polity matters. He was now concerned — some would say obsessed — with order, orthodoxy, and authority; and when he felt his New Light and Free Will opponents were mounting a major offensive against him, he struck back with vigour and with self-righteous wrath. In the process, he encouraged the fragmenting of the New Light movement into bitter and often warring Calvinist and Free Will Baptist factions. After September 1803, Lydia Randall disappears from the religious life of the Cornwallis-Horton community. She represented, some would say symbolized, in a very real sense, the Antinomian, anarchical extreme to be found in the Allinite legacy in Nova Scotia.

239. Fally Harding, the sister of Harris Harding, was the youngest child of Israel Harding (?-1794) and Sarah Harris.

240. David Harris (1756-1848) was the youngest son of Lebbeus Harris (1713-1792) and of his second wife Eliphal. He married Sarah Travis of Saint John, N.B. Related to Harris Harding, David Harris became a New Light preacher and a Baptist. Walter Bates, Sheriff of Kings County, New Brunswick, wrote the following in 1799 about David Harris preaching in the Sussex area:

341

He was a notorious preacher who came into the parish of Sussex and told the people he had come to them by an irresistable call from Heaven to offer salvation in Sussex that night, and that if he disobeyed the call the very stones would rise up against him. (Burnett Collection, Hartland, New Brunswick)

Harris continued to preach in the Horton area until, at least, the outbreak of the War of 1812.

241. Nancy Brown may have been the daughter of Darius Brown.

242. James DeWolf was the son of Simeon DeWolf (1719-1780) and Susanna Douglas who were married on July 23, 1741, in Connecticut. James was an immersed member of the Cornwallis New Light Church and he married in 1790 Nancy Lawrence, the daughter of the Rev. Dr. William Lawrence of Massachusetts, distinguished Harvard graduate and first minister of the First Congregational Church, Lincoln.

1791
September-December

243. David George was a Black Loyalist Baptist preacher in Shelburne. A former slave, born in "about 1742", he came to Nova Scotia in 1782 from South Carolina and was an unusually effective preacher among Whites and Black alike. In 1792, together with over 1,000 other Blacks, he left Nova Scotia for Sierra Leone where he eventually died. There apparently was little, if any, racial prejudice shown by the early New Lights who were convinced that Black and White were "all one in the Lord."

244. Frederick Fitch was the son of Ebenezer Fitch and Lydia Fisk who had left Connecticut in 1765 to settle first in Amherst and then in the Cannan area of Horton Township. Fitch was not a member of the Cornwallis New Light Church; in 1799 he was converted during a revival and was baptized and became a member of the Horton Baptist Church.

245. Daniel Shaw was a native of Scotland who died at the age of 80 at Millstream, near Sussex New Brunswick, on May 26, 1838. He was a very influential Free Christian Baptist preacher at a crucial stage of that denomination's formative development in early nineteenth century New Brunswick. He was an early member of the Cornwallis New Light Church and was expelled

in 1804 largely because of Edward Manning's bitter opposition. Shaw, an ardent advocate of Alline's "Free Will theology," was condemned on August 11, 1804, because the Church "believ'd him to be currupt in principal & practice." (Cornwallis Church Records, B.H.C. A.U.A.). Like his close associate John Pineo, Shaw, considering himself to be an unreconstructed Allinite, emphasized that "the Scriptures was no rule without the teachings of the Spirit & that it was a dead matter but it was a rule a testimony of Jesus but that it was no rule for him without the Spirit." On September 8, 1804 Shaw was formally excommunicated in the hope, according to the Church Clerk, "that it may be a warning to us all."

Forced out of his home church, Shaw itinerated widely especially in New Brunswick. His preaching style was unusual; he did not shout and whine in typical Yankee New Light fashion. Rather, he yelled out his words in a thick Scottish accent; the speed of his delivery was such and the accent so pronounced that often, especially when he was agitated, his audience would not be able to understand him. But, despite this, he was regarded as an unusually gifted preacher. He organized at least seven Free Christian Baptist Churches in New Brunswick, at Upper Sussex, Millstream, Lower Hampstead, one on the Oromocto River, another on the Nashwaak, and two others at South Hampton and Wakefield. Shaw was assisted in his work by Clark Alline. a nephew of Henry Alline.

Shaw seemed to love controversy and like Henry Alline he was not afraid to shatter existing Churches into what he considered to be pure and impure segments. Shaw detested Calvinist Baptists like Edward Manning who in turn detetested him, regarding him as a dangerous schismatic. For years Manning urged the rapidly proliferating churches in his denomination to keep clear of his Free Will nemesis, Daniel Shaw. (Burnett Papers).

246. William Alline Sr. (1714-1799) was the father of Henry Alline. Like his son and his son's New Light disciples, William expressed himself in what might be referred to as a distinctive stream-of-consciousness rhetorical style. After hearing of the death of Henry, William wrote the following letter on June 29, 1784 to the Reverend David McLure:

Dear Friend I rec^d yours [of] April 29, 1784 and take it very kind of you to Let me know how my Dear Child Departed this life and it is Some relaafe to me under my troble that it pleased God to cast him upon one who Wasse so kind to him. the Lord Reward you he will Reward you. no a Cup of Cold water to one of the least of Christ'[s] Disciples Shall be forgot by our Dear Lord. O what a kind friend is our Blessed Jesus. it Supports me under my troble. I know that all his Dealings is in Love. than the Cup that my Heavenly father gives me to Drink, Shall I not Drink it? he is gone to that Everlasting Rest, to to the home of Everlasting Love. he has acted Like one ever Since he knew the Lord Which is aboute Nine years Lik one that had a great work to Du and but a Short time to du it in and it has pleased God so to Bless his Labours that there has ben a great Work in this Land. Blessed be the Lord. Oh for ever Blessed be his Name. he has not Left us Dear S^r . many poor Sinners have Ben Brought to tast the Sweets of Redeeming Love and to Drink from the Living Stremes that make glad the City of our God. in falmouth and winser Since Last fall Some Littel Children [have been] Lisping out the Love of Jesus. O my Dear Brother in Christ Let us and all the followers of the Lamb praise this Blessed Jesus. why this is our god our frind and father. is he my father and frind? O can it Can it Can it be? is his grace so free and his Love so unbonded? it is a free Salvation free for all that will. O what a god. free Grace Will be the Everlasting Song. I hope to bear apart with you to join the throng of the Redeemed in the most Exalted notes of praise thro a never ending Eternity. the Lord Grant it for his name Sake. their is one thing in providence that is Dark to me. this is when it has pleased god to raise up a faithfull Sarvent they are often taken away in the midst of their work I know it has ben Said that it is some times in Judgment to a people who have Long Resisted his grace but that is not the thing With us. if you be so kind to inlighten me in this you will Oblige me. I think I have a Right to ask the Watchman and as you S^r are a minister of Christ I hope you Will answer me in this matter. S^r I wrote to you by the w[ay?] of Boston some time ago which I hope you R[ec'd?] as to what my Sone Left. I hope Cosen Alline will take the Care of them espetily his papers. as for the Hymns I am in

344

Some hope of Geting them printed in Boston and if you Can be any help I hope you wont be Backward Remember [us] in your prayers. may the Love of God be With you. my Wife joins with me in Love to you & yours.
Will m Alline
S r It is Desier that all Charges be payd and that Grave Stons be got and I have Desired Cosin Alline to Do it. falmouth June 29 1784. (Dartmouth University Archives).

1792

247. Nabby may have been one of the nine children of Darius Brown and Rachel Bass. Or she may have been the step-daughter of Mr. James Brown who married, after December, 1789, Mrs. Samuel Witter Jr. widow of Samuel Witter Jr. Sarah Witter had been born on February 4, 1775.

248. Eunice Hamilton, born on May 18, 1777, was the daughter of Samuel Hamilton and Sarah Davison who were married on July 11, 1771. Sally was probably Sabra, born on May 14, 1780.

249. Mrs. Edward (Sarah) DeWolf was married to Edward Dewolf, son of Nathan DeWolf (1720-1789) and his first wife. Sarah Brown DeWolf, born in 1739, was a member of the Cornwallis New Light Church; she was married in 1773, had eleven children, and died in 1819.

250. There is no available information concerning Hannah Potter; she may have been the daughter of Henry and Martha Potter of Cornwallis.

251. Lavinia Brown, of Kings County, was the wife of Thomas Brown.

1793

252. Fally Bent

253. Fally Bent

254. Dorcas Prentice

255. There is no information about this woman.

256. It is of some interest that in 1796, in Liverpool, Harding confessed that he had impregnated Hetty Harrington. On September 28 he married her and it was reported that six weeks later a child was born to the couple.

345

257. Manning was trained in surveying. He was probably referring to the reaction to New Dispensationalism and to the rumours about Harris Harding.

258. H. Alline, *Hymns and Spiritual Songs* (Boston, 1786) p. 14-15. The final three stanzas are missing from the Bennett version as is the title but they are included here in square brackets. A similar policy has been followed for the remaining Alline hymns and spiritual songs found in the Bennett volume. It should be pointed out that in the manuscript version usually the title was omitted as was most of the punctuation. In addition, the two versions differ fundamentally in terms of capitalization policy.

259. p. 31-32.

260. p. 69-70. The last two verses were not included in the Bennett volume.

261. p. 82.

262. p. 85.

263. p. 115-116.

264. p. 122.

265. p. 135-136.

266. p. 138-9. The final two stanzas are not in the Bennett manuscript.

267. p. 184-185. The 1786 printed version's title does not have the word *"free."*

268. p. 196-197. The last line of stanza 4 and the following two stanzas are missing in the Bennett volume.

269. Two verses, verses XII and XIII, of Alline's published *Hymns and Spiritual Songs*, p. 199-200, are not included in this manuscript version.

270. p. 201-202. The last four verses are not included in the manuscript version.

271. p. 207-208. The first five stanzas are missing in the Bennett collection.

272. p. 220.

273. p. 233.

274. p. 235.

Spiritual Songs

301. Alline's disciples, it has already been pointed out, were eager to emulate their master, almost in every respect. They composed these and other spiritual songs not only to show contemporary Nova Scotians that they were faithfully following their master but also to underscore their own spirituality. The hymns were the outward visible sign of the working of the Holy Spirit in their lives. For "without the Spirit", according to the New Lights, even the Scriptures were "a dead letter." (Cornwallis Church Records, B.H.C. O.U.A.)

302. These verses were probably composed by Benjamin Cleaveland. They are not to be found in either of Alline's two volumes of *Hymns and Spiritual Songs.*

303. Alline, *The Anti-Traditionalist*, p. 50-54. All material in square brackets is from the *Anti-Traditionalist* and is inserted, either after the inaccurate Bennett transcription of a word or phrase or, if a sentence or two, where they belong in the text. Apart from these minor differences the Bennett version is a remarkably accurate transcription of the printed *Anti-Traditionalist*. Throughout this section, as was the case with the section dealing with Alline's *Hymns and Spiritual* I have not added the punctuation from the printed version of Alline's treatises, sermons, or *Journal*. Nor have I noted every variance in capitalization or spelling.

304. From the *Anti-Traditionalist*, p. 34. This final line is missing from the Bennett version.

305. From the *Anti-Traditionalist*, p. 36.

306. Alline, *A Sermon On a Day of Thanksgiving Preached at Liverpool on the* 21st of November, 1782, p. 15.

307. H. Alline, *A Sermon On a Day of Thanksgiving Preached at Liverpool on the 21st of November, 1782* (Halifax). The Bennett version, apart from spelling, punctuation, capitalization, and two different words ("Clods" on line 4 rather than "cloths" and "Abstract" on line 20 rather than "Attract") is the same as the Henry Alline printed version.

308. Alline, *Journal*, p. 105. I have included in square brackets words or lines from the *Journal* not to be found in the manuscript version. Where the sense of a sentence might not be clear I have added the entire line from the *Journal*.

309. The Reverend David McClure to William Alline, North

Hampton, New Hampshire, April 29, 1784. This version of the McClure letter to Henry Alline's father is, on the whole, spelling, capitalization, and punctuation aside, quite similar to the letter included in Alline's *Journal.* See J. Beverley and B. Moody (eds), *The Journal of Herny Alline* (Hantsport, 1982), pp. 219-222. The first paragraph of the *Journal* letter is not included nor is the last paragraph and the funeral description. Moreover, there is an interesting difference in the description of Alline's last words. The *Journal* version reads, "In this state he lay about two hours in great distress for breath, and the last intelligible sentence he spoke was in the strain of his general conversation in these words. Now I rejoice in the Lord Jesus.

And between three and four o'clock in the morning he breathed out his soul with the arms of Jesus, with whom he longed to be."

The *Journal* version which is similar to the Handley Chipman manuscript version is probably the original. The Bennett letter seems to have been a slightly altered version of the original. The material in square brackets if from the printed *Journal* version.

Footnotes to
Appendix I

310. Ebenezer Hobbs, a resident of Argyle, was one of Alline's teen-age converts. On July 21, 1782, Simeon Perkins of Liverpool noted in his *Diary* "one Ebenezer Hobbs of Argyle, a Lad of about 17 years, made prayer and Exhortation at an Evening meeting. He is thought to be too Young for a Teacher." See D.C. Harvey (ed.) *Diary of Simeon Perking, 1780-1789* (Toronto, 1958), p. 146. Nothing else is known of Hobbs' post-Alline career. This letter is to be found in the B.H.C., A.U.A.

311. The Prescott letters are to be found in the "Memoir of Mrs. Charlotte Boyle," *The Baptist Missionary Magazine.* Vol. II, No. 1 (January, 1835), pp. 3-4.

312. Nancy Lawrence (1764-1807) was born in Lincoln, Massachusetts and married James DeWolf, a widower, in 1790. Her father, the Reverend William Lawrence (1723-1780), was an eminent Congregational minister who had opposed, throughout his life, religious enthusiasm of any kind.

Sometime in 1788 or in early 1789 Nancy came to Granville, near Annapolis to visit her Loyalist brother William and sister-in-law who had recently moved to the township. While in Granville Nancy became an ardent New Light having been profoundly influenced by Harris Harding and Joseph Dimock in particular. She felt compelled to share immediately her new found faith with her friends and her family; and it was a faith not insignificantly shaped by Henry Alline's theology.

Nancy had been overwhelmed by "the riches of free grace" to such an extent that without her mother's consent she abandoned her spinster status in December for marriage to a widower with three young children. Her husband James DeWolf, a merchant from Horton, had according to Nancy "a double claim to my affections, for he loves Jesus, we have a spiritual union that earth nor Hell can never dissolve which will outlive time and exist to all Eternity." After briefly describing her "deceit" to her mother and requesting her "forgiveness" in a letter written on January 5, 1791, Nancy DeWolf quickly turned her attention to what mattered most to her — the salvation of her family and friends. Nancy's obviously distraught mother — a traditional Congregationalist — must have been both angered and amazed to have been instructed by her daughter to tell all their Lincoln neighbours that "they must be born again or I shall be eternally separated from them." "Tell them", she informed her mother "tis not for any merit or worthiness in me that the

Lord hath chosen me, no tis free Grace, free Grace and it is free for them as me". "Give my love to Bulkly Adams and wife," she went on "tell him he must forsake all for Christ or He is lost for ever, remember me to all my friends tell them that the friendship of the world is emnity with God, that my soul loves and longs for their redemption."

Nancy DeWolf, by her conversion and her marriage, had obviously declared her independence of her mother and her family. Though happily married, at least for the first few years of her marriage, Nancy found herself estranged from her family — a family which was unable to condone either her religious enthusiasm or her secret marriage to an older man. There is a sense of despair and acute concern in her letter written on May 2, 1793 to her mother. "Tis a year and half since I received a line from the family," she complained "and have only heard from you but once" since early 1790. "I want exceedingly to hear from each one of the family" she confessed, "sometimes my heart forebodes a thousand evils, and imagination points distress and horor around that dwelling where first I received the ellemental life." Eighteen months later, on October 9, 1794, Nancy, informed her mother:

> Tis now almost three years since I received a line from any of the family, I conclude you have entirely cast me of[f], but God is my refuge, my refuge, my fortress, high tower and exceeding great reward. He will not leave me nor forsake me.

Nancy still had not heard from her family on April 17, 1795. Her mother, however, was constantly bombarded in the few letters written by Nancy with Allinite statements such as "O that you may have an interest in that Lamb which was slain from before the foundation of the world."

Sometime between April 1796 and November 1798, the DeWolf family moved from Horton — the Allinite New Light heartland — to Liverpool, where the Reverend John Payzant, Alline's brother-in-law, was the Congregational minister. During this period, Nancy evidently lost much of her religious enthusiasm. Her mind, she graphically observed "was caried away, captive into Babalon" and her "harp was hung upon the willows." She now never mentioned "Experimental religion" in her letters to her mother. Rather, she complained bitterly about her poor health and the frequent absences from

Liverpool of her husband. "There is nothing but an sciety [anxiety] and trouble in this life," she moaned "and tho we are prospered in our outward circumstances beyond our expectations yet it appears to me all is Vanity and Vexation of Spirit."

All was "Vanity and vexation of Spirit" for Nancy DeWolf until Liverpool's "Great Reformation." Until the early months of 1807, she was evidently far more interested in Liverpool's economic prospects than she was in evangelical Christianity. Then she experienced a profound spiritual revitalization; she had discovered the pristine purity of her earlier New Light faith.

Like many other Nova Scotians in the first decade of the nineteenth century, Nancy DeWolf had experienced first the ecstacy of regeneration and then the slow and almost inexorable slide to religious apathy and indifference. And then came the revival to be followed, for many, but not for Nancy, by declension and then another outburst of spiritual revitalization.

In early February, 1807, Nancy, together with hundreds of her Liverpool neighbours, were caught up in what the Reverend John Payzant described as "a wonderful moving (among the people) of the power of God." For almost two months, Nancy DeWolf attended special revival meetings at least "four or five times a week." And by the first week of April, she had, she was certain, rediscovered the magic of her earlier faith during what she called "a day of Penticost." She wrote to her sister:

it is thought their is five Hundred brought to the knowledge of the truth. I could write a volum but I am affraid I shall frighten you, for I was so far from enjoying religion when I was with you. My mind was carried away captive into Babalon and how could I sing one of Zion's songs in a strange land? My harp was hung upon the willows, but O my sister I can bless God their is a Glorious reallity in experimental Religion. I can say this night with the energy of truth that I am a living witness for the cause of Christ, that we must be born again or never enter the kingdom of Heaven, that we must be slain by the law and made or live by grace. O that it might spread from shore to shore that the knolege of the Lord might cover the earth as the waters do the seas.

353

For a two week period, Nancy observed, "it was a sabath all over Liverpool, all Labour ceased, vessels stopt loading, stores were shut up and all were enquiring what they should do to be saved." The enthusiasm, energy and confidence of the young converts struck a particularly responsive chord in Nancy as she remembered those days and months — some two decades earlier — when she, too, had been absolutely certain about the "Glorious reallity" of "experimental Religion". When she heard the young Liverpool converts witness to their faith she heard her own voice echo from what seemed to be a distant past. She knew the words — she knew the phrases — and she understood the complex nature of the concern — for these were all once uniquely hers. What reverberated through her mind, richocheting wildly into the darkest corners of her guilt, were the familiar — the painfully familiar — reminders of a past when she was convinced that she had been suddenly and marvellously, by the ravishing power of the Holy Spirit, "reinstated in the Image of God." In March and April, 1807, the present was collapsed into the past, as Nancy DeWolf confronted the bitter depths of her back-sliding. "God has redeemed my soul", she was told, over and over again, by scores of young people, "He has taken me out of the Horrible Pit and mirey clay and put a new song into my mouth, even praise to God." "Come my dear friend," she was urged "share a part their is room enough in my fathers kingdom."

It is clear that Nancy DeWolf's experience was not a unique one. Many Nova Scotians, in the post-Revolutionary period, experienced the ecstacy of conversion, and then the prolonged despair associated with back-sliding. Some, during frequent revivals which affected their communities, would emulate Nancy DeWolf. These people, in a very real sense, were not re-converted but rather were revived. For some, their being regularly revived from what they described as a state of "spiritual stupor" became the essence of their religious experience. Outside stimulii, they felt, were needed to keep the evangelical cause alive; their inner resources appeared to be totally inadequate to accomplish this end. Dependence merely bred further dependence. And this too would become a distinguishing feature of both Nova Scotia and Maritime Evangelical religious culture. (This discussion of Nancy (Lawrence) DeWolf is based upon her letters in the DeWolf-Lawrence Correspondence, located in the American Antiquarian Society, Worchester, Mass.).

313. Probably the sister of Nancy Lawrence.

314. Julia Bass, the daughter of Sally Bass.

315. Dr. William Lawrence and his wife lived at Granville. They moved from Nova Scotia in the 1790s to Fort Edward, New York, and were visited by the Reverend Joseph Dimock in 1797 (See G.E. Levy (ed.) *The Diary of Joseph Dimock* (Hantsport, 1979), pp. 29-30.

316. B.H.C., A.U.A., J.M. Cramp, "History of the Maritime Baptists" pp. 41-43.

317. Mr. Jeremiah Sabine or Sabean, born Feb. 17, 1717, in Connecticut, immigrated to Argyle, Nova Scotia in 1762 and to the Sissiboo River in 1765. Sabine had at least eleven children some of whom became active Baptists.

318. Mr. Foot, either Isaac or Samuel, sons of Captain Zechariah Foot, a native of Salem, Massachusetts, who immigrated to Nova Scotia in 1769 and who died in 1784.

319. Cramp, pp. 40-41.

320. Mr. Thompson. Perhaps Samuel Thompson, the Anglican Loyalist who married Elizabeth Purdy on August 24, 1786.

321. Enoch Towner was a Loyalist who after his conversion was ordained a New Light Baptist minister in 1799 at Sissiboo, now Weymouth. After seven years there he was called to the Argyle Church and in 1816 he returned to Weymouth where he remained until 1825 when he moved to Westport where he died in June, 1828. Towner was a very effective preacher during Nova Scotia's "Great Reformation", 1805-1808 but during his latter years he was something of a spent force.

322. Cramp, pp. 52-57. The *** are from Cramp.

323. There is a gap in the account.

324. John Bradshaw was the son of Abraham Bradshaw, a native of Massachusetts who died in February 1791.

325. Cramp, pp. 54-55.

326. *Ibid.*, p. 55.

327. A section of the letter is probably missing.

328. M. Richey, *A Memoir of the Late Rev. William Black* (Halifax, 1839) pp. 160-172.

329. P.A.N.S. MG1 No. 100, pp. 428-431.

330. The Reverend Jacob Bailey (1731-1808), Anglican priest, Loyalist, and writer, arrived in Halifax with his family, on June 21, 1779. He moved to Cornwallis and after spending three years there moved permanently to Annapolis Royal. Bailey had considerable contact with New Lights and he hated them with a passion. His acerbic narrative verse, though distorted by his finely developed bitter despair and his lack of empathy for religious enthusiasm, nevertheless, does convey some critical truths about the New Lights.

331. pp. 19-20, 23, 24-29, 30-31, 32, 33, 35, 36, 37.

332. *Jeremaih* XXIII, 21. *Ezek.* XXII. 28.

333. Hoc genus hominum eo periculosius est, quod humanis cupiditatibus praetexunt autoritatem Dei; et sub imagine pietatis invehunt pietatis exitium.

    Erasmi Ecclesiastes

    [This kind of person is the more dangerous in that he clothes the authority of God with human desires and under the appearance of piety brings about the destruction of piety.

    Erasmus] This translation is not to be found in the original pamphlet.

334. *John* IV. I.

335. *John* V, 43.I.

336. ....There is nothing new under the sun. If some persons in our days, make pertensions to inspiration and a divine commission, and in consequence of them, invade the ministerial office — if their fancied inspirations are attended with screaming, violent agitations, and uncouth gesticulations — and if, several weak, ignorant people are hereby seduced, and brought under delusion: We need not be surprised; for this has happened a thousand times before, besides the instances now produced. Nor is this any more an impeachment of true, rational religion, than counterfeit coin is of true money. Against this infirmity, or disease of our common nature, which has been manifested by individuals in every country, and of every religion, we should guard ourselves by unprejudiced reason, and by the instructions of Holy Scripture, which was mercifully given for that purpose, and to make us wise to salvation....Last summer, a woman among the sect of New Lights in this Province, commenced Prophetess. Her name is Sara Bencraft. She

prophecied that on a certain day, the Devil would come, and carry off bodily a man, whom she named — but the prophecy was not fulfilled.

337. *Philip* I, 15, etc.

338. Public Archives of Nova Scotia, MG 1. Vol. 93a.

INDEX

359

360